PAST, PRESENT, AND FUTURE

PAST, PRESENT, AND FUTURE

A READING-WRITING TEXT

JOAN YOUNG GREGG
New York City Technical College

JOAN RUSSELL
New York City Technical College

WADSWORTH PUBLISHING COMPANY
Belmont, California
A Division of Wadsworth, Inc.

To our parents
Mollie Silverman and Harry Silverman,
Sylvia and Harry Young

English Editor: Kevin Howat
Production Editor: Gary Mcdonald
Designer: Cynthia Bassett
Copy Editor: Jonas Weisel
Cover Illustrator: Lucy H. McCargar

Photo Credits: NASA: Pp. 1, 91, 332; John Edelmann Galleries: P. 2; Ravinder
Nanda: P. 2; Serena Nanda: Pp. 2, 15, 57, 77, 83, 122, 174, 295, 303, 310, 328; Tony
Gahan: Pp. 9, 21; U. S. Dept. of Interior: P. 20; United Nations: Pp. 45, 53, 107, 121,
166, 171, 191, 203, 217, 229, 250, 290, 313; Canadian Government: P. 53; Hawaii
Visitors Bureau: Pp. 68, 74; Joan Gregg: P. 86; IBM: P. 102; UNESCO: Pp. 121, 191;
Bernard Krauss: Pp. 135, 188, 199, 313; Raymond Kennedy: P. 137; New York Public
Library: P. 142; American Book Company: P. 150; Gunther Holtorf: P. 158; Almasy-
Vauthey: P. 191; David Klein: P. 201; Courtesy of Joan Russell: P. 227; Eliza Pacheco:
Pp. 230, 238; Chicago Historical Society: P. 253; Vassar: P. 260; Solomon D. Butcher
Collection: P. 269; Nebraska State Historical Society: P. 269; John Gregg: Pp. 275,
283; CUNY/Steve Gerardi: P. 294; Simone Larive: P. 320; International Ladies
Garment Workers Union: P. 345

Printed in the United States of America

4 5 6 7 8 9 10—87 86 85

ISBN 0-534-01218-3

Library of Congress Cataloging in Publication Data

Gregg, Joan Young.
    Past, present, and future.
    1. English language—Text-books for foreigners.
I. Russell, Joan, date.   II. Title
PE1128.G66 1982   428.2′4   82-11083
ISBN 0-534-01218-3

PREFACE

This text is designed for college students at the low intermediate level of academic reading and expository writing in English as a second language (ESL). Through extensive writing and composition exercises students will develop competence in expressing their ideas, describing their environment, and narrating personal events using the basic English structure and sentence patterns.

The readings in this text are thematically related within each of the three Units. The themes of the reading selections are also the subject of the accompanying writing and composition assignments. Vocabulary is recycled throughout the Units, and students are provided with an academically oriented information base for oral and written work.

The text has been organized to provide maximum flexibility. The A and B sections of each chapter cover the same topics and writing targets but use different passages, vocabulary, and exercises. The A sections treat the topics from a cross-cultural perspective; the B sections offer an American perspective. Each section provides 45 to 60 semester hours of instruction for a total of 90 to 120 hours. Alternate chapters may be used for ESL laboratory assignments, extra credit work, additional semester hours, or a second term of instruction.

Each Unit has its own Review, which includes vocabulary work, reading comprehension, and composing assignments.

THE FOLLOWING ORGANIZATION IS USED IN EACH CHAPTER OF THE TEXT

Prereading

Varied cognitive tasks introduce each chapter and provide motivation for the reading passage and comprehension exercises. A New Word list directs attention to the words that are the basis for the Vocabulary exercises. It is useful for the instructor to pronounce these words aloud with the students. Students should underline these words as they occur in the reading passage and use their dictionaries as necessary to find the meanings.

Reading

Each of the reading passages develops one aspect of the Unit's theme. Each passage is followed by a comprehension or summarization exercise.

Vocabulary

Each Vocabulary section offers a variety of tasks focusing on the New Word list. This section includes a special Word Family activity for vocabulary enrichment.

Reading Comprehension

In this section students practice finding main ideas, significant details, and supporting examples, as well as answering both information and inference questions.

Writing Exercises

These exercises focus on verb formation and sentence-writing skills appropriate to this level, such as word order, subject-verb agreement, use of complementary tenses, article use, and punctuation.

Composing

The composing tasks provide a foundation for the development of college level composition skills. The material in this section helps students generate and organize paragraphs on topics related to the readings.

Unit Review

There are three Unit Reviews, each of which encompasses the work of the six preceding chapters (both A and B parts together). The Unit Reviews provide a summary of the basic skills presented in the chapters.

Appendices

Appendix A contains the Basic Terminology for English Language Study and a list of commonly used irregular verbs. Appendix B contains the Paragraph Correction Symbols sheet.

CONTENTS

UNIT II: LANGUAGE   121

**Chapter Eight A
Brides and Grooms   273**

**Chapter Eight B
Men's and Women's Roles:
A Changing View   293**

**Chapter Nine A
Focus on the Family   312**

**Chapter Nine B
Dual-Career Families   331**

NOTES TO THE INSTRUCTOR

To acquaint students with the textbook and to provide an overview of the sections in each chapter, the instructor should read the Preface of the textbook with the class. The instructor should also point out Basic Terminology for English Language Study, Appendix A, and have the students read it carefully at the beginning of and throughout the semester; these terms are used in the text and will be mentioned often in class. Since verbs are one of the major problems for ESL students, the Verb Summary deserves special attention, and students should be reminded to refer to it for error correction. If the instructor intends to utilize the Paragraph Correction Symbols sheet, Appendix B, he or she should review this with the class.

The instructor should determine beforehand which set of chapters, the A or the B, will be used as the primary text for the class. Students ought to read and work on Chapter 1 entirely in class; they should complete and discuss each exercise before moving on to Chapter 2. Throughout this process the instructor might read the explanations and directions for each exercise aloud as the students follow in their texts. The instructor will have his or her own preference for following this practice throughout the book.

It will be noted that the reading passages in Units I and II are structurally simple, allowing the student to gain confidence in handling the information and responding correctly to the reading comprehension questions. A more complex form of reading passage is presented in Unit III, with a correspondingly higher level of reading comprehension questions. By this time the student should be ready for the structures as they relate to the readings and reading questions, as well as for the writing exercises requiring them.

USING THE TEXT

In using the text, students should be directed to complete all exercises on a separate sheet of notebook paper, except where stated otherwise. This will foster careful writing habits and will make the correction of homework assignments more convenient. When assigning a particular exercise, whether for homework or class work, the instructor should go over the example or first item with the students so that they know what is required and have an opportunity to ask questions.

Vocabulary

In the area of Vocabulary the instructor may introduce several useful exercises to help students expand their productive, as well as their receptive, lexicon. For example, the instructor may assign small group paragraph composition that utilizes five to eight words from the New Word lists. The instructor may have the groups choose the words themselves or may offer sets of words from which each group must choose one. Or the instructor may ask pairs or groups of students to choose a photograph and to write sentences about it so as to incorporate vocabulary from the text. Representative paragraphs may then be put on the board or dittoed for class evaluation and correction.

Aural and Oral Work

Aural comprehension exercises eliciting either oral or written responses should supplement the text as time is available. All such supplementary material ought to be thematically related to the lesson at hand. Instructors may wish to use the alternate section of the text for this purpose, or they may wish to extract and adapt paragraphs from newspapers and magazines. The following activities are among those that have proved most useful:

1. The instructor reads a passage as a form of "lecturette." Students take notes of the main ideas and significant details in order to respond to appropriate questions either orally or in writing.
2. The instructor reads a paragraph for Oral Cloze. The entire paragraph should be read aloud three times; then the paragraph is read aloud with every ninth or tenth word deleted. Students must write a semantically and syntactically correct word for each blank.
3. The instructor dictates a passage either in its entirety or with blank spaces to be filled in by the students. A dictation of this kind may focus on target structures. It is especially effective when it uses student paragraphs.
4. The instructor dictates without articulating sentence boundaries. Students must then punctuate and capitalize the paragraph correctly.
5. In groups, or as individuals in front of the class, students present three-minute talks on assigned topics. Speakers formulate questions for listeners to answer, or listeners may ask speakers questions.

Writing Exercises

The Writing Exercises present brief but clear explanations of target structures and sentence patterns and provide sentence pattern work through appropriately sequenced tasks. The Writing Exercises may be expanded by using the text's photographs or other theme-related pictures or reality as their basis.

The reconstruction of short paragraphs or groups of related sentences with the aid of key words or subject-verb kernels is a useful task for integrating and reinforcing sentence-building skills. Instructors may read the paragraph to the students several times or present it to them in written form for several readings. The instructor then elicits the key words or subject-verb kernels from the students and puts these on the board. The students are assigned the task of reconstructing the material based only on the words on the board. This activity is best done in pairs or small groups. Another useful activity is to have students read passages from supplementary material to extract particular target structure to be incorporated into their own sentence composition. For example, students may be asked to extract pronouns and categorize these as subjects, objects, or possessives; their composition objectives would be to write a brief paragraph utilizing pronouns and to categorize and explain these in the same way.

A similar activity asks students to list all words ending with *s* according to whether they are noun plurals, third-person verbs, possessives, or simple spellings. Students are then asked to employ several of each category in their own paragraphs and explain their use.

Composing

If time permits, the instructor may conduct prewriting activities such as brainstorming, class discussion of assigned topics, or group or class writing of an outline or even a model paragraph. Formal paragraph writing may be done at home or in class. It is interesting for students to read their paragraphs to a partner before handing them in, and this practice reinforces the sense that writing is done to communicate with other people.

Students want and appreciate a clear and thorough location (not correction) of errors in their writing. Instructors may wish to mark the symbols from the Paragraph Correction Symbol sheet in the margin or in the body of the paper, or they may simply circle or underline the points at which errors occur and leave it to the student to identify the correction needed. Students should spend a few minutes correcting their paragraphs as soon as the assignments have been returned. This step of the writing process may be done in pairs so that each student reads his or her paper aloud to the other and has pencil in hand to make corrections. Pair correction adds an aural and oral dimension to composition and reinforces the idea that writing is communication with another. Paragraphs that need extensive correction should be completely rewritten.

Group Work

Many of the activities in the text lend themselves to pair or group work. Pair work is usually most conveniently performed by students sitting next to each other. For group work involving three to five students, however, the instructor has a number of options. Groups may be formed on the basis of students' strengths or weaknesses, or random groups may be formed by the count-off system, alphabetical order, or proximity. In acquainting students with group work, instructors can help them feel more comfortable the first time or two by assisting with the moving of chairs, introducing students to each other, and encouraging pair or group members to sit facing each other. Group activities may procede in various ways. All the items in a particular task may be assigned to each group, or different groups may be assigned different items. Time limits should be announced and adhered to. During the period the instructor should circulate to see that work is moving along at a satisfactory pace and that everyone is participating. In the plenary period following the group work, students must rearrange their chairs so that they are once more able to focus on the board, the instructor, and the other students.

Since the Unit Reviews include exercises in reading, vocabulary, and writing, they may be assigned as tests when a Unit has been completed. The Unit Reviews include general information from both A and B sections of the text and therefore are suitable for use no matter on which section the class is working. Because the book has perforated pages, the Unit Reviews can easily be removed and handed in for correction and grading.

ACKNOWLEDGMENTS

It gives us great pleasure to acknowledge the contributions of our colleagues at New York City Technical College who have provided us with valuable insights in language skills instruction. We would also like to acknowledge our colleagues in TESOL who have been so generous in sharing their ideas at conferences and in publications. We are especially thankful to Beth Pacheco for her helpful suggestions for revising parts of the manuscript.

We are grateful to Kevin Howat, Cynthia Bassett, and Gary Mcdonald at Wadsworth Publishing Company for their generous assistance. We also thank Jonas Weisel for his careful copy editing. Reviewers to whom we are thankful for their constructive suggestions are Tom Bambrey, University of Denver; Dennis Chowenhill, Chabot College; Jean Zukowski Faust, University of Arizona; Naguib Greis, Portland State University; Dale Myers, University of Tennessee at Knoxville; Roger Owens, California State University at Dominguez Hills; Barbara Rolland, University of Wisconsin; Walter Sherwood, Sacramento City College; Peter Silva, Contra Costa College; and Marcie Williams, Michigan State University.

For their photographs we would especially like to thank Serena Nanda, Tony Gahan, Bernhard Krauss, Simone Larive, Ravinder Nanda, John Gregg, John Edelmann, Raymond Kennedy, and David Klein.

To our husbands, John and Alfred, who have experienced the pleasures of learning a second language, and to Paisley, who is about to begin this adventure, we also dedicate this text.

UNIT I

OUR PHYSICAL WORLD

The Earth as seen from the moon

CHAPTER ONE A

ARCHEOLOGY: UNCOVERING THE PAST

PREREADING

Class Discussion. These pictures show things from earlier times. How are they similar to things that people use today? How are they different?

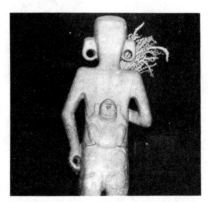

Pre-Columbian fertility god, *circa* 1500

Chinese man's court robe, *circa* 1800

Doric Temple, Athens, Greece, Fifth Century B.C.

What are some ways that we can find out about the past?

New Words.   Try to understand the meanings of these words as they are used in the reading passage. Use a dictionary when necessary.

secret	object	examine
archeologist	inform	splendid
discover	accurate	produce
	special	

READING

Bringing the Past to Life

[1]   Our earth is very old. It holds many secrets about life in the past. Archeologists dig in the ground and bring out these secrets. They discover objects thousands of years old that inform us about how people lived long ago.

[2]   Archeologists work in all parts of the world. Some work in their own countries and others are invited to dig in foreign lands. They set up field camps at sites in Mexico, Italy, China, and the United States. There are famous ruins in Greece, Egypt, and Turkey where archeologists continue to make important discoveries. Archeologists dig in the countryside or beneath city streets. Some Americans do underwater archeology. Wherever they work, all these men and women use their skills to bring the past to life.

[3]   In order to get accurate information about the past, archeologists must work very carefully. Before they begin to dig, archeologists draw maps and plans of the ground. An archeologist always digs slowly, using special tools such as picks and brushes. He or she makes notes about each discovery and marks the discovery on a map. Afterward the archeologists wash all the objects or brush them clean. Then they examine them and take photographs of them.

[4]   Archeologists discover different kinds of objects that tell us how the people in the past lived. In many places tools for hunting and farming are often uncovered. Pots, dishes, jars, and other items of daily use lie among the ruins. In addition to household objects, archeologists find children's toys and games and jewelry made of stone beads or bone. In the palaces of kings and queens there are splendid objects of gold and silver, wall paintings, statues of important people, and other works of art. When archeologists dig up the graves of soldiers, they usually find weapons near the bodies. From temples and shrines, they bring out objects of religious meaning.

[5]   Sometimes archeologists find writing on stone, clay, or bone objects. There are many types of texts: business letters from merchants to customers; school exercises in language and mathematics; government regulations and codes of law;

reports of armies in battle; poems and stories about heroes, gods, and goddesses. Writing of the past always helps the archeologist understand the culture and customs of the people.

[6]   The earth produces information of other times, of life and death, war and peace, work and play, and of gods and human beings. Were these ancient people very different from us? What do you think?

Summary Completion.   Fill in the blank spaces with the correct word from the reading passage.

The earth holds many secrets about the (1) _life in the past_. Archeologists bring the past to (2) _life_ . They use special (3) _tools_ in their work. They uncover objects that tell us how (4) _the people_ lived long ago. The writing of the past helps archeologists (5) _understand_ the people's culture and customs. These people of the past weren't very (6) _different_ . from us.

VOCABULARY

1. **Expanding Vocabulary.**   Circle the number of the word that is closest in meaning to the given word.

    a. secrets   (1) sentences   (2) paintings   (3) hidden things
    b. objects   (1) countries   (2) items   (3) people
    c. archeologist   (1) a person who studies the past   (2) a person who teaches English   (3) a person who lives in Mexico
    d. discover   (1) find   (2) draw   (3) bring
    e. examine   (1) live   (2) wash   (3) look closely at
    f. splendid   (1) careful   (2) beautiful   (3) slow
    g. produces   (1) brings out   (2) uses   (3) takes
    h. inform   (1) go inside   (2) dig   (3) tell about
    i. special   (1) secret   (2) careful   (3) particular
    j. accurate   (1) correct   (2) different   (3) old

2. **Using Vocabulary.**   Fill in the blanks in the following sentences with one word from the preceding list of given words. Each word may be used only once.

    a. There are many different _items_ in my kitchen such as pots, pans, and dishes.

b. Students try to get ___correct___ answers to their math problems.

c. An apple tree always ___produces___ fruit in the fall.

d. Children often tell each other ___their secrete___ .

e. Does the dentist use X rays to ___examine___ your teeth?

f. Teachers should ___tell___ students about their grades.

g. There is a ___Archeologist___ name for people who study the past.

h. You can ___find___ the meaning of words in a dictionary.

i. My sister has a ___beautiful___ gold necklace.

3. **Word Families.**   Study the following lists.

Type of Work	Person Who Does That Type of Work
archeology	archeologist
art	artist
science	scientist
writing	writer
teaching	teacher
photography	photographer

Sentence Completion.   Choose the correct word in parentheses to fill in the blank space in each sentence.

a. (archeology, archeologist) An ___archeologist___ digs in the earth to find hidden objects.

b. (Writing, Writer) ___Writing___ is also an important part of an archeologist's work.

c. (Farming, Farmer) ___Farming___ was the most usual type of work in the past.

d. (art, artist) Pablo Picasso was a famous Spanish ___artist___ .

e. (art, artist) His ___art___ is famous all over the world.

f. (psychology, psychologist) A ___psychologist___ studies the human mind.

g. (teaching, teacher) Some archeologists also enjoy ___teaching___ in universities.

h. (photography, photographer) A good _photographer_ always takes clear, interesting pictures.

READING COMPREHENSION

1. **Understanding the Text.**   Follow the directions for each item.

   a. Mark the following sentences *True* or *False* according to the information in the reading passage. Underline the part of the passage where you find your information.

   (1) Archeologists work only in the United States. __F__   2

   (2) Archeologists use special tools in their work. __T__   3

   (3) In the past there were kings and queens in some countries. __T__ 4

   (4) People of the past did not attend school. __F__   5

   (5) Archeologists paint pictures on palace walls. __F__ 5

   b. Circle the letter of the correct answer.

   (1) In Paragraph [1], the last sentence, *they* refers to

      a. secrets.   **b.** archeologists.   **c.** objects.

   (2) In Paragraph [2], the last sentence, the word that could take the place of *men and women* is

      a. Americans.   **b.** countries.   **c.** archeologists.

   (3) In Paragraph [3], the last sentence, *them* refers to

      a. tools.   **b.** photographs.   **c.** objects.

   (4) In Paragraph [4], the fourth sentence, the word that could take the place of *In addition to* is

      a. Below.   **b.** Without.   **c.** Besides.

   (5) In Paragraph [5], the second sentence, the word *texts* means the same as

      a. customs.   **b.** writing.   **c.** bone objects.

   (6) In Paragraph [6], the words in the pairs *life and death, war and peace, work and play, gods and human beings*

      a. are the same in meaning.   **b.** are opposite in meaning.
      c. refer only to the past.

2. **Answering Information Questions.**   Write the answers to the following questions in complete sentences.

    a. Name three countries where archeologists work. *Mexico - Italy - China .*

    b. Name two special tools archeologists use. *Picks & brushes .*

    c. Do archeologists dig slowly or quickly? *slowly .*

    d. What objects of daily use lie among the ruins? *Pots, dishes , jars ..*

    e. What kind of objects do archeologists usually discover in the graves of soldiers? *weapons .*

    f. Where do archeologists sometimes find writing? *stone , clay or bone objects*

3. **General and Specific Words.**   A general word is a word used for a large group or class of things. A specific word is used to give us a special detail or example of a more general word.

General word: people	**General word: student**
Specific word: king	**Specific words: archeology student**

    a. For each set of words, mark *G* next to the more general word(s) and *S* next to the more specific word(s). The first one is done for you.

        (1) tool __*g*__   **(2)** country __*G*__   **(3)** notebook __*S*__

                brush __*S*__   China __*S*__   book __*G*__

        (4) ball __*G*__   **(5)** chair __*G*__   **(6)** women __*G*__

                doll __*G*__   furniture __*G*__   queens __*S*__

                toy __*G*__

        (7) business letters __*S*__

                writing __*G*__

                school lessons __*S*__

    b. In the blank space write a general word that names the group of specific words. The first one is done for you.

        (1) picks   shovels   brushes __*tools*__

        (2) Mexico   China   Italy   Colombia __*Country*__

        (3) chairs   tables   beds   bookcases __*object*__

        (4) farmers   soldiers   kings   queens __*titles people*__

(5) dress   hat   shirt   pants _____ *clothes* _____

(6) notes   letters   compositions _____ *writing* _____

c. The topic of a paragraph or a passage is the general idea or general subject. We use general words to talk about topics.
    Circle the correct answer for the following items.

(1) The topic of the whole reading passage in this chapter is

   a. archeologists and the past.
   b. archeologists find gold and silver.
   c. archeologists in Mexico.

(2) The topic of Paragraph [2] is

   a. what American archeologists do.   b. digging in Turkey and Greece.
   c. where archeologists work.

(3) The topic of Paragraph [3] is

   a. using brushes and picks.   b. what archeologists draw.
   c. how archeologists dig.

(4) The topic of Paragraph [4] is

   a. archeologists' discoveries.   b. children's games.
   c. kings and queens of the past.

(5) The topic of Paragraph [5] is

   a. writing of the past.   b. letters and stories.
   c. stone, clay, and bone.

WRITING EXERCISES

Sentence Kernels

1. **Verbs.**   The verb is the heart of the English sentence. There cannot be an English sentence without a complete main verb. The main verb is the word that tells us the state of being, the feeling, or the action of a person, place, or thing.

> **An archeologist *digs* in the ground.**

Archeologists sometimes find the bones of people who died long ago. Here is an ancient grave uncovered in Tikal, Guatemala.

Recognizing Verbs.   Underline the verbs in the following sentences.

a. The earth holds many secrets about the past.
b. An archeologist writes everything in a notebook.
c. Archeologists discover objects of gold and silver.
d. They never keep these objects for themselves.

2. **Subjects.**   The subject of a sentence answers the question, *Who* or *what* is doing the verb action?

An archeologist **digs in the ground. (Who digs?)**

Recognizing Subjects.   Go back to sentences *a, b, c,* and *d*. Circle the subject of each underlined verb.

Identifying Verbs and Subjects.   Read the following paragraph carefully. Find the complete main verb in each sentence. Put each verb in the Verb column of the chart that follows. Then find the subject of each verb. Put the subject in the Subject column. The first one is done for you.

(1) Professor Ortiz teaches archeology in Mexico City. (2) He has permission to dig in certain areas of the city. (3) His students help him in

the field. (4) They follow his instructions carefully. (5) They receive course credit for their work. (6) The professor writes a report about their discoveries at the end of the dig.

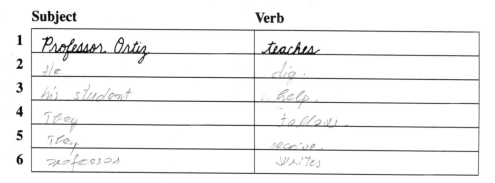

	Subject	Verb
1	*Professor Ortiz*	*teaches*
2	*He*	*dig.*
3	*his student*	*help.*
4	*They*	*follow.*
5	*They*	*receive.*
6	*professor*	*writes*

Simple Present Tense

The Simple Present tense is used to talk about things that are generally true. It is also used to talk about things that people usually do (not what they are doing right now). All the verbs in your Verb column are in the Simple Present tense.

> **Archeologists *dig* in the ground. (This is something they usually do.)**

Study the following Simple Present tense forms.

	Singular	Plural
First Person	I dig	An archeologist and I dig We dig
Second Person	You dig	You dig
Third Person	An archeologist digs He/She/It digs	Archeologists dig They dig

Notice that only the Third Person Singular form has the extra *s* at the end.

1. **Sentence Completion.**   Write the correct verb form in parentheses in the blank space. First you must find the subject. Is the subject singular or plural? Choose the verb that agrees in number with its subject.

Iris Love is a famous archeologist. She (work, works) __*works*__
(1)

in Turkey. Many archeologists (dig, digs) __*dig*__ with
(2)

her. They (bring, brings) _____*bring*_____ the past to life. But Iris
                              (3)
Love also (discover, discovers) _____*discovers*_____ the past of New
                                        (4)
York City. She sometimes (dig, digs) _____*digs*_____ in Central
                                              (5)
Park. Many secrets of New York City (lie, lies) _____*lie*_____
                                                      (6)
in the earth of Central Park.

2. **Scrambled Sentences.**   The words in each item form a complete English
   sentence, but they are out of order. Rewrite the words in the correct order so
   they form a correct sentence. Punctuate the sentence. Remember to look for
   the verb first. Then find its subject.

| ground | . | archeologists | maps | the | draw | of |

Archeologists draw maps of the ground.

---

a. everything   an archeologist   .   writes   in a notebook
b. us   .   tell   archeologists   a lot   the past   about
c. the past   us   .   informs   the present   about
d. find   sometimes   archeologists   .   bodies   dead
e. gods   students   and   goddesses   about   .   like
   stories

3. **Controlled Writing.**   Rewrite the following paragraph. Change the subject
   Paula and Brian to the singular subject *Paula*. Change the pronoun *they* to
   she. Change all the verbs to the Third Person Singular. Your first sentence
   will be the following: *My friend Paula is an archeologist.*

> My friends Paula and Brian are archeologists. They know a lot about
> the past. Every summer they dig in Turkey. Usually they find pieces of
> pots and dishes, but sometimes they discover gold and silver objects.
> Paula and Brian always send me splendid photographs of Turkey. They
> want me to visit them in Turkey one summer. They want me to dig with
> them.

Plurals

An archeologist is one person. *Archeologist* is singular. *Archeologists* refers to
more than one person. *Archeologists* is plural.

1. **Regular Plurals.**   Most regular plurals are formed by adding *s* to the singular form.

Singular	Plural
a map	maps
a boy	boys

Regular plurals of words ending in *y* preceded by a consonant are formed by changing the *y* to *i* and adding *es*.

Singular	Plural
a library	libraries

Regular plurals of words ending in *sh* or *s* are formed by adding *es* to the singular form.

Singular	Plural
a class	classes
a wish	wishes

Fill in the blank spaces with the correct singular or plural form.

Singular	Plural
a secret	*secrets.*
a goddess	*goddesses.*
Tool.	tools
a body	*bodies*
a piece	*pieces*
_____	objects
a toy	*toys*
a country	*countries.*

_____game_____   games

a dish   _____dishes._____

a story   _____stories._____

a brush   _____brushes._____

_____place_____   places

When we write about objects in the singular, we use the indefinite article *a* or *an* in front of them. When we write about plural objects, we do not use *a* or *an*.

2. **Irregular Plurals.**   Irregular plurals do not follow one pattern. Study the following list of irregular plurals.

Singular	**Plural**
a man	men
a woman	women
a child	children

Sentence Completion.   Choose the correct word in parentheses to fill in the blank space in each sentence.

a. (place, places) Archeologists go to many _____places_____ to dig in the earth.

b. (child, children) Many _____children_____ like to dig in the park.

c. (object, objects) An archeologist is happy to find a gold _____ in the earth.

d. (man, men) Most _____men_____ a thousand years ago were farmers.

e. (body, bodies) Archeologists sometimes find a dead _____body_____ when they dig in the earth.

f. (map, maps) Archeologists make careful _____map_____ of the places where they dig.

g. (woman, women) A _____woman_____ of the past usually made her own clothing.

h. (story, stories) Do you like to read _____stories_____ about men and women of the past?

i. (piece, pieces) Chinese people of the past often wrote on _Pieces_ of bone.

Prepositions *To* and *From*

Prepositions are short but important words in English. They show the relationships among things, people, and places. The words *to* and *from* are prepositions. They tell us in which direction things or people move. *To* usually shows a forward direction. *From* often has the meaning of away or out of.

> **Iris Love comes *from* New York. She goes *to* Turkey in the summer.**

1. **Recognizing Prepositional Phrases.**   A prepositional phrase is a group of words that begins with a preposition. Prepositional phrases with *to* or *from* usually include places or people. Listen carefully and read the following paragraph silently as your instructor reads it aloud. Underline the prepositional phrases with *to* or *from*. The first one is done for you.

> Archeologist Iris Love comes from New York. She often goes to Turkey in the summer. She gives careful directions to her workers. The workers bring maps and tools to the field. They bring objects from the earth to the laboratory. Ms. Love sends objects from the field to Turkish museums. We learn a lot about the past from these objects.

2. **Answering Questions with Prepositional Phrases.**   Write the answers to the following questions in complete sentences. Underline the prepositional phrases in your answers.

    a. What country do you come from?
    b. Where do you often go on a nice day?
    c. Is the plane ride from New York to London one hour or six hours?
    d. Do you walk or ride to work?
    e. Do you send many letters to your relatives?
    f. Do you walk home from school alone or with friends?
    g. At what time do you go to school?

Adverbs of Frequency

The words *always, usually, often, sometimes, rarely,* and *never* tell us how often we do things or how often things happen. Study the following chart.

The desert sands covered the Egyptian Sphinx many times in the past. The ancient legend says that the Sphinx asked travelers the following riddle: What walks on four legs in the morning, two legs in the afternoon, and three legs in the evening? Can you guess the answer? What stories do you know about ancient monuments in your country?

always	usually	often	sometimes	seldom rarely	never
100% of the time		less than half of the time			none of the time

1. **Dictation.**   Write each sentence as your instructor dictates it.

    a. I always like to read about the past.
    b. My friend sometimes digs in Mexico.
    c. She rarely finds gold and silver objects.
    d. She often discovers dishes in the earth.
    e. She never keeps any objects for herself.

2. **Sentence Building.**   Make a complete sentence using the words in each set. Add as many words as you need to make a correct, interesting sentence. Do *not* change the form or the order of the given words.

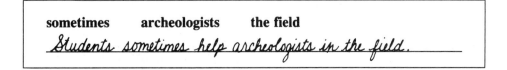

sometimes   archeologists   the field

Students sometimes help archeologists in the field.

    a. often   in Mexico   summer

    b. archeologists   rarely   articles of clothing   the earth

    c. usually   wash   the   in   laboratory

    d. always   examines   carefully

    e. sometimes   discovers   paintings   statues

3. Sentence Composing. Write a complete sentence following the directions for each item. The first one is done for you.

    a. Tell when you usually eat lunch.

        I usually eat lunch at 1 p.m.   .

    b. Tell where children often play.

    c. Tell what you sometimes find in your pocket.

    d. Tell what piece of clothing you rarely wear in winter.

    e. Tell whether you usually watch TV or listen to the radio at night.

    f. Tell what an artist always needs.

    g. Tell where a scientist sometimes works.

Punctuation and Capitalization

In English every new sentence begins with a capital letter. Every complete sentence ends with a period. The names of countries, states, and cities begin with capital letters. Punctuate and capitalize the following paragraph.

       my friend is an archeologist every summer he digs in mexico or colombia he digs for objects from the past he usually finds pots and dishes sometimes he finds gold and silver next summer i am going to mexico with him we will look for interesting discoveries in the earth

Only one English pronoun is always capitalized. It is capitalized at the beginning of a sentence and within the sentence. Do you know which pronoun this is? Can you find it in the paragraph? Did you capitalize it?

COMPOSING

Read this paragraph about a daily schedule.

       Archeologists usually have a busy day. They eat breakfast at 6:00 A.M. Then they go to work in the field. They usually dig until 11:00 A.M. Then they have a lunch break. They often eat lunch with other archeologists. At 6:00 P.M. they go to their rooms. They sometimes study the objects in the evening. They always go to sleep late.

Notice that specific times of the day follow the preposition *at: at* 6:00 A.M.; *at* 11:00 A.M.; *at* 6:00 P.M. Use such expressions in your own paragraph.

Notice the use of the word *then*. When one thing happens after another, we use the word *then* to introduce the second thing. Use the word *then* in your paragraph.

1. **Developing a Paragraph.**

   a. Use the following words to write a paragraph about your daily schedule. Use the paragraph about an archeologist's day to guide you.

      I   busy   day / I   breakfast   A.M. / go   school / Usually   until   A.M. (noon) / I   a lunch break   / often lunch   friend (alone) / I   home   P.M. / Sometimes homework (watch TV) *in the* evening   / always   to sleep late (early)

   b. Now rewrite your paragraph from Exercise *a* about your best friend, your child, or your sister or brother. Use the appropriate singular pronouns and verb forms. Add three new sentences to the paragraph.

2. **Composing a Paragraph.**

   a. In Paragraph [3] of the reading passage you are told about the steps archeologists follow when they work in the field. Compose a paragraph that describes the steps you take to do a certain activity. Here are some suggestions for topics: washing a car, dressing a baby, making a sandwich, buying a new pair of shoes, taking a photograph.

   b. To practice writing in the Third Person Singular, rewrite your paragraph using another person such as your brother, father, or sister as the subject.

CHAPTER ONE B

GEOLOGY: ROCKS REVEAL THE PAST

PREREADING

Class Discussion. The time line on page 19 shows plants and animals from the early period of life on earth to the present.

How long ago was the Age of Dinosaurs? What kind of living things existed before the dinosaurs? Which appeared first on earth: mammals or flowering plants? In what era did human life appear on earth?

New Words. Try to understand the meanings of these words as they are used in the reading passage. Use a dictionary when necessary.

extraordinary	protect	fragment
active	machinery	related
proper	discovery	behavior
fragile	skeleton	

READING

Skeletons of America's Past

[1]   Fossils are the remains of plants and animals of past eras. Fossils give us a picture of early human life. They also show us a picture of life millions of years before the existence of human beings. At that time extraordinary reptiles called dinosaurs were active on the earth. Geologists working in the United States often find the fossil bones of dinosaurs.

[2]   Some geologists spend time in western states like New Mexico, Texas, or Wyoming, digging for dinosaur bones. They climb over the rocks looking for proper places to dig. When they see signs of fossils in the area, they start the

Time Line

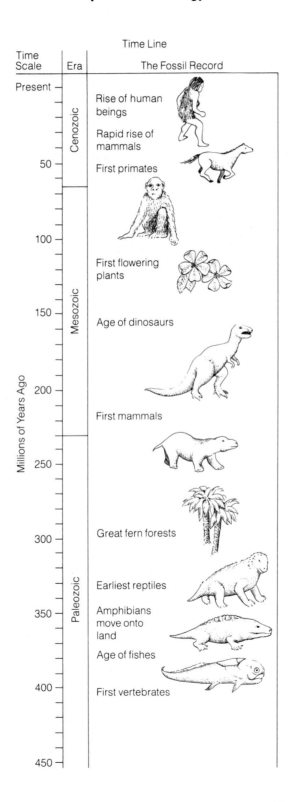

Time Scale	Era	The Fossil Record
Present	Cenozoic	Rise of human beings
		Rapid rise of mammals
50		First primates
100	Mesozoic	First flowering plants
150		Age of dinosaurs
200		First mammals
250	Paleozoic	
300		Great fern forests
		Earliest reptiles
350		Amphibians move onto land
		Age of fishes
400		First vertebrates
450		

Millions of Years Ago

Geologists work carefully because fossil bones are very fragile. Here an American geologist starts the difficult work of cutting into stone. Write five sentences about this picture using words from the New Word list.

difficult work of cutting into stone. They work carefully because fossil bones are very fragile. As the fossils appear, the geologists put paper and paint over them to protect them. Then they cut away the rocks in large pieces. They use heavy machinery to remove the rocks from the ground. Geologists have an active life. By hard work they often make exciting and important discoveries.

[3]   Geologists look over their discoveries in a museum laboratory. With the help of technicians they fit all the fossils together properly for careful study. Sometimes the rocks reveal whole dinosaur skeletons. Some of them are eighty-five feet long and eighteen feet high. Some dinosaur skeletons have wing bones and look like strange birds. Other skeletons look like giant fish. But geologists usually find only fragments of the reptiles, such as heads, teeth, feet, and tails. They sometimes discover eggs four and a half inches long, but they rarely find the fossils of babies.

[4]   Geologists try to find out how dinosaurs lived. They study the size of the teeth, feet, and brain. Then they compare the dinosaurs with related living reptiles such as crocodiles, alligators, and turtles. They also compare them with elephants because of their great size. They study the eating habits, movements, and intelligence of these living animals. In this way geologists are able to understand something about the behavior of dinosaurs.

[5]   Dinosaurs are extinct; they are gone forever. But we can see their bones and learn about their life habits in such places as the American Museum of Natural History in New York City, the Los Angeles Museum in Los Angeles, California, or the Natural History Museum in Chicago, Illinois. Geologists do an extraordinary job of showing us America's past from a few pieces of rock.

Summary Completion.   Fill in the blank spaces with the correct word from the reading passage.

Fossils show us a picture of life millions of years before (1) _____ beings. Geologists often find the fossils bones of (2) _____ . They go out west to look for proper places to (3) _____ . By hard work they often make exciting and (4) _____ discoveries. Geologists look over their discoveries in a (5) _____ laboratory. They fit all the fossils (6) _____ for careful study. Geologists compare the dinosaurs with related living (7) _____ . We learn about the life (8) _____ of dinosaurs when we visit a natural history museum.

VOCABULARY

1. **Expanding Vocabulary.**   Replace the italicized word(s) in each sentence with a word from the New Word list.

    a. The western states are the best places for the *new finding* of fossil bones.

    b. Even a *broken piece* of rock can be important to a geologist.

Geologists lead an active life. Does this look like interesting work to you? Discuss why or why not.

c. Sometimes geologists find not the *bone structure* of a dinosaur but only its footprints in the ground.

d. Geologists use *mechanical equipment* to lift the heavy rocks into trucks.

e. Laboratory technicians can't remove the *delicate* fossils from the rocks without the *right* tools.

f. Fossil bones don't show the *conduct* of dinosaurs, but they give us an idea of how they did things.

g. The crocodile is the living reptile most closely *connected* to the dinosaur.

h. After reptiles lay their eggs, they cover them up with dirt to *guard* them.

i. Dinosaurs were often *in motion,* looking for food, fighting other animals, and building nests for the eggs.

j. The elephant is a very large animal, but some dinosaurs were *exceptional* in size.

2. Using Vocabulary.   Follow the directions for each item.

a. Each sentence uses an antonym, or word that is opposite in meaning, from a word in the New Word list. Substitute an antonym from the New Word list for the italicized word in each sentence so that the sentence makes sense.

(1) Fossil eggs are very *strong*.

(2) A geologist is a *lazy* person.

(3) It is important to look for *unsuitable* places to dig for fossil bones.

(4) Everyone enjoys seeing the skeletons of *common* animals in the museum.

(5) When baby reptiles come out of their eggs, they run away and hide to *hurt* themselves.

b. Draw a line from each item in Column A to the related item in Column B. Then rewrite each complete item as a sentence.

A	**B**
(1) *Skeletons* of humans and animals	**(a)** are *related* by marriage
(2) Scientists make many great *discoveries*	**(b)** you can study its *behavior*
	(c) are bodies without flesh or skin
(3) A woman and her husband	**(d)** that help people live a better life
(4) If you have a dog or a cat,	**(e)** we must be careful not to get hurt
(5) The *fragments* of a rock	**(f)** can tell us a lot about the past
(6) When we use *machinery,*	

3. Word Families.   Study the following lists.

Type of Work	Person Who Does That Type of Work
science	scientist
geology	geologist
astronomy	astronomer
history	historian
mathematics	mathematician
teaching	teacher

Sentence Completion.   Choose the correct word in parentheses to fill in the blank space in each sentence.

a. (Teaching, Teacher) _____ is an important part of a geologist's work.

b. (anthropology, anthropologist) An _____ studies the behavior and beliefs of people, past and present.

c. (Biology, Biologist) _____ is the study of plant and animal life.

d. (history, historian) An _____ is a person who studies and writes about the past events of a country and its people.

e. (science, scientist) Biology, chemistry, geology, and astronomy are all parts of the general subject called _____ .

f. (Astronomy, Astronomer) _____ is the science of the stars and the planets.

g. (Mathematics, Mathematician) _____ is a difficult subject for some students.

READING COMPREHENSION

1. Understanding the Text.   Follow the directions for each item.

   a. Mark the following sentences *True* or *False* according to the information in the reading passage. Underline the part of the passage where you find your information.

      (1) Some geologists dig for fossil bones in Texas. _____

      (2) Geologists remove heavy rocks by themselves. _____

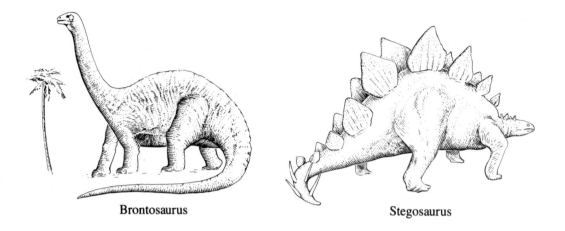

Brontosaurus   Stegosaurus

(3) Geologists find only whole dinosaur skeletons. _____

(4) Baby dinosaur fossils are rare. _____

(5) A turtle's behavior is related to a dinosaur's behavior. _____

(6) Dinosaurs are active on the earth today. _____

b. Circle the letter of the correct answer.

(1) In Paragraph [1], the third sentence, *they* refers to

    a. geologists.   **b.** fossils.   **c.** human beings.

(2) As the fossils appear, the geologists

    a. climb over them.

    b. cut them in large pieces.

    c. protect them.

(3) In Paragraph [3], the fourth sentence, *some of them* refers to

    a. skeletons.   **b.** feet.   **c.** rocks.

(4) According to Paragraph [3],

    a. dinosaurs rarely had babies.

    b. all dinosaurs had wings.

    c. some dinosaurs looked like birds or fish.

(5) In Paragraph [4], the last sentence, the expression *In this way* means

    a. by working hard.

    b. by making comparisons.

    c. by using machinery.

(6) From Paragraph [5] we learn that

    a. all reptiles are extinct.

    b. dinosaurs live in the Los Angeles Museum.

    c. there are dinosaur exhibits in many American museums.

2. **Answering Information Questions.** Write the answers to the following questions in complete sentences.

    a. What are fossils?

    b. Name two western states where geologists dig for fossils.

    c. How do geologists protect the fossils?

    d. What do geologists use to remove the rocks from the ground?

    e. Where do geologists look over their discoveries?

    f. Do geologists compare dinosaurs with monkeys or elephants?

    g. Are dinosaurs living animals, or are they extinct?

    h. Name one museum where you can learn about dinosaurs.

3. **General and Specific Words.** A general word is a word used for a large group or class of things. A specific word is used to give us a special detail or example of a more general word.

> **General word: animal**
> **Specific word: dinosaur**
>
> **General word: teacher**
> **Specific words: geology teacher**

    a. For each set of words mark *G* next to the more general word(s) and *S* next to the more specific word(s). The first one is done for you.

      (1) state __*G*__   (2) head _____   (3) 85 feet _____

           Wyoming __*S*__   body _____   size _____

      (4) Boston _____   (5) alligator _____   (6) toes _____

           city _____   reptile _____   tails _____

           Chicago _____   turtle _____   fragments _____

      (7) eating habits ____   (8) geologist _____

           thinking _____   scientist _____

           behavior _____

b. In the blank space write a general word that names the group of specific words. The first one is done for you.

(1) dinosaurs   turtles   crocodiles   alligators *reptiles*

(2) New York   Chicago   Los Angeles   Dallas _____

(3) 4½ inches wide   16 feet long   25 feet high _____

(4) astronomer   biologist   chemist   geologist _____

(5) Wyoming   Texas   California   Florida _____

(6) eating   fighting   laying eggs   thinking _____

(7) a car motor   a tractor   factory tools _____

c. The topic of a paragraph or passage is the general idea or general subject. We use general words to talk about topics.

Circle the correct answer.

(1) The topic of the whole passage in this chapter is

    a. geologists' work with dinosaur fossils.

    b. the hard life of geologists.

    c. fossil bones in Texas.

(2) The topic of Paragraph [2] is

    a. how geologists use heavy machinery.

    b. how geologists paint dinosaur fossils.

    c. how geologists dig for dinosaur fossils.

(3) The topic of Paragraph [3] is

    a. dinosaur fossil discoveries.

    b. fragile dinosaur eggs.

    c. strange birds in the laboratory.

(4) The topic of Paragraph [4] is

    a. discovering living reptiles.

    b. comparing elephants and dinosaurs.

    c. understanding dinosaur behavior.

(5) The topic of Paragraph [5] is

    a. cities to visit in the United States.

    b. places to learn about dinosaurs.

    c. things to do in Chicago.

WRITING EXERCISES

Sentence Kernels

1. **Verbs.**   The verb is the heart of the English sentence. There cannot be an English sentence without a complete main verb. The main verb is the word that tells us the state of being, the feeling, or the action of a person, place, or thing.

A geologist *sends* fossil bones to a museum.

Recognizing Verbs.   Underline the verbs in the following sentences.

   a. Fossils give us a picture of early human life.
   b. Geologists climb over the rocks.
   c. They send fossil bones to a museum.
   d. A technician removes the bones from the rocks.
   e. We see dinosaur skeletons in the museum.

2. **Subjects.**   The subject of a sentence answers the question, *Who* or *what* is doing the verb action?

A geologist puts paint and paper over the bones. (Who puts?)

Recognizing Subjects.   Go back to sentences *a, b, c, d,* and *e.* Circle the subject of each underlined verb.

Identifying Verbs and Subjects.   Read the following paragraph carefully. Find the complete main verb in each sentence. Put each verb in the Verb column of the chart that follows. Then find the subject of each verb. Put the subject in the Subject column. The first one is done for you.

   (1) My friend Charles takes courses in geology. (2) He goes to Texas in the summer with other students. (3) They dig for fossils in the rocks. (4) They always take the fossil bones to the museum. (5) Sometimes Charles helps the technicians in the laboratory. (6) All the students return to school at the end of the summer.

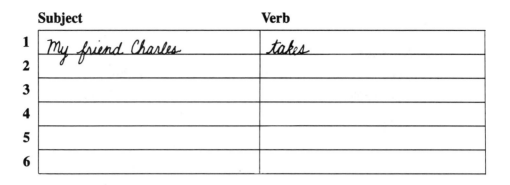

	Subject	Verb
1	My friend Charles	takes
2		
3		
4		
5		
6		

Simple Present Tense

The Simple Present tense is used to talk about things that are generally true. It is also used to talk about things that people usually do (not what they are doing right now). All the verbs in your Verb column are in the Simple Present tense.

> **Geologists *protect* the bones with paint and paper. (This is something they usually do.)**

Study the following Simple Present tense forms.

	Singular	Plural
First Person	I protect	A geologist and I protect We protect
Second Person	You protect	You protect
Third Person	A geologist protects He/She/It protects	Geologists protect They protect

Notice that only the Third Person Singular form has the extra *s* at the end.

1. **Sentence Completion.**   Write the correct verb form in parentheses in the blank space. First you must find the subject. Is the subject singular or plural? Choose the verb form that agrees in number with its subject.

   Dr. Edwin H. Colbert is an important American geologist. He sometimes (teach, teaches) _____ a course in geology at
   (1)
   Columbia University in New York. But he (do, does) _____
   (2)

most of his work in Arizona, where he (live, lives) _____ .
(3)

He and other scientists (collect, collects) _____ dino-
(4)

saur fossils in the United States. But they also (go, goes) _____
(5)

to Europe, Africa, and Asia to collect them. Dr. Colbert (study, studies)

_____ the fossils and (write, writes) _____
(6)   (7)

books about them. His wife, Margaret Colbert, (draw, draws) _____
(8)

pictures for his books. The pictures (give, gives) _____
(9)

us a very good idea of how dinosaurs looked.

2. **Scrambled Sentences.**   The words in each item form a complete English sentence, but they are out of order. Rewrite the words in the correct order so they form a correct sentence. Punctuate the sentence. Remember to look for the verb first. Then find its subject.

---

discoveries	and	.	a geologist	important	makes
exciting					

A geologist makes important and exciting discoveries.

---

a. spend   some   .   time   geologists   in Texas

b. whole   sometimes   finds   skeletons   .   a geologist

c. dinosaurs   with   compare   .   they   reptiles   living

d. us   the past   about   fossils   things   .   many
   tell

e. learns   in a museum   dinosaurs   .   a person   about

3. **Controlled Writing.**   Rewrite the following paragraph. Change the subject *Teresa and Steven* to the singular subject *Teresa*. Change the pronoun *they* to *she*. Change all the verbs to the Third Person Singular. Your first sentence will be the following: *My friend Teresa is a geology student.*

My friends Teresa and Steven are geology students. In the summer they usually go to Wyoming to look for fossils. They collect the fossils and bring them to a museum. Teresa and Steven study the fossils in the laboratory. Sometimes they do different jobs to help the geologists. They have an interesting time in Wyoming. They always write to tell me about their extraordinary discoveries.

Plurals

A geologist is one person. *Geologist* is singular. *Geologists* refers to more than one person. *Geologists* is plural.

1. **Regular Plurals.**   Most regular plurals are formed by adding *s* to the singular form.

Singular	Plural
a piece	pieces
a toy	toys

Regular plurals of words ending in *y* preceded by a consonant are formed by changing the *y* to *i* and adding *es*.

Singular	Plural
a discovery	discoveries

Regular plurals of words ending in *f* or *fe* are formed by changing the *f* or *fe* to *v* and adding *es*.

Singular	Plural
a knife	knives

Note that the plural of the words *belief*, *chief*, and *roof* are formed by adding *s* only.

Fill in the blank spaces with the correct singular or plural form.

Singular	Plural
a rock	_____
_____	wives
a fossil	_____
a city	_____

_____	bones
_____	babies
_____	animals
a life	_____
a fragment	_____
a university	_____
_____	toes
an activity	_____
_____	leaves
a shelf	_____

When we write about objects in the singular, we use the indefinite article *a* or *an* in front of them. When we write about plural objects, we do not use *a* or *an*.

2. **Irregular Plurals.** Irregular plurals do not follow one pattern. Study the following list of irregular plurals.

Singular	**Plural**
a mouse	mice
a tooth	teeth
a foot	feet

Sentence Completion.   Fill in the blank spaces in the following paragraph with the correct item from the Key. The first one is done for you.

Scientists spend _many hours in laboratories_ . They have to
                              (1)
work hard to make _____ . But if a sci-
                              (2)
entist works _____ during the day, he or
                              (3)
she can sometimes find time to do _____
                                            (4)
such as running or playing tennis. _____
                                                  (5)
like New York _____ sometimes run or
                              (6)
play tennis before or after work. But they try to protect themselves because
they can hurt _____ . They try to lead
                              (7)
_____ .
            (8)

Key

(1) **a.** many hour in a laboratories

　　b. many hour in laboratory

　　c. many hours in laboratories

(2) **a.** an important discoveries

　　b. an important discovery

　　c. important discovery

(3) **a.** in a university

　　b. in a universities

　　c. in university

(4) **a.** different activity

　　b. different activities

　　c. a different activities

(5) **a.** In large city

　　b. In a large cities

　　c. In a large city

(6) **a.** scientists and other instructors

　　b. scientist and other instructors

　　c. a scientists and other instructor

(7) **a.** fragile bone in their arm and foot

　　b. fragile bones in their arms and feet

　　c. a fragile bones in their arms and feet

(8) **a.** safe, active life

　　b. a safe, active life

　　c. a safe, active lives

Prepositions *To* and *From*

Prepositions are short but important words in English. They show the relationships between things, people, and places. The words *to* and *from* are prepositions. They tell us in which direction things or people move. *To* usually shows a forward direction. *From* often has the meaning of away or out of.

> **Dr. Colbert comes** *from* **Arizona. He goes** *to* **different western states in the summer.**

1. **Recognizing Prepositional Phrases.**   A prepositional phrase is a group of words that begins with a preposition. Prepositional phrases with *to* or *from* usually include places or people. Listen carefully and read the following paragraph silently as your instructor reads it aloud. Underline the prepositional phrases with *to* or *from*. The first one is done for you.

   The geologist Edwin H. Colbert comes <u>from Arizona</u>. He goes to different western states in the summer. He also goes to other countries. He collects fossils from all those places. He often goes to New York, where he talks to the geology students at Columbia University. Other students from all over the city also attend his lectures about fossils. He shows the fossils to them. The students learn a lot of interesting information from him and from his collection of fossils.

2. **Sentence Building.**   Draw a line from the item on the left to the correct prepositional phrase on the right. Then rewrite each complete item as a sentence.

a. I use soap to remove the dirt	to school by train
b. On weekends I often go	from my clothing
c. Foreign students get help	to laboratory technicians
d. My daughter borrows interesting books	from geology books
e. I write letters about my activities	to a museum
f. Every morning I go	from her school library
g. Geologists give careful directions	from New York to Chicago
h. We learn a lot about the past	to my family back home
i. It takes only two hours to fly	from their advisors and teachers

Adverbs of Frequency

Adverbs of frequency tell us how often we do things or how often something happens. The words *always, usually, often, sometimes, rarely,* and *never* are adverbs of frequency. Study the following chart.

always	usually	often	sometimes	rarely	never
100% of the time		less than half of the time			none of the time

1. **Dictation.**   Write each sentence as your instructor dictates it.

   a. My friend often finds fossils in the rocks.

   b. She always brings them to a museum.

   c. Sometimes she discovers whole skeletons.

   d. She rarely finds plant fossils.

   e. She usually writes me long letters.

   f. She never brings the fossils home.

2. **Sentence Building.**   Make a complete sentence using the words in each set. Add as many words as you need to make a correct, interesting sentence. Do *not* change the form or the order of the given words.

   > **often   dinosaurs   museums**
   >
   > *People often look at dinosaurs in American museums.*

   a. sometimes   summer   in Texas

   b. usually   paint   paper   bones

   c. rarely   fossils   babies

   d. often   machinery   remove   rocks

   e. always   rocks   museum

3. **Sentence Composing.**   Write a complete sentence following the directions for each item. The first one is done for you.

   a. Tell where you sometimes study your English lessons.

   I sometimes study my English lessons in the library.

   b. Tell when you usually go to bed.

   c. Tell what you always do in the evening.

   d. Tell what you often do on weekends.

   e. Tell what friend you never see during the week.

   f. Tell where you rarely eat lunch.

Punctuation and Capitalization

In English every new sentence begins with a capital letter. Every complete sentence ends with a period. The names of countries, states, and cities begin with capital letters. Punctuate and capitalize the following paragraph.

my   friend   patricia   is   a   geologist   every   summer   she   goes   out   west   to   wyoming   or   montana   she   looks   for   fossils   in   the   rocks   she   usually   discovers   animal   bones   sometimes   she   finds   plant   fossils   she   never   finds   human   fossils   in   that   part   of   the   united   states   i   am   interested   in   her   work   she   and   i   often   visit   the   museum   in   chicago   where   we   both   live

Only one English pronoun is always capitalized. It is capitalized at the beginning of a sentence and within the sentence. Do you know which pronoun this is? Can you find it in the paragraph? Did you capitalize it?

COMPOSING

1. **Developing a Paragraph.**

   a. First read the following paragraph. Do not fill in any blank spaces. Then read the paragraph again. For each numbered blank space, choose the correct sentence from the Key. Write that sentence in the blank space. Make sure you read the words before and after the blanks carefully so that your choices make sense. When you have finished filling in the blanks, write a title for the whole paragraph on the line provided.

   Geologists have an active life. They teach in colleges and universities during the school year. _____
   _____ . They also work in the science laboratory. _____
   _____ . In the evening they often go to
   (2)
   meetings. Sometimes they meet in a museum for a special lecture with other geologists. _____ .
   (3)
   On weekends they usually write reports or mark papers. But they also find time to do other activities. _____
   (4)
   _____ . Some of them play tennis or run in the park.
   _____ . During the
   (5)
   school year geologists work hard and play hard. They always enjoy themselves.

   Title: _____

Key

(1) a. They give lectures about different kinds of rocks and fossils.

b. They talk about the behavior of their children.

(2) a. They help their students to use English grammar properly.

b. They show their students the proper way to remove fossils from rocks.

(3) a. They usually finish their meeting at 3 P.M.

b. They usually go home at 10 or 11 P.M.

(4) a. They visit friends and relatives or go to parties.

b. They read books about rocks and mark exams.

(5) a. Others never have any fun.

b. Others swim at a health club.

b. When the following sentences are put in order, they will make up a paragraph about how one geologist spends his year. Rewrite these sentences in correct order and paragraph form. Your first sentence will be the following: *Professor Grayson has a very full schedule during the year.*

(1) During the nice spring weather he often takes his students on field trips to look for fossils.

(2) At the end of the summer Professor Grayson sends the fossils that they have gathered to a museum.

(3) From September to January he teaches geology to three sections of undergraduate students.

(4) He begins his year with the fall semester at college.

(5) Between fall and spring semesters Professor Grayson prepares lecture notes for his new classes.

(6) In the summer months he and some of his students dig for dinosaur bones in Texas.

2. Composing a Paragraph.

a. Think about all the things you do during the week and on weekends. Write a paragraph about your active life. Use the paragraph about geologists to guide you. Use the Simple Present tense in your sentences. Use adverbs of frequency in some of your sentences. Begin your paragraph with the following sentence: *I have an active life.*

b. To practice writing in the Third Person Singular, rewrite your paragraph using another person such as a friend or a relative as the subject.

CHAPTER TWO A

GEOGRAPHY: A STUDY OF EARTH

PREREADING

Class Discussion. What do the picture below and those on page 38 show? How do these things help you? When do you use them?

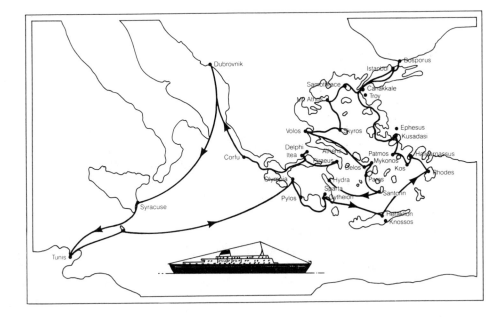

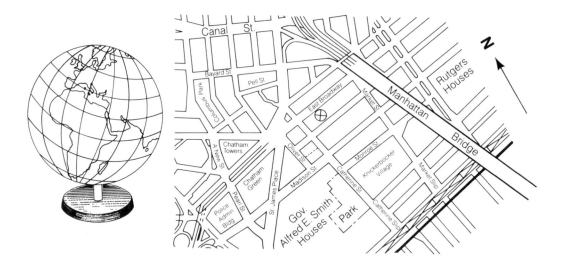

Look at the map of the world in the back of the book. Find your native country. How long does it take to fly from your native country to your new country? What other countries do you fly over? Which bodies of water do you fly over?

New Words.   Try to understand the meanings of these words as they are used in the reading passage. Use a dictionary when necessary.

basic	describe	population
surface	climate	dependent (on)
area	vegetation	serious

READING

The World We Live In

[1]   A knowledge of geography is basic for understanding the world around us. Geography is a study of the earth's surface. It informs us about all the land areas and bodies of water. It describes the climate and vegetation all over the world. It gives us details about the world's population. When we study geography, we use an atlas, or book of maps.

[2]   Maps show us large land areas. There are six main continents on the map. They are Asia, Europe, Africa, North America, South America, and Australia. There are many countries on these continents. For example, Canada, the United States, and Mexico are in North America. Brazil, Peru, and Ecuador are in South America. Italy, Denmark, and Greece are in Europe. Burma, India, and China are in Asia. Turkey is in both Europe and Asia. Kenya, Liberia, and Egypt are African countries. Australia is the only country on the continent of Australia.

[3]   There are many bodies of water on the earth's surface. Looking at the

map, we see that about three-fourths of the earth is water. The largest water bodies are the oceans. The three main oceans are the Pacific, the Atlantic, and the Indian. The Pacific Ocean is the largest body of water on earth. There are smaller bodies of water called seas, such as the Mediterranean Sea, the Caribbean Sea, and the South China Sea. There are thousands of islands in all the oceans and seas.

[4]   Climate is an important part of geography. The areas around the equator, or the middle of the earth, are always hot and wet. Java, for example, an island in the South China Sea, isn't far from the equator. So Java's climate is tropical all year long. The areas far from the equator are always very cold. The coldest climates are in areas close to the North and South Poles. Some areas aren't very hot or very cold. The climate of most European countries is temperate.

[5]   Vegetation is dependent on the climate. The different areas of the earth produce different kinds of vegetation. In tropical climates there is a lot of jungle vegetation. The trees produce fruit and seeds. In very cold climates there isn't any vegetation. In temperate climates the most important foods are rice, corn, and wheat. Rice, corn, and wheat are the basic foods of most people in the world.

[6]   There are now over three billion people on the earth. The population grows larger every year. People are dependent on vegetation. In some areas of the world there aren't enough basic foods for all the people. Overpopulation is a serious problem in these places. We learn many important facts about the world's population from the study of geography.

Summary Completion.   Fill in the blank spaces with the correct word from the reading passage.

(1) _geography_ is the study of the earth's surface. There are six main (2) _continents_ on the map. About three-fourths of the earth is (3) _water_ . (4) _Climate_ is an important part of geography. (5) _Vegetation_ is dependent on the climate. The world's (6) _population_ grows larger every year. In some areas there aren't enough basic (7) _food_ . This is a serious (8) _problem_ . We learn many (9) _important_ facts from the study of geography.

VOCABULARY

1. **Expanding Vocabulary.**   Circle the number of the word that is closest in meaning to the given word.

   a. area   (1) object   (2) region   (3) atlas

   b. surface   (1) inside   (2) map   (3) outside

c. basic   (1) most important   (2) oldest   (3) best
d. describe   (1) discover   (2) tell about   (3) pronounce
e. serious   (1) difficult   (2) special   (3) small
f. population   (1) number of places   (2) number of objects   (3) number of people
g. vegetation   (1) plant life   (2) animal life   (3) gold and silver
h. climate   (1) warm clothing   (2) weather conditions   (3) continent
i. dependent on   (1) free from   (2) different from   (3) supported by

2. **Using Vocabulary.**   Fill in the blanks in the following sentences with one word from the New Word list.

a. Geography books _____ different countries and people of the world.

b. The Caribbean Islands have a hot __*climat*__ all year long.

c. Children are __*dependent*__ on their parents for food.

d. In some countries the problem of overpopulation is very __*serious*__ .

e. The __*surfact*__ of the earth isn't flat.

f. Food, clothing, and houses are __*basic*__ needs of life.

g. Greece has a __*area*__ of nearly nine million people.

h. What kind of __*vegetation*__ grows well in your country?

3. **Word Families.**   A noun is the name of a person, place, or thing. An adjective describes a noun. It tells what kind of person, place, or thing. Adjectives and nouns are related to each other in meaning, but they usually have different forms.

He lives in the *south*.
            (noun)

***Southern Italy* has a *hot climate*.**
(adjective) (noun)   (adjective)(noun)

(What part of Italy? *southern*. What kind of climate? *hot*.)

Notice that in English adjective-noun combinations the adjective always goes before its noun. Study the following lists.

Noun	Adjective
Asia	Asian
Africa	African
China	Chinese
Greece	Greek
(the) south	southern
(the) north	northern
seriousness	serious
importance	important
difference	different

Sentence Completion.   Choose the correct word in parentheses to fill in the blank space in each sentence.

a.   (Africa, African) Liberia is an _African_ country. Kenya is also a country in _Africa_ .

b.   (difference, different) An atlas shows us _different_ areas of the world. Is there a _difference_ in the size of Europe and the size of Asia?

c.   (importance, important) The passage tells about the _importance_ of climate. Wheat is an _important_ food in temperate climates.

d.   (north, northern) Norway and Sweden are countries in _northern_ Europe. Spain isn't in the _north_ of Europe.

e.   (Mexico, Mexican) Corn is a basic _Mexican_ food. The people of _Mexico_ use it in many different ways.

f.   (wetness, wet) Java has a hot and _wet_ climate. Wheat doesn't grow there because of the _wetness_ .

g.   (seriousness, serious) Do you see the _seriousness_ of war? What are some other _serious_ problems in the world today?

READING COMPREHENSION

1.   **Understanding the Text.**   Follow the directions for each item.

a.   Match the topics listed in Column B with the paragraph number in Column A. Place the correct letter next to the paragraph number. Refer back to the passage as often as necessary.

A		B	
Paragraph [1] _d_		**a.**	bodies of water
Paragraph [2] _e_		**b.**	population of the earth
Paragraph [3] _a_		**c.**	climate in different areas
Paragraph [4] _c_		**d.**	the study of geography
Paragraph [5] _f_		**e.**	land areas
Paragraph [6] _b_		**f.**	vegetation of different climates

b. Circle the letter of the correct answer.

(1) The main topic of the whole passage is

    a. land areas and bodies of water.

    b. the study of geography.

    c. climate and vegetation in different areas.

(2) In Paragraph [1], the third, fourth, and fifth sentences begin with *it*. *It* refers to

    a. maps. **b.** geography. **c.** the earth's surface.

(3) According to Paragraph [2],

    a. Brazil is a continent.

    b. Canada and the United States are on the same continent.

    c. India and Peru are on the same continent.

(4) According to Paragraph [3],

    a. there is more water than land on the earth.

    b. seas are larger than oceans.

    c. there is more land than water on the earth.

(5) According to Paragraph [4],

    a. the climate of Java is temperate.

    b. most of Europe is hot and wet.

    c. most of Europe isn't very hot or very cold.

(6) According to Paragraph [6],

    a. the population of the earth stays the same every year.

    b. the population of the earth is larger now than in the past.

    c. the population is large in all areas of the world.

Rice is a basic food of many people in the world. Here, Indonesian women plant rice, the most important grain in Southeast Asia. Describe the different kinds of dishes prepared from grain in your culture.

   c. Using the information in Paragraphs [4] and [5], draw a line connecting the places on the left to the words on the right.

North and South Poles   fruit and seeds
Europe   no vegetation
Java   wheat and corn

   d. Mark *True* or *False* next to each statement. Underline the part of the passage where you find your answer.

    (1) We need maps to study the earth's surface. ____

    (2) Turkey is on two continents. ____

    (3) The largest bodies of water are seas. ____

    (4) There are many islands in the world. ____

    (5) The climate near the equator is temperate. ____

    (6) In temperate climates the earth produces wheat. ____

    (7) Everyone in the world has enough food. ____

2. Answering Information Questions.   Write the answers to the following questions in complete sentences.

   a. What is geography?

   b. How many main continents are there on the map?

   c. Name two countries in South America. *Brazil . peru*

   d. How much of the earth is water? *3/4 .*

   e. Is the Pacific Ocean larger or smaller than the Atlantic Ocean? *larger .*

   f. Where are the coldest climates? *North & south poles .*

   g. What is vegetation dependent on? *the climate.*

   h. Name the basic foods of most people in the world. *wheat rice corn.*

   i. Does the population of the earth grow larger or smaller every year?   *.*

3. **Identifying Main Ideas.** A main idea states the topic of a passage. It also tells something important about the topic. A main idea sentence is a general statement. It helps the reader to understand the writer's basic idea. Look for the main idea sentence in the following paragraph.

> The Pacific Ocean is the largest body of water in the world. It is seven thousand miles long. It is ten thousand miles wide. It takes many hours to fly over it in an airplane. The Pacific Ocean is also the deepest body of water. It is almost seven miles deep at its deepest part.

Underline the first sentence. It tells you the main idea of this paragraph. It tells the topic: *the Pacific Ocean*. It also tells something important about the topic: *The Pacific Ocean is the largest body of water in the world*. The first sentence is the most general statement in this paragraph.

Read the next paragraph and underline the sentence that contains the main idea.

> Water rises from the oceans and seas. It goes up into the air. The winds bring the wet air over the land areas. Then the water falls on the earth as rain. Oceans and seas produce the water we need to grow food.

The last sentence tells the topic: *oceans and seas*. It also tells something important about oceans and seas: *They produce the water we need to grow food*. The last sentence is the main idea sentence.

Circle the correct answer for each of the following questions.

   a. Which sentence tells the main idea of Paragraph [2]?

     (1) the first sentence   **(2)** the fifth sentence   **(3)** the last sentence

   b. Which sentence tells the main idea of Paragraph [3]?

     (1) The Pacific Ocean is the largest body of water on earth.

     (2) There are many bodies of water on the earth's surface.

     (3) There are thousands of islands in all the oceans and seas.

c. Which sentence tells the main idea of Paragraph [4]?

    (1) The areas around the equator are always hot and wet.

    (2) Some areas aren't very hot or very cold.

    (3) Climate is an important part of geography.

d. Which sentence tells the main idea of Paragraph [5]?

    (1) The different areas of the earth produce different kinds of vegetation.

    (2) The trees produce fruit and seeds.

    (3) Rice, corn, and wheat are the basic foods of most people in the world.

e. Which sentence tells the main idea of Paragraph [6]?

    (1) There are now over three billion people on the earth.

    (2) The population grows larger every year.

    (3) We learn many important facts about the world's population from the study of geography.

f. The main idea of the whole passage is the first sentence in

    (1) Paragraph [1].   **(2)** Paragraph [2].   **(3)** Paragraph [4].

In many parts of the world people like these Kurdish women still grind grain by hand.

WRITING EXERCISES

Simple Present Tense of *To Be*

The Simple Present tense of *to be* connects the subject with the rest of the sentence to show the existence of a person, place, or thing. It also describes or gives information about a person, place, or thing.

France *is* in Europe. (shows existence)
Gold and silver *are* metals. (describes or gives information)

Study the Simple Present tense forms of the verb *to be*.

	Singular	Plural
First Person	I am (I'm)	My friend and I are We are (We're)
Second Person	You are (You're)	You are (You're)
Third Person	A friend is He is (He's) She is (She's) It is (It's)	Friends are They are (They're)

The negative forms are *am not (I'm not), are not (aren't),* and *is not (isn't).*

1. **Sentence Kernels with *To Be*.**   Number each sentence in Paragraph [4]. There are eight sentences. In the following chart fill in the verb of each sentence in the Verb column. Then fill in the subject in the Subject column. Mark *S* if the kernel is singular. Mark *P* if the kernel is plural. The first one is done for you.

	Subject	Verb	S/P
Sentence 1	Climate	is	S
2	equators	are	P
3	island climate	isn't . is	S - s
4	Areas	are	P
5	climat.	are	P
6	arcas	aren't	P
7	climate	is	S
8			

2. **Sentence Completion.** Fill in the correct form of the verb *to be* in the following sentences. The first sentence in each pair is positive. The second sentence in each pair is negative. The first one is done for you.

a.   An atlas __*is*__ a book of maps. It __*isn't*__ an archeology book.

b.   Continents __are__ land areas. They __aren't__ countries or cities.

c.   The earth __is__ mostly water. It __isn't__ mostly land.

d.   European climate __is__ temperate. It __isn't__ like the climate of Java.

e.   Meat __is__ a basic food in some countries. It __isn't__ a basic food for most people in the world.

f.   The Hawaiian Islands __are__ in the middle of the Pacific Ocean. These islands __aren't__ part of a mainland area.

g.   All of us __are__ dependent on basic foods. We __aren't__ dependent on vegetation such as sugar, coffee, or tea.

There Is or There Isn't and There Are or There Aren't

When the subject of the verb *to be* is not a specific person or thing, we usually use the expression *there is* or *there are* + a noun. The negative forms are *there isn't* and *there aren't*.

	Verb	**Subject**	**Rest of Sentence**
There	is	a map	on the wall.
There	isn't	any vegetation	at the North Pole.
There	are	mountains	in Switzerland.
There	aren't	any people	in some areas of the world.

The subject is not *there*. The subject comes after the verb. When the subject is plural, the verb must be plural.

1. **Sentence Completion.**   In the following paragraph fill in the blank spaces with *there is* or *there are*. Use the negative where the directions say so. The passage is about Switzerland, a country in Europe.

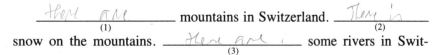

__There are__ mountains in Switzerland. __There is__
(1)   (2)
snow on the mountains. __There are__ some rivers in Swit-
(3)

zerland. ___*There are*___ also lakes. (negative) ___*there aren't*___
(4)   (5)
any dry areas. (negative) ___*There isn't*___ many people. (nega-
(6)
tive) _____ much land to grow food. But _____
(7)   (8)
enough food for all the people there.

2. **Matching.**   Draw a line matching the words on the left to the information
on the right. Then write the combined items as complete sentences.

a. There are   any vegetation in very cold climates
b. There is   six main continents on the map
c. There aren't   only one country on the Australian continent
d. There isn't   enough basic foods in some areas

When you have completed the sentences, put the subjects and verbs in the
correct places in the following chart. Mark *S* for singular and *P* for plural
sentences.

		Verb	**Subject**	**S/P**
Sentence a.	**There**	*are*		
b.	**There**			
c.	**There**			
d.	**There**			

3. **Sentence Composing.**   Write the answers to the following questions in complete sentences. Use *there is, there isn't* or *there are, there aren't* in your
answers. The first one is done for you.

a. Are there any students from Greece in your class?
    There aren't any students from Greece in my class.
b. How many people are there in your family?   2.
c. Is there a Spanish store in your neighborhood?
d. Are there any Chinese restaurants near your school?
e. Is there an atlas in your classroom?
f. How many books are there on your desk?
g. Are there any maps in your kitchen?

To Be + Adjective + Noun

Study the sentences in the chart.

Subject	Verb	Article	Adjective	Noun
Sweden	is	a	northern	country.
Sugar	isn't	an	important	food.
Wheat and rice	are		basic	foods.
Java and Borneo	aren't		dry	areas.

Adjectives don't change for plural nouns. Adjectives never add an *s* for plural nouns. Do we use the article *a* or *an* for plurals?

1. **Sentence Building.**   Draw a line from the subject on the left to the correct adjective-noun phrase on the right.

Subject	Adjective-Noun
a. An atlas	important city
b. I	basic food
c. Burma	serious problem
d. Overpopulation	cold area
e. Norway	deep body of water
f. Rice	careful worker
g. The North Pole	foreign student
h. The Pacific Ocean	northern country
i. New York	Asian country
j. An archeologist	special book

Now write a complete sentence with the Simple Present tense of the verb *to be*, using your matched items. Your first sentence will be the following: *An atlas is a special book.*

2. **Sentence Building with Plurals.**   Now rewrite each sentence from Exercise 1 using the following plural subjects.

   a. Atlases *are special books*
   b. We *are foreign students*
   c. Burma and China *an Asian country*
   d. Overpopulation and sickness *are*
   e. Norway and Sweden *are northern country*
   f. Rice and wheat *are basic food*
   g. The North and South Poles *an cold area*
   h. The Pacific and Atlantic Oceans *deep bodies*
   i. New York and Hong Kong *are important city*
   j. Archeologists *an serious problems*

Your first sentence will be the following: *Atlases are special books*. Remember that the article *a* or *an* is not used with plurals.

Prepositions *In* and *On*

Prepositions of Place.   *In* and *on* are prepositions of place. *In* tells you that someone or something is inside or within a place. *On* tells you that someone or something is on top of or on the surface of a place. Prepositions + places are called *prepositional phrases*. These phrases answer the question, *Where?*

Identifying Prepositional Phrases of Place.   The following prepositional phrases are taken from Paragraph [2] of the reading passage. Complete the list with the prepositional phrases of place from Paragraphs [3] and [4].

on the map   in North America
on these continents   in Europe
on the continent of Aus-   in both Europe and Asia
tralia

_____   _____

_____   _____

                                         _____

Prepositions of Time.   Some prepositional phrases with *in* and *on* tell us about time. They answer the question, *When?*

Identifying Prepositional Phrases of Time.   In the following sentences underline the prepositional phrases that answer the question, *When?* The first one is done for you.

a.   Archeologists usually study in the laboratory <u>in the evening</u>.

b.   <u>On July 4</u> Americans have a special holiday.

c.   There is usually snow <u>on mountains</u> even <u>in summer</u>.

d.   Many people like to go to the sea in August.

e.   Careful workers always get to work on time.

f.   In hot climates people often take a long rest in the afternoon.

g.   On the weekend we sometimes visit one of the museums in the city.

h.   In the past there were statues of gods and goddesses in many houses.

1.   **Paragraph Completion.**   Complete the given sentences with a prepositional phrase of place or time.

The living room in my apartment is very comfortable. There are pictures _____ (1) . There is a rug _____ (2) . There is a lamp _____ (3) . _____ (4) I usually sit _____ (5) and talk or read. There are books _____ (6) . _____ (7) my friends often visit me. There is always a lot of food _____ (8) . I like to put flowers _____ (9) of the table. Then the air _____ (10) always smells sweet.

2. **Adding Adjectives.**   Look back over the completed paragraph. Add an adjective in front of one noun in each sentence.

> Colorful
> **There are ⌃pictures <u>on the wall.</u>**
>   blue
> **There are pictures <u>on the ⌃wall.</u>**

3. **Sentence Combining.**   The first sentence in each group states the subject. The second sentence states the adjective. The third sentence states the place *where* or the time *when*. Place the adjective in the correct order, and add the prepositional phrase to make one complete sentence. Leave out any unnecessary words.

> **(1) There are students.**
> **(2) The students are French.**
> **(3) The students are in my class.**
> *There are French students in my class.*

  a. (1) There are objects.
     (2) The objects are ancient.
     (3) The objects are in the earth.

  b. (1) There are mountains.
     (2) The mountains are high.
     (3) The mountains are in Switzerland.

   c. **(1)** There are cities.

       (2) The cities are important.

       (3) The cities are in each country.

   d. **(1)** There are books.

       (2) The books are interesting.

       (3) The books are in the library.

   e. **(1)** There is a holiday.

       (2) The holiday is Irish.

       (3) The holiday is on March 17.

   f. **(1)** There are islands.

       (2) The islands are beautiful.

       (3) The islands are in the Caribbean Sea.

   g. **(1)** There are children.

       (2) The children are hungry.

       (3) The children are in many areas of the world.

   h. **(1)** There are news programs.

       (2) The news programs are special.

       (3) The news programs are in the evening.

   i. **(1)** There are oceans.

       (2) The oceans are large.

       (3) The oceans are on the earth's surface.

   j. **(1)** There is snow.

       (2) The snow is deep.

       (3) The snow is on the mountains.

   k. **(1)** There are problems.

       (2) The problems are serious.

       (3) The problems are in our cities.

Punctuation: Question Marks

A question mark (?) is placed after a sentence that asks a question.

   Information questions answer *who, what, where, when, how, which,* or *why.*
Yes or *no questions* can be answered with a yes or no.

Punctuating a Paragraph.   Read the following paragraph and punctuate it correctly.

This snow-colored polar bear lives near the North Pole where it is very cold. Since there is no vegetation there, polar bears live on fish. Write some sentences that describe the special kinds of food other animals eat.

Each country has a capital city The capital is the center of government Maps usually show capital cities with a star What is the capital of France The capital of France is Paris Quito is the capital of Ecuador and Lima is the capital of Peru Where is Tokyo Tokyo is in Japan Is Tokyo the capital of Japan Do you live in the capital city of this country

Capitalization of Proper Nouns

The names of all specific places are capitalized. The names of all continents, countries, cities, oceans, mountains, and so on are proper nouns. They are capitalized. The adjectives made from proper nouns are also capitalized.

Punctuation and Capitalization.   Correctly punctuate and capitalize the following paragraph.

most people in the united states and canada speak english we sometimes call these two places anglo-america most people in mexico, the caribbean islands, and south america speak spanish, french, or portuguese we often call these places latin america there are many latin americans in new york and los angeles are you from a latin american country do some of

your   classmates   speak   spanish   or   french   what   countries   are
they   from

COMPOSING

1.   Developing a Paragraph.

a. For each paragraph write a main idea sentence in the space provided.

(1) _____

In one part of Switzerland the people speak Italian. In another part
they speak French. In a third part the people speak Romansh. In the
area of Switzerland near Germany the people speak German.

(2) _____

It is warm in southern France most of the year. There isn't much rain.
There isn't any snow near the sea. The air is always fresh. The sun
usually shines all day. The evenings are cool.

(3) _____

There are books about geography. There are atlases. There are math
and science books. There are also storybooks. School children use
the library a lot. Adults also find good books to read there.

(4) _____

Rice grows well in northern Italy. Farmers plant wheat in the central
areas of the country. They also grow corn and barley. In the south
there are many fruit trees. Olive trees grow well in many parts of
Italy.

b. Combine the following sentences into longer, more interesting statements
to form a paragraph about Mexico. Leave out all the unnecessary words.
Rewrite your complete new paragraph on a separate sheet of paper.

(1) I like to visit Mexico.

(2) (because) There are many beautiful places there.

(3) There are mountains.

(4) The mountains are high.

(5) The mountains are near the ocean.

(6) The ocean is the Pacific.

(7) The ocean is on the west coast of Mexico.

(8) There is also jungle.

(9) The jungle is in the center of Mexico.

(10) There are/ruins in the jungles.

(11) The ruins are ancient. *Indian*

(12) The ruins are Indian.

(13) Vera Cruz is a city in Mexico.

(14) Vera Cruz is on the east coast of Mexico.

(15) Vera Cruz has a climate.

(16) The climate is tropical.

(17) There are beaches in Vera Cruz.

(18) The beaches are splendid.

(19) There are so many places in Mexico.

(20) These are places to enjoy.

2. **Composing a Paragraph.**

   a. The following questions are about you and your native country. Answer each question with a complete sentence. Write your answers in the form of a paragraph on a separate sheet of paper. You may add more sentences about the geography of your country if you wish.

      (1) What is your name?

      (2) Where are you from?

      (3) Where is your country?

      (4) What is the capital city of your country?

      (5) What kind of climate does your country have?

      (6) What are some of the basic foods?

      (7) Is there a large population or a small population?

      (8) Where do the people go on vacation in your country?

      (9) On vacation do you like to go to the ocean or to the mountains?

   b. In a paragraph similar to the one about Mexico, describe some of the beautiful places to visit in your native country or in the area where you are now living. Think about such natural features as mountains, bodies of water, forests, and beaches.

CHAPTER TWO B

THE UNITED STATES: LAND OF MANY CULTURES

PREREADING

Alphabetizing. The people of the United States come from many different cultural backgrounds. The following is a partial list of these cultures. Rewrite this list in alphabetical order. Number the items from 1 to 22.

Mexican	Japanese	Iranian	Russian
Greek	Lebanese	Chinese	Dutch
Indian	Hungarian	British	Scandinavian
Creole	Hispanic	Vietnamese	Polynesian
African	Polish	Filipino	
French	Eskimo	Italian	

Are the people from your background listed here? Tell how your culture celebrates the New Year.

New Words. Try to understand the meanings of these words as they are used in the reading passage. Use a dictionary when necessary.

ancestor	celebrate	ceremony	occasion
immigrant	native	delicious	ancient
preserve	descendant	skillful	

READING

Hawaiian Feasts and Festivals

[1]   The United States is a land of many cultures. Its people come from different homelands. They bring their own customs from all parts of the world. Many people follow the traditions of their ancestors in their new homeland. The

The United States is a land of many cultures. Its people come from many different homelands.

United States is a richer and more interesting country because of its immigrants and their way of life.

[2]   When people come to a new land, they like to preserve their traditions and pass them on to their children. So, many Americans continue to speak their native languages in addition to English. They cook food in their own way. They celebrate the holidays and festivals of their native culture. They have their own religious ideas. They have different ways of thinking about life and death.

[3]   Hawaii is America's island state far out in the Pacific Ocean. Many of Hawaii's people are descendants of immigrants from different parts of Asia. Most of these Asians are of Japanese ancestry. The parents and grandparents of other Hawaiians came from China, the Philippine Islands, and Korea. In addition, there are some Polynesians in Hawaii. Their ancestors came to Hawaii thousands of years before any other people. Hawaii is rich in traditions. Hawaiians are Americans, but they have preserved the ceremonies of their homelands.

[4]   People from all over Hawaii come to see the Japanese O-bon Festival in memory of dead relatives and friends. This is an important part of the Buddhist religion. The O-bon ceremonies take place in July and August on Oahu, the main island of Hawaii. There is music of drums and flutes in the courtyards of Buddhist temples. Men and women, wearing traditional clothing called *kimonos,* do the folk dances of their ancestral land. In the evening the people go to the seashore. They place paper lanterns on hundreds of tiny wood boats. These lights lead the souls of the dead across the dark waters to rest until the next year.

[5]   Chinese-Hawaiians have their own way of celebrating the past. For the Moon Festival in mid-August, Chinese stores sell delicious round cakes filled with meat. On the night of the full moon, families get together in a garden or open-air space to eat these cakes and drink tea. The cakes are the same shape as the bright moon they see in the sky. Then the people remember how their ancestors won a war by sending secret messages to each other in round cakes. The Moon Festival is important because it helps Chinese-Hawaiians to recall the story of their brave ancestors.

[6]   The Hawaiian Islands are also rich in Polynesian traditions. The Polynesians love the sea. They are skillful swimmers, sailors, and fishermen. Some of the young men still catch fish with spears, as their great-grandfathers did. Sometimes they have a fishing party, called a *hukilau.* All the neighbors help catch fish with big nets. Then they cook the fish on the beach. On special occasions there is a *luau,* an outdoor feast under the trees. The food is cooked in an underground oven, or *imu,* and the people sit on the ground to eat in the style of their ancestors. At the end of a *luau* there is hula dancing. The graceful movements of the dance tell stories about the early Polynesians' long trip over the dangerous waters of the Pacific Ocean to find the beautiful islands of Hawaii.

[7]   Hawaii is only a small state of the United States. But its ancient traditions give it an important place in the American family of cultures. The richness of the United States comes from the gifts of other lands.

Summary Completion.   Fill in the blank spaces with the correct word from the reading passage.

The United States is a land of many (1) _____ . People like to preserve their traditions and pass them on to their (2) _____ . Many of Hawaii's (3) _____ are descendants of immigrants from Asia. They have preserved the ceremonies of their (4) _____ . The Japanese celebrate the O-bon Festival in memory of dead (5) _____ and friends. Chinese-Hawaiians eat cakes the same shape as the bright (6) _____ to recall the story of their ancestors. The islands are also rich in Polynesian (7) _____ . The *luau* is a (8) _____ under the trees with hula dancing afterward. Hawaii's ancient traditions have an important place in the (9) _____ family of cultures.

VOCABULARY

1. **Expanding Vocabulary.**   Choose the best word from the New Word list to fill in the blank space in each sentence.

   a. In the United States we _____ Independence Day on July 4. It is always a happy _____ .

   b. The Chinese are _____ cooks. They can prepare _____ meals quickly and easily.

   c. Folk tales and legends are stories that _____ traditions from times long ago. These _____ stories help people understand their past.

   d. An American bride usually wears a white dress for her wedding _____ .

   e. An _____ to the United States can learn to speak English by attending classes. Many foreign students learn English in school but still speak their _____ language at home.

   f. An _____ on my father's side was a soldier in the War of 1812. My mother is a _____ of a famous Dutch astronomer of the seventeenth century.

2. **Using Vocabulary.**   Follow the directions for each item.

   a. Circle the events that might call for a *ceremony*.

   a graduation   a national holiday   a summer vacation

   a death in the family   a grammar test

   b. Circle the items that would be good to *preserve*.

   trash   works of art   crime

   family photographs   peace   broken dishes

   c. Underline the sentences that explain why people might *celebrate* a special *occasion*.

      (1) They get a raise in salary.
      (2) They pass all their final exams.
      (3) They finish reading a good book.
      (4) They lose their house keys.
      (5) They win a free trip to Mexico.

   d. Circle the letter of the item that best completes the following sentences.

      (1) Chicken is *delicious*

         a. if you don't pay a lot for it.
         b. if you cook it with spices.
         c. if you buy it in the morning.

      (2) In *ancient* times

         a. everyone talked about the moon landing of 1969.
         b. people watched TV.
         c. there weren't any cars, trains, or planes.

      (3) Some people leave their *native* land

         a. to study in another country.
         b. to see the place where they were born.
         c. to visit a friend down the street.

      (4) If you want to learn more about your *ancestors*

         a. you can read about them in a newspaper.
         b. you can ask older relatives about them.
         c. you can look them up in the phone book.

      (5) Your *descendants* will be

         a. your brothers, sisters, and cousins.

    b. your grandparents, great-grandparents, and so on.

    c. your children, grandchildren, and so on.

e. Circle the words that are related in meaning to the word *immigrant*.

    imagination   immigration   immigrate   energy   migrate

3. **Word Families.**   A noun is the name of a person, place, or thing. An adjective describes a noun. Adjectives and nouns are related to each other in meaning, but they usually have different forms.

She is from *Hawaii*.
     (noun)

***Hawaiian men* are *excellent swimmers*.**
 (adjective) (noun)   (adjective) (noun)

(What kind of men? Hawaiian. What kind of swimmers? excellent.)

Notice that in English adjective-noun combinations, the adjective always goes before its noun. Study the following lists.

Noun	**Adjective**
America	American
Korea	Korean
(the) east	eastern
(the) west	western
richness	rich
tradition	traditional
culture	cultural

Sentence Completion.   Choose the correct word in parentheses to fill in the blank space in each sentence.

a. (west, western) California is a _____ state.

b. (culture, cultural) Mexican cowboys went to Hawaii and introduced the knowledge of horses from their own _____ .

c. (America, American) There are fifty stars on the _____ flag, one for each state.

d. (tradition, traditional) The _____ gift to visitors in Hawaii is a long necklace of flowers, called a *lei*.

e. (ancestor, ancestral) Many Americans save money to take a trip to their
_____ homeland.

f. (kindness, kind) Visitors to Hawaii always find _____
and friendly people to welcome them.

g. (Hawaii, Hawaiian) *Aloha* is the _____ word for welcome or good-bye.

h. (Korea, Korean) There aren't many people from _____
in Hawaii, but their number is growing every year.

i. (richness, rich) Immigrants from Scandinavia, Portugal, Spain, Ireland,
and Holland have added to the _____ of life in Hawaii.

READING COMPREHENSION

1. **Understanding the Text.**   Follow the directions for each item.

a. Mark the following sentences *True* or *False* according to the information
in the reading passage. Underline the part of the passage where you find
your answer.

(1) Many Americans follow the customs of their ancestors. _____

(2) Americans speak only English. _____

(3) Hawaii is a state of the United States. _____

(4) Many Hawaiians are of Asian ancestry. _____

(5) The O-bon ceremonies are part of the Christian religion. _____

(6) At the Moon Festival, Chinese-Hawaiians eat a large meal in a restaurant. _____

(7) The movements of the hula dance describe stories of the past. _____

b. Circle the letter of the correct answer.

(1) The topic of Paragraph [2] is

a. celebrating a holiday.
b. preserving traditions.
c. cooking in the United States.

(2) According to the information in Paragraph [3], most Asians in Hawaii

a. are of Chinese ancestry.

b. are from the mainland of the United States.

c. are descendants of immigrants from Japan.

(3) In Paragraph [3], the sixth sentence, the word *Their* refers to

   a. Filipinos.

   b. Koreans.

   c. Polynesians.

(4) The Polynesians were

   a. the first people in Hawaii.

   b. the last people to arrive in Hawaii.

   c. immigrants from Europe.

(5) The Japanese celebrate the O-bon Festival

   a. with a feast in a garden.

   b. with music and folk dancing.

   c. with a boat trip to Japan.

(6) In Paragraph [4], the last sentence, the words *these lights* refers to

   a. *kimonos*.

   b. wood boats.

   c. paper lanterns.

(7) The topic of Paragraph [5] is

   a. an important Chinese celebration.

   b. the full moon in Hawaii.

   c. delicious Chinese food.

(8) The ancient Chinese won a war

   a. by filling round cakes with meat.

   b. by using round cakes to send messages.

   c. by making cakes in the shape of the moon.

(9) According to the information in Paragraph [6], the Polynesians in Hawaii

   a. never do things as their ancestors did.

   b. catch fish only with spears.

   c. continue to practice some ancient customs.

(10) A *hukilau* and a *luau* are examples of

   a. Hawaiian dances.

     b. Polynesian traditions.

     c. Hawaiian flowers.

2. **Answering Information Questions.** Write the answers to the following questions in complete sentences.

     a. When did the ancestors of the Polynesians come to Hawaii?

     b. Is the O-bon Festival a part of the Buddhist religion or the Hindu religion?

     c. When do the O-bon ceremonies take place?

     d. What dances do men and women do during the O-bon Festival?

     e. What kind of cakes do Chinese stores sell for the Moon Festival?

     f. In what month is the Chinese Moon Festival?

     g. How do all the neighbors help catch fish for a *hukilau?*

     h. What is an *imu?*

     i. What happens at the end of a *luau?*

3. **Identifying Main Ideas.** A main idea states the topic of a passage. It also tells something important about the topic. A main idea is a general statement. It helps the reader to understand the writer's basic idea. Look for the main idea sentence in the following paragraph.

> The Honolulu Academy of Arts is the cultural center of Hawaii. There you can see Chinese paintings by Ma Fen and other masters. There are works by skillful Japanese artists. The Academy also has fine examples of Buddhist religious art. In addition, it has the best collection of Korean pottery outside of Asia.

Underline the first sentence. It tells you the main idea of this paragraph. It tells the topic: *the Honolulu Academy of Arts.* It also tells something important about the topic: *The Honolulu Academy of Arts is the cultural center of Hawaii.* The first sentence is the most general statement in this paragraph.

    Read the next paragraph and underline the sentence that contains the main idea.

> Kim Fong is Chinese, Polynesian, and Portuguese. Daniel Sato is part Japanese, part Korean, and part French. Josie Hall's grandparents came to Hawaii from Spain, and her father is from San Francisco. John Doi's father is a Filipino immigrant, and his mother is part Irish and part Norwegian. In Hawaii there are many people of mixed ancestry such as these.

The last sentence tells the topic: *people of mixed ancestry.* It also tells something important about the topic: *There are many people in Hawaii of mixed ancestry.* The last sentence is the main idea sentence.

Circle the correct answer for each of the following questions.

a. Which sentence tells the main idea of Paragraph [3]?

   (1) the first sentence   **(2)** the third sentence   **(3)** the last sentence

b. Which sentence tells the main idea of Paragraph [4]?

   (1) the first sentence   **(2)** the second sentence   **(3)** the third sentence

c. Which sentence tells the main idea of Paragraph [5]?

   (1) the third sentence   **(2)** the fourth sentence   **(3)** the last sentence

d. Which sentence tells the main idea of Paragraph [6]?

   (1) The Hawaiian Islands are also rich in Polynesian traditions.

   (2) They are skillful swimmers, sailors, and fishermen.

   (3) All the neighbors help catch fish with big nets.

WRITING EXERCISES

Simple Present Tense of *To Be*

The Simple Present tense of *to be* connects the subject with the rest of the sentence to show the existence of a person, place, or thing. It also describes or gives information about a person, place, or thing.

Hawaii *is* in the Pacific Ocean. (shows existence)
Turtles and alligators *are* reptiles. (describes or gives information)

Study the Simple Present tense forms of the verb *to be*.

	Singular	**Plural**
First Person	I am (I'm)	The teacher and I are We are (we're)
Second Person	You are (You're)	You are (You're)
Third Person	The teacher is He is (He's) She is (She's) It is (It's)	Teachers are They are (They're)

The negative forms are *am not (I'm not), are not (aren't),* and *is not (isn't).*

1. Sentence Kernels with *To Be*.   Read the following paragraph and number each sentence.

Hawaii is the fiftieth state of the United States. But it isn't part of the mainland. The state of Hawaii is a chain of islands in the Pacific Ocean. The islands are the tops of great underwater mountains. The mountain tops are quite high in some parts of the islands. Mauna Kea, the highest mountain, is almost fourteen thousand feet. Some areas aren't very mountainous. The farms are in the lowlands.

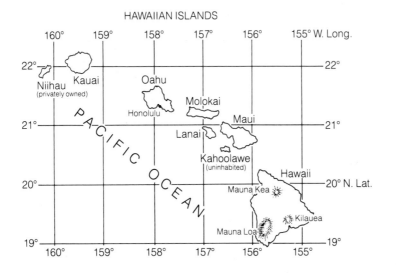

In the following chart fill in the verb of each sentence in the Verb column. Then fill in the subject in the Subject column. Mark *S* if the kernel is singular. Mark *P* if the kernel is plural. The first one is done for you.

	Subject	**Verb**	**S or P**
Sentence 1	Hawaii	is	S
2			
3			
4			
5			
6			
7			
8			

Now write sentences using these subject-verb kernels without looking back at the paragraph.

2. **Sentence Completion.**   Fill in the correct form of the verb *to be* in the following sentences. The first sentence in each pair is positive. The second sentence in each pair is negative. The first one is done for you.

   a. The weather ___*is*___ warm in most parts of Hawaii. It ___*isn't*___ warm high up in the mountains.

   b. Thanksgiving Day _____ a holiday in the United States. It _____ a holiday in other countries.

   c. The Philippine Islands _____ in the Pacific Ocean. They _____ far from the Asian mainland.

   d. English _____ difficult for some people. It _____ difficult for me.

   e. Crocodiles _____ reptiles. They _____ warm-blooded animals.

   f. I _____ only in my first year of college. I _____ ready to graduate.

   g. Fossils _____ fragile. They _____ easy to find.

There Is or There Isn't and There Are or There Aren't

When the subject of the verb *to be* is not a specific person or thing, we usually use the expression *there is* or *there are* + a noun. The negative forms are *there isn't* and *there aren't*.

	Verb	Subject	Rest of Sentence
There	is	a festival	in August.
There	isn't	any snow	in the lowlands.
There	are	beaches	all along the coast.
There	aren't	any roads	on some parts of the islands.

The subject is not *there*. The subject comes after the verb. When the subject is plural, the verb must be plural.

The graceful movements of the hula dance tell stories of Hawaii's past. The *lei* and *ti* leaf skirt are part of the traditional Hawaiian ceremonial dress. Describe a traditional dance in your culture.

1. **Sentence Completion.** In the following paragraph fill in the blank spaces with *there is* or *there are*. Use the negative where the directions say so. The passage is about Niihau, one of the Hawaiian Islands.

_____ only three hundred people on Niihau. (nega-
        (1)
tive) _____ any airplane service to the island. (nega-
        (2)
tive) _____ any visitors, except those who are invited
        (3)
by the people living there. _____ lots of sheep, horses,
                                        (4)
and wild pigs, but (negative) _____ any dogs. The peo-
                                        (5)
ple can't do farming because (negative) _____ much
                                                    (6)
water. _____ a public school for the children, but young
            (7)
people must leave Niihau if they want to continue their education. Many
of them return because _____ peace on the island. (neg-
                                    (8)
ative) _____ any policemen or private telephones. The
        (9)
people on Niihau want to preserve their ancient way of life.

2. **Matching.**   Draw a line matching the words on the left to the information on the right. Then write the combined items as complete sentences.

   a. There are   any farms high up in the mountains
   b. There is   many people of Japanese ancestry in Hawaii
   c. There aren't   much water on Niihau
   d. There isn't   music of drums and flutes during the O-bon Festival

   When you have completed the sentences, put the subjects and verbs in the correct columns in the following chart. Mark *S* for singular, and *P* for plural sentences.

		Verb	Subject	S/P
Sentence a	**There**			
b	**There**			
c	**There**			
	There			

3. **Sentence Composing.**   Write the answers to the following questions in complete sentences. Use *there is, there isn't* or *there are, there aren't* in your answers. The first one is done for you.

   a. How many states are there in the United States?

   There are fifty states in the United States.

   b. Is there a map of Hawaii in this book?
   c. How many verbs are there in this sentence?
   d. Are there any Portuguese students in your class?
   e. Is there any water on the moon?
   f. Are there any dinosaur fossils in the museum?
   g. How many ounces are there in a pound?

To Be + Adjective + Noun

Study the sentences in the chart.

Subject	Verb	Article	Adjective	Noun
A geologist	is	an	active	person.
Japan	isn't	a	large	country.
Polynesians	are		skillful	fishermen.
Dogs and cats	aren't		extraordinary	animals.

Adjectives don't change for plural nouns. Adjectives never add an *s* for plural nouns. Do we use the article *a* or *an* for plurals?

1. **Sentence Building.** Draw a line from the subject on the left to the correct adjective-noun phrase on the right.

	Subject	**Adjective-Noun**
a.	Japanese	delicious fruit
b.	A lion	small state
c.	Gold	serious student
d.	An apple	difficult subject
e.	*Aloha*	Asian language
f.	Hawaii	expensive metal
g.	I	American city
h.	Mauna Kea	wild animal
i.	Los Angeles	Polynesian word
j.	Chemistry	high mountain

Now write a complete sentence with the Simple Present tense of the verb *to be,* using your matched items. Your first sentence will be the following: *Japanese is an Asian language.*

2. **Sentence Building with Plurals.** Now rewrite each sentence from Exercise 1 using the following plural subjects.

a.	Japanese and Chinese	f.	Hawaii and Delaware
b.	Lions and tigers	g.	My brother and I
c.	Gold and silver	h.	Mauna Kea and Mauna Loa
d.	Apples and oranges	i.	Los Angeles and New York
e.	*Aloha* and *hukilau*	j.	Chemistry and astronomy

Your first sentence will be the following: *Japanese and Chinese are Asian languages.* Remember that the article *a* or *an* is not used with plurals.

Prepositions *In* and *On*

Prepositions of Place. *In* and *on* are prepositions of place. *In* tells you that someone or something is inside or within a place. *On* tells you that someone or something is on top of or on the surface of a place. Prepositions + places are called *prepositional phrases*. These phrases answer the question, *Where?*

Identifying Prepositional Phrases of Place.   Answer the following questions with a prepositional phrase of place with *in* or *on*. You will find the answers in the reading passage. The first one is done for you.

   a. Where is Hawaii? *in the Pacific Ocean*

   b. Where do the O-bon ceremonies take place? _____

   c. Where do the people dance to the music of drums and flutes?

       _____

   d. Where do the Japanese place paper lanterns? _____

   e. Where do Chinese families get together for the Moon Festival?

       _____

   f. Where do Polynesians have a *hukilau?* _____

   g. Where do Polynesians cook food for a *luau?* _____

   h. Where do people sit to eat at a *luau?* _____

Prepositions of Time.   Some prepositional phrases with *in* and *on* tell us about time. They answer the question, *When?*

Identifying Prepositional Phrases of Time.   In the following sentences underline the prepositional phrases that answer the question, *When?* The first one is done for you.

   a. Some geologists work in Texas <u>in the summer</u>.

   b. Hawaii became the fiftieth state on August 21, 1959.

   c. Many shops in my neighborhood are open on Sunday.

   d. There are many visitors in Hawaii in the winter.

   e. In the morning I sometimes have breakfast in a coffee shop.

   f. On special occasions we go to an expensive restaurant.

   g. The new semester usually begins in the middle of September.

   h. I would like to visit Asia sometime in the future.

1. Sentence Composition.   Study the following list of prepositional phrases of time and place.

   a. on Saturday night   **b.** in my English class   **c.** in the evening

   d. in the library   **e.** in the summer   **f.** in my native country

   g. on my street   **h.** on my birthday   **i.** on a rainy day

Write a sentence for each prepositional phrase in the list.

> **I usually meet my friends on Saturday night.**
> **There are many interesting geology books in the library.**

2. **Pair Dictation.**   Select three correct sentences from Exercise 1. Dictate these sentences to a partner. Then take dictation of three sentences from him or her.

3. **Sentence Combining.**   The first sentence in each group states the subject. The second sentence states the adjective. The third sentence states the place *where* or the time *when*. Place the adjective in the correct order, and add the prepositional phrase to make one complete sentence. Leave out any unnecessary words.

---

(1) **There is a restaurant.**
(2) **The restaurant is Chinese.**
(3) **The restaurant is in my neighborhood.**

There is a Chinese restaurant in my neighborhood.

---

a. (1) There are bowls.
    (2) The bowls are wooden.
    (3) The bowls are on the table.

b. (1) There are animals.
    (2) The animals are wild.
    (3) The animals are on some of the Hawaiian Islands.

c. (1) There are paintings.
    (2) The paintings are Chinese and Japanese.
    (3) The paintings are in the Honolulu Academy of Arts.

d. (1) There are workers.
    (2) The workers are skillful.
    (3) The workers are in my native country.

e. (1) There is a festival.
    (2) The festival is Polynesian.
    (3) The festival is in October.

f. **(1)** There is a holiday.

   (2) The holiday is American.

   (3) The holiday is on July 4.

g. **(1)** There are bones.

   (2) The bones are fragile.

   (3) The bones are in our body.

h. **(1)** There are seashells.

   (2) The seashells are beautiful.

   (3) The seashells are on the beach.

i. **(1)** There are dances.

   (2) The dances are traditional.

   (3) The dances are on special occasions.

j. **(1)** There are activities.

   (2) The activities are cultural.

   (3) The activities are on the weekends.

k. **(1)** There is an elephant.

   (2) The elephant is newborn.

   (3) The elephant is in the zoo.

Punctuation: Question Marks

A question mark (?) is placed after a sentence that asks a question.

   Information questions answer *who, what, where, when, how, which,* or *why.*
Yes or *no questions* can be answered with a yes or no.

Punctuating a Paragraph.   Read the following paragraph and punctuate it correctly.

   The mainland of the United States has four borders   Canada is on
the north   Which country is on the southern border of the United States
Mexico is on the southern border   Is the Atlantic Ocean to the east or to the
west   It is to the east   Where is the Pacific Ocean   The Pacific Ocean is on
the western border   Do you live near one of the borders of the United States

Early Hawaiians used outrigger canoes like this one to sail the Pacific Ocean.

Capitalization of Proper Nouns

The names of all specific places are capitalized. The names of all continents, countries, states, cities, oceans, mountains, and so on are proper nouns. They are capitalized. The adjectives made from proper nouns are also capitalized.

Punctuation and Capitalization.   Correctly punctuate and capitalize the following paragraph.

many people in the united states are bilingual they can speak english and the language of their ancestors some people in the city of new orleans, louisiana, speak french and english some people in the states of minnesota and wisconsin still speak swedish, german, and other european languages many people of mexican ancestry live in the southwest near the rocky mountains they know spanish very well are there many americans of asian ancestry what are some asian languages which languages do the people of hawaii speak do you know any polynesian words

COMPOSING

1. Developing a Paragraph.

   a. For each paragraph write a main idea sentence in the space provided.

      (1) _____

During the Aloha Festival, Polynesians wear traditional clothing of skins and feathers. The people act out stories of Hawaii's past. You can watch boat races and other sports contests. There is hula dancing. Everyone wears long necklaces of flowers called *leis*.

      (2) _____

Some of the workers make beautiful bowls and plates of wood. Many Hawaiians are skillful at weaving things from leaves and grass such as mats, bags, baskets, and hats. There are excellent workers who make articles of bone and shells. In some workshops the people make *leis* of silk or paper.

A visitor to Hawaii can try *kim chee,* a Korean vegetable dish. Japanese raw fish, called *sashimi,* is delicious. The Chinese make excellent dumplings filled with meat. You can have a fine meal of Polynesian roast pork. **(3)** _____

_____

   b. Combine the following sentences into longer, more interesting statements to form a paragraph about a festival in New Orleans. Leave out all unnecessary words. Rewrite your complete new paragraph on a separate sheet of paper.

      (1) New Orleans is a city.

      (2) New Orleans is in Louisiana.

      (3) There is a festival there.

      (4) The festival is exciting.

      (5) The festival is in the winter.

      (6) The festival is called Mardi Gras.

      (7) During Mardi Gras there is dancing.

      (8) The dancing is in the streets.

      (9) The dancing is all day and night.

     (10) The people wear masks.

     (11) The masks are interesting.

(12) The masks are to cover their faces.

(13) Everyone enjoys eating the food.

(14) The food is delicious.

(15) The food is Creole.

(16) The food is outdoors or in restaurants.

(17) New Orleans is a place to visit.

(18) The place is extraordinary.

(19) The time to visit is during the Mardi Gras celebration.

2. **Composing a Paragraph.**

   a. Write a paragraph describing a holiday, festival, or special occasion that is celebrated in your native culture. Use some of the following sentences to guide you in your description. Use correct paragraph form.

   (1) Tell the name of the holiday.

   (2) Tell where it takes place.

   (3) Tell when it takes place.

   (4) Tell the reason for the celebration.

   (5) Tell what the people wear.

   (6) Tell what kind of music and dancing there is, if any.

   (7) Tell what other activities there are during the day or at night.

   (8) Tell how people feel during the celebration.

   b. Food and drink are a special part of many celebrations. Write a paragraph in which you describe some special foods and drinks that are part of a celebration in your culture.

CHAPTER THREE A

SAVING OUR PLANET EARTH

PREREADING

Class Discussion. Study the following entry from the *Webster's New World Dictionary,* pocket-size edition:

> *pre.dict* (pri-dikt′), v.t. & v.i. [LL. *prae,* -before + *dicere,* tell], to make known beforehand; foretell; prophesy—predict′ a-ble, adj.—prediction, n.

What does the dictionary tell you about the entry word? What do the abbreviations mean?

Describe what you see in these pictures. Discuss these and other methods of predicting the future. How may predictions help us plan our future?

New Words.   Try to understand the meanings of these words as they are used in the reading passage. Use a dictionary when necessary.

travel	variety	explore
necessary	crowded	scientific
environment	universe	suitable
destroy	observe	

READING

Steps to the Future

[1]   Nine planets move around the sun. But the Earth has the best position among the planets. It doesn't travel too near or too far from the sun. It receives the necessary amount of heat and light. The air around the Earth keeps out the sun's dangerous rays. The sun dries up some of the ocean water, but the air turns it into rain. Sun, air, and water give us the change of seasons from autumn and winter to spring and summer. The Earth becomes green with vegetation. Without the Earth's special environment, there would be no life. If we change this environment, we may destroy some of the life on Earth.

[2]   The Earth is 4½ billion years old. At first it was a dead object of rock, without air or water. Now the Earth is the home of a variety of living things. All the varieties of plants and animals are dependent on the sun, on air and water, and on each other. The sun will shine for millions of years into the future. But will we be able to keep the Earth a special place among the planets?

[3]   The future of the Earth doesn't look bright. By the year 2000 there will be over six billion people on our planet. Even the farming areas of the world will be crowded with people. So farmers won't have a lot of land to grow food or to keep many animals. In twenty years bad air will produce more serious health problems. Chemicals will kill more fish in our rivers, lakes, and oceans. If we cut down too many trees, then many birds and wild animals won't have a home. We will destroy our environment if we don't plan for the future.

[4]   Scientists are discovering more about the universe and the Earth's place in it. They know that the Earth is only a tiny object among billions of others. They can observe new and dying stars through telescopes. They listen to radio signals from objects in deep space. They also send spaceships to explore the planets closely. According to the scientific information, no other planet but Earth has the air, water, and vegetation necessary for life. The scientific exploration of space is an important step to the future of the Earth. Learning about climate and conditions on other planets may instruct us in how to take better care of this one.

[5]   Space scientists are hopeful about the future. They are planning new projects such as building space stations near the Earth. They will observe the stars and planets from these stations. They will also study biology, medicine, and

chemistry there. They hope to find new ways of making the Earth a more healthful and comfortable place to live.

[6]   Someday astronauts, or space explorers, will travel to the moon again. The moon is a lifeless world, as the Earth once was. The astronauts will dig in the rocks below the moon's surface for signs of past life. Perhaps they will discover water in the rocks. Then they can grow some vegetation in a laboratory. Maybe later the vegetation will produce air in the moon's environment. Right now life on the moon seems difficult and dangerous. But perhaps in the future astronauts can change the environment to make it more suitable for scientific work. From their discoveries we can learn to make a safer environment for life on Earth.

[7]   Space explorers see the Earth as a beautiful planet in the sky. We must not destroy it by being careless. The Earth is our only home, and we should plan now for its future. It is necessary for people to live here in peace and work together for a better Earth and a brighter future.

Summary Completion.   Choose the correct word from the columns following the paragraph to fill in each blank space in the paragraph.

The Earth is the only (1) _____ *planet* _____ with an environment of air, water, and vegetation. All life is dependent (2) _____ *on* _____ these things. In the future there will be more (3) _____ problems on Earth. Perhaps we (4) _____ have all the varieties of living things. (5) _____ are discovering important information about the universe. The exploration of space may (6) _____ *teach* _____ us how to take better care (7) _____ the Earth. Astronauts will do (8) _____ work on the moon someday. Perhaps their work will help us (9) _____ our environment. We must all plan (10) _____ for a brighter future.

(1) star, planet
(2) from, on
(3) serious, splendid
(4) don't, won't

(5) Farmers, Scientists
(6) teach, learn
(7) leave blank, of

(8) crowded, dangerous
(9) save, destroy
(10) after, now

VOCABULARY

1. **Expanding Vocabulary.**   Choose the best word from the New Word list to fill in the blank space in each sentence.

a. Tokyo, Japan, with a population of over nine million people, is one of the most _____ cities in the world.

b. People all over the world want a better _____ for themselves and their children.

c. We must be careful not to _____*destroy*_____ life by using dangerous chemicals.

d. Spaceships send important _____ information about the planets back to the Earth.

e. In most countries there is a greater _____ of fruit and vegetables in summer than in winter.

f. On certain nights of the year we can easily _____ the planets Venus, Mars, and Jupiter in the sky.

g. Someday astronauts will walk around and _____ the oldest areas of the moon, the highlands.

h. The area around the South Pole doesn't have a _____ climate for growing food.

i. There are millions of stars in the _____ much bigger and brighter than our sun.

j. It is _____ for the governments of the world to make stronger laws against bad air and dirty water.

k. It takes 365 days for the Earth to _____ completely around the sun.

2. **Using Vocabulary.**   Each of the following sentences includes a word from the New Word list. Circle the number of the sentence that would correctly follow the given sentence.

a. It is difficult to read *scientific* reports about stars and planets.

   (1) Scientists use everyday language in their reports.
   (2) Scientists use a special vocabulary and mathematical signs.
   (3) Scientists describe the universe in an interesting way.

b. Bad air can *destroy* great paintings, statues, and buildings of the past.

   (1) The objects of the past will always remain the same.

(2) In the future we won't be able to see these things.

(3) People don't care about the art of the past.

c. The best place to *observe* the stars is high up on a mountain.

(1) The air is clear and there are no city lights.

(2) Mountain climbing is good for your health.

(3) You can't see the stars without a telescope.

d. Babies need a warm family *environment* to give them a safe feeling.

(1) They like to play with toys.

(2) They don't care about the things around them.

(3) They need love and care from parents and relatives.

e. Capital cities are often *crowded* with cars, buses, and taxis.

(1) Sometimes you can't cross the streets.

(2) It's easy to walk in these cities.

(3) There are many government office buildings.

f. Perhaps astronauts will *explore* Mars someday.

(1) They can't land on Jupiter.

(2) They will read about it in books.

(3) They will go over the surface carefully for signs of life.

g. On the African continent there are many *varieties* of wild animals.

(1) All the elephants look the same.

(2) You can see elephants, lions, and zebras.

(3) You can see tigers and lions in the zoo.

h. The Earth *travels* around the sun at eighteen miles per second.

(1) It certainly moves very fast.

(2) Mars is the nearest planet to the Earth.

(3) It takes about three days to go from the Earth to the moon.

i. Many people can't find *suitable* apartments in large cities.

(1) The apartments are large and filled with light.

(2) The apartments aren't far from the trains and buses.

(3) The apartments are too small and too expensive.

j. Special clothing is *necessary* for traveling to the moon.

(1) A person doesn't have to wear it.

(2) A person would die without it.

(3) Nobody wants to wear it.

k. The Earth is only one tiny object in the *universe*.

(1) There are many moons around the large planet Jupiter.

(2) Mercury is smaller than the Earth.

(3) There are billions of stars, comets, and other objects in deep space.

3. **Word Families.**   Some English adjectives can be formed by adding the suffix *-less* to a noun. The suffix *-less* means without.

The moon is a world without *life*. (*Life* is a noun.)
The moon is a *lifeless* world. (*Lifeless* is an adjective.)

Study the following list of nouns and adjectives.

Nouns	Adjectives
life	lifeless
air	airless
hope	hopeless
care	careless
tree	treeless
home	homeless
pain	painless
sleep	sleepless

Sentence Completion.   Choose the correct word in parentheses to fill in the blank space in each sentence.

a. (home, homeless) We can see _____ cats in some neighborhoods at night.

b. (sun, sunless) During the winter in North America there are many _____ days.

c. (pain, painless) Do you usually have _____ during your visit to the dentist?

d. (meat, meatless) If farmers don't keep a lot of animals, people will eat many _____ dinners.

Health problems are caused by smoke from cars, factories, and homes. Describe the air, water, and other features of your environment. What health problems may these cause?

e. (hope, hopeless) We must all have _____ that the future will be brighter.

f. (star, starless) In the past men couldn't sail their ships across the ocean without a _____ to help them.

g. (sleep, sleepless) Scientists spend _____ nights watching the stars through telescopes.

h. (water, waterless) Scientists used to think there were rivers on Mars, but now they know that the planet is _____ .

i. (tree, treeless) A traveler will see a _____ environment at the North and South Poles.

j. (care, careless) We must treat the Earth with ____*care*____ or we will destroy it.

k. (life, lifeless) Where there is ____*life*____ , there is hope.

READING COMPREHENSION

1. Understanding the Text.   Follow the directions for each item.

a. Mark *True* or *False* next to each statement. Underline the part of the reading passage where you find your answer.

(1) The Earth is one of nine planets around the sun. _____

(2) Rain comes from ocean water. _____

(3) The Earth was always suitable for life. _____

(4) Air and water problems will be worse in the future. _____

(5) Spaceships explore the stars closely. _____

(6) All the planets have air and water. _____

(7) There is life on the moon. _____

(8) Discoveries on the moon may help us have a better Earth. _____

b. Circle the letter of the correct answer.

(1) According to the information in Paragraph [1],

    a. all of the sun's rays are dangerous.

    b. the Earth has four seasons.

    c. the Earth travels very close to the sun.

(2) According to the information in Paragraph [2],

    a. the Earth was lifeless 4½ billion years ago.

    b. the sun will die out soon.

    c. the Earth has only a few kinds of living things.

(3) In Paragraph [2], the last sentence, *a special place* means

    a. a place with an environment for living things.

    b. a place without air or water.

    c. a place around the sun.

(4) In the future, according to Paragraph [3],

    a. people will have a lot of space to live in.

    b. there won't be any water in the rivers, lakes, and oceans.

    c. people won't have too much food to eat.

(5) In Paragraph [4], the sixth sentence, the expression *no other planet but Earth* means

    a. besides the Earth.

    b. sometimes the Earth.

    c. only the Earth.

(6) The exploration of space is important because

    a. it may teach us how to take better care of our Earth.

    b. the Earth is 4½ billion years old.

    c. scientists don't know anything about the universe.

(7) Scientists are hopeful that space stations

    a. will help in the study of archeology.

    b. will be for the good of the Earth.

    c. will be near the Earth.

(8) In Paragraph [6], the fifth sentence, *Then* refers to the time

    a. after the astronauts discover water in the rocks.

    b. before they discover water in the rocks.

    c. right after they arrive on the moon.

(9) The main idea of Paragraph [6] is stated in

    a. the second sentence.

    b. the third sentence.

    c. the last sentence.

(10) The topic of the entire reading passage is

    a. building space stations.

    b. saving the Earth's environment.

    c. living on the moon.

2.   Answering Information Questions.   Write the answers to the following questions in complete sentences.

  a. What keeps out the sun's dangerous rays?

  b. What are all plants and animals dependent on?

  c. How many people will there be by the year 2000?

  d. Will the air be better or worse in twenty years?

  e. Name three ways scientists have of finding out about the universe.

  f. Will space stations be near the Earth or far away?

  g. Where will the astronauts dig on the moon?

3.   Identifying Specific Information.   Specific information sentences give the details or facts in a paragraph. These sentences support the main idea of a paragraph. Details and facts explain the main idea sentence by answering the questions *why, when, where, how, what, who,* and *which* about the main idea. Specific information sentences can also give examples of, or reasons for, something or give a time order of when things happen.

    Reread Paragraph [5] of the reading passage. The first sentence is the main idea sentence. The next three sentences give specific information that supports the main idea. They all tell specifically why scientists are hopeful about the future.

Many species of animals—like this white tiger at the New Delhi, India, zoo—are dying out because of changes in the environment.

Answer the following questions by referring back to the reading passage. Follow the directions for each item.

a. Write the number of the sentence in the blank space. The first one is done for you.

(1) In Paragraph [1] which sentence answers the question, *How many* planets? _Sentence 1_____

(2) In Paragraph [2] which sentence answers the question, *How old* is the Earth? _____

(3) In Paragraph [2] which sentence answers the question, *How long* will the sun shine? _____

(4) In Paragraph [3] which sentence answers the question, *What* will kill more fish? _____

(5) In Paragraph [4] which sentence answers the question, *Who* uses telescopes? _____

(6) In Paragraph [4] which sentence answers the question, *Which* planet has the air and water necessary for life? _____

(7) In Paragraph [5] which sentence answers the question, *Where* will scientists build space stations? _____

(8) In Paragraph [6] which sentence answers the question, *What kind of* world is the moon? _____

(9) In Paragraph [7] which sentence answers the question, *When* should we plan for the Earth's future? _____

b. The main idea of Paragraph [3] is that the future doesn't look bright. Then the paragraph gives specific examples of the problems. Match the details by drawing a line from the items on the left to the appropriate item on the right.

chemicals   homeless birds and animals

overpopulation   serious health problems

bad air   little land to grow food

not enough trees   dead fish

c. The following information from Paragraph [6] tells specific facts about the astronauts' work on the moon in the future. Arrange these sentences in the correct time order by writing a number from 1 to 5 in each blank space. The first thing that happens will be number 1.

(1) Maybe later the vegetation will produce air. _____

(2) They will dig in the rocks below the moon's surface. _____

(3) Then they can grow some vegetation. _____

(4) Perhaps they will discover water in the rocks. _____

(5) The environment may become more suitable for work. _____

WRITING EXERCISES

Future Tense with *Will* + Basic Form of Verbs

Will + the basic form of a verb is one way of expressing action that will be completed in the future. This form usually expresses opinions, beliefs, or hopes about the future. It also expresses the idea of determination, promise, or inevitability.

> **I think it will rain. (opinion)**
> **Spring will come again. (inevitability)**
> **I will see you at 6 P.M. (promise)**

Study the following Future tense forms.

	Singular	**Plural**
First Person	I will travel (I'll travel)	My friend and I will travel We will travel (We'll travel)
Second Person	You will travel (You'll travel)	You will travel (You'll travel)
Third Person	A scientist will travel He/She/It will travel He'll/She'll/It'll travel	Scientists will travel They will travel (They'll travel)

Notice that the auxiliary verb *will* never changes its form. Notice also that the main verb that follows *will* is always in its basic form. The negative form of the Future tense is *will not (won't)*.

1. **Recognizing Verb Forms.**   Read Paragraph [3] again. Underline each complete verb form of the Future tense.

    Circle the two time expressions that signal the Future tense. Can you tell why the first sentence uses the Simple Present tense, not the Future?

2. **Controlled Writing.**   Rewrite the following paragraph. Pretend that the paragraph is a prediction about the future of New York City. Change the name *Rome* to *New York*. Change the Present tense verbs to the Future tense in each sentence. Your first sentence will be the following: *New York will have a new law.*

    Rome, Italy, has a new law. The government doesn't allow cars in special areas of the city. The people of Rome and visitors from other cities explore these areas freely. The streets are crowded with people. There isn't any noise of car engines. The people walk around slowly and stop to look at interesting buildings or shop windows. They sit outside and have coffee or ice cream without smelling bad air. The children of Rome play ball in the middle of the street. They ride their bicycles without danger. There is a very pleasant environment in these areas of Rome.

3. **Scrambled Sentences.**   Rewrite the following mixed-up sentences so that they form correct English sentences. Remember to look for the complete verb first. Then look for the subject.

    a. moon   water   will   on   perhaps   .   discover
    astronauts   the

| b. | will | millions | sun | of | . | shine | for | the |

years

c.	environment	we	our	?	destroy	special	will
d.	have	many	a	.	birds	won't	home
e.	a lot of	won't	.	food	there	be	years	in

twenty

Simple Present Tense Negative Forms

The negative form of the Simple Present tense is the auxiliary verb *don't + base verb* for all persons, singular and plural except the Third Person Singular. The Third Person Singular forms the negative by *doesn't + base verb*.

I (You, We, They) *don't travel* **by bus very often.**
The planet Venus *doesn't have* **a suitable environment for life.**
He (She, It) *doesn't predict* **the future.**

---

1. **Sentence Composing.**   Write the answers to the following questions in complete sentences. Use the Simple Present tense negative form of the verb in each question. The first one is done for you.

   a. Does our future look bright?

   Our future doesn't look bright.

   b. Does the Earth travel too near the sun?

   c. Do the other planets have the air and water necessary for life?

   d. Do archeologists keep any ancient objects for themselves?

   e. Does Java have a temperate climate?

   f. Does clean air produce health problems?

   g. Does the sun travel around the Earth?

   h. Does your teacher come from Turkey?

   i. Do astronauts wear ordinary clothes on the moon?

2. **Identifying Subjects and Verbs.**   Check your answers to the questions in Exercise 1. In the following chart put the subject of each sentence in the Subject column, the auxiliary verb in the Auxiliary column, and the base verb in the Base Verb column. Check the last column if the subject and verb are Third Person Singular. The first one is done for you.

	Subject	Auxiliary	Base Verb	Third Person Singular
a	*Our future*	*doesn't*	*look*	
b				
c				
d				
e				
f				
g				
h				
i				

3. **Sentence Completion.**   Fill in the blank space with the negative form of the same Simple Present tense verb in the first sentence of each pair. The first one is done for you.

   a. Astronauts *eat* special food in a spaceship. They _*don't eat*_ with knives, forks, or spoons.

   b. The Earth *has* air and water. The other planets _*doesn't*_ these basic things.

   c. The sun *shines* brightly. The planets _____ with their own light.

   d. My family and I *travel* in the summer. We _____ during the school year.

   e. Peru *produces* gold. It _____ as much gold as South Africa.

   f. An old photograph of Saturn *shows* the rings around the planet. But it _____ all of Saturn's moons.

   g. The writer Lawrence Maisak *describes* the moon's environment in easy-to-read books. He _____ it in scientific language.

Linking Verbs + Adjectives

   Linking verbs are used to describe how a subject might *be, become, feel, seem, look,* or *appear.* A linking verb connects a subject with an adjective.

> **Some drivers** *are careless.*
> **Foreign students sometimes** *feel lonely.*
> **Our future** *doesn't look bright.*
> **The problem** *seems hopeless.*

1. **Recognizing Linking Verbs + Adjectives.**   Listen carefully as your instructor reads the following paragraph. Underline the complete linking verb forms and their adjectives.

   Scientists describe these interesting details about the moon. The moon looks bright in the night sky, but it doesn't have its own light. The sun's rays are strong and dangerous on the moon's surface. Everything appears gray in the sharp light. The surface isn't smooth. There are rocks everywhere. In between the small rocks the soil is fine and dusty. There are mountains in some areas, but they don't seem high. The moon is light for half a month. Then it becomes dark for half a month. During the long night, the sky around the moon is bright with stars. The moon is peaceful. The astronauts' footsteps will remain in the soft dust of the moon for millions of years.

2. **Sentence Composing.**   Write a complete sentence following the directions for each item. Use a linking verb + adjective for each answer. The following adjectives will help you write your sentences. The first one is done for you.

noisy	comfortable	splendid	busy
messy	serious	tired	easy
crowded	hungry	bright	

Apollo II astronaut Edwin E. Aldrin, Jr., leaves his footprints on the surface of the moon. They will remain in the soft dust for millions of years.

a. Describe how your living room looks after a party.

My living room looks messy after a party.

b. Tell how the stores are at Christmastime.

c. Describe how the moon appears in the night sky.

d. Tell how the exam seems when you know all the answers.

e. Tell how the health problems are in the world today.

f. Describe how wild animals look when they can't find food.

g. Tell how you don't feel on a long bus ride.

Singular Possessives

> **an astronaut's clothing (the clothing of an astronaut)**
> **Java's climate (the climate of Java)**
> **the archeologist's shovel (the shovel belonging to the archeologist)**
> **a bird's nest (the nest of a bird)**

The *apostrophe + s* ('s) form is used to show that one person, place, or thing has or owns another noun.

1. **Dictation.** Write the following sentences from your instructor's dictation. All the sentences have a singular possessive form.

   a. Some of the sun's rays are dangerous.

   b. An atlas tells us about the world's population.

   c. Will scientists find water under the moon's surface?

   d. Love is necessary in a child's environment.

   e. Do you ever visit your friend's family?

2. **Rewriting Sentences.** Rewrite each sentence, changing the italicized expressions to singular possessives in the *apostrophe + s* form. The first one is done for you.

   a. *The job of an archeologist* is very interesting.

   An archeologist's job is very interesting.

   b. We often listen to *the problems of a friend.*

   c. Objects from the earth tell us about *the past of a country.*

   d. It is difficult to read *the reports of a scientist.*

   e. Foreign students learn a lot from *the explanations of the instructor.*

    f. Sometimes I use *the telescope belonging to my father* to observe the stars.

    g. There are always many students in *the office of the advisor.*

    h. *The laws of the city* against smoking on buses are very strict.

3. **Sentence Completion.** Choose the correct word from the following list to fill in the blank space in each sentence. Change the noun before each blank space to the singular possessive form to show the correct relationship between the two nouns. The first one is done for you.

footsteps	jewelry	power	office
toys	environment	brother	mistakes

    a. All of us can help make the earth's *environment* _____ better.

    b. My mother's *jewelry* _____ is very expensive.

    c. I always get nervous sitting in the doctor 's *office* _____ .

    d. Archeologists sometimes find a child 's *Toys* _____ .

    e. The instructor will correct a student 's *mistakes* _____ .

    f. Maria's *brother* _____ wants to be an astronaut.

    g. A spaceship 's *power* _____ comes from special engines.

    h. The astronaut 's *footstep* _____ on the moon will be clear for millions of years.

Prepositional Phrases With *At*

1. *At* **with Phrases of Time.** The preposition *at* is used with a point of time such as a specific hour of the day or with a general period of time.

He always gets up *at 7:30*. (specific time)
I'll visit my aunt *at Thanksgiving*. (general period of time)
***At dinner time* we all talk about the day's events. (general period of time)**

Note that we say *at night*, but *in the morning, in the afternoon, in the evening*.

Sentence Completion. Fill in the blank spaces with *at, in,* or *on* to complete the prepositional phrase of time.

    a. I'll go to Paris sometime ___*in*___ the spring.

    b. ___*in*___ the afternoon I attend school, but ___*at*___ night I relax.

c. The restaurants are always crowded _____at_____ lunchtime.

d. I spend a lot of time shopping _____ Saturdays.

e. _____ the end of the semester I'll get a part-time job.

f. The French have a special holiday _____ July 14.

g. My friend from Spain will arrive _____ August.

h. My mother usually eats lunch _____ noon and dinner _____ 7:00.

i. We never eat much _____ breakfast time, but we have a large meal _____ the evening.

2. *At* **with Phrases of Place.**   The preposition *at* also refers to an area or place. It shows closeness of position or point of contact with a place.

She sits *at her desk* and studies.
He'll meet his friends *at the seashore.*

We also use *at* for arrival with the words *airport, station, terminal, someone's house, the theater, school,* and so on.

The plane will arrive *at O'Hare airport* in an hour.
The guests will arrive *at Mary's house* soon.

Another important use of *at* is with a specific street address.

Paula lives *at 46 Riverside Drive.*

Other useful phrases of place are *at work* and *at home.*

My brother has to be *at work* by eight o'clock.
I usually study *at home* on Sundays.

Sentence Composing. Write the answers to the following questions in complete sentences. Use a prepositional phrase with *at* in each answer, and underline the prepositional phrase of place. The following list will help you write your sentences. The first one is done for you.

Pennsylvania Station	party	specific street address
library	uncle's house	desk
beach	home	health club

a. Where will you meet your friend tomorrow?

I'll meet my friends <u>at the library</u> tomorrow.

b. Where do you usually eat lunch on Sundays?

c. Where do you like to spend the summer?

d. Where does your friend usually play tennis?

e. Where will the train from Chicago arrive?

f. Where will your friends dance on Saturday night?

g. Where do you live?

h. Where does your instructor sit?

COMPOSING

1. **Developing a Paragraph.**

   a. *Outlining*.   Making an outline of a paragraph helps the reader understand the writer's main idea and how the idea is developed with specific information details. Outlining is also important for writing your own compositions. It helps you organize your thoughts before writing a paragraph.

   An outline begins with the complete main idea sentence. Then specific information is written in brief note form.

   Read the following paragraph. Fill in the main idea sentence of the paragraph on the lines that follow. Then in the spaces following the main idea fill in the specific information in short note form. Two of the details are done for you.

   Some people are predicting that by the year 2000 there will be many good solutions to the world's problems. People will use sun and wind power to heat homes and run factories. Farmers will be able to grow food in very dry and cold areas of the world. There will be fast public transportation and fewer private cars. Then cities will have more open spaces with trees instead of parking lots. There will be stronger laws against the use of dangerous chemicals. Scientists will find cures for serious illnesses. Life may be more pleasant in the future.

Main Idea: _____

_____

Details: _____

_____

fast public transportation – fewer cars

_____

cures for serious illnesses

Now copy the main idea sentence from your outline on a separate sheet of paper. Without looking at the paragraph, use just your outline to complete a paragraph with your own sentences. You will have seven sentences in your paragraph.

b. When the following sentences are put in order, they will make up a paragraph about a couple's plans for taking an evening plane from New York to Paris. Rewrite these sentences in correct time order and paragraph form. Your first sentence will be: *Ilsa and Edward expect to have an easy and comfortable flight to Paris.*

(1) After the movie, they'll try to sleep.

(2) The plane will leave on time at 8 P.M.

(3) Then Edward will buy some magazines to pass the time.

(4) They will arrive at Kennedy Airport at 6 P.M.

(5) At about nine o'clock the stewards will serve dinner.

(6) The plane will land in Paris at 8 A.M.

(7) They'll board the plane a half hour before takeoff.

(8) After dinner Ilsa and Edward will watch a movie.

(9) In the morning the captain will announce the landing.

(10) They'll be finished checking their bags by 6:30.

2. Composing a Paragraph.

a. Imagine that a friend is going to visit you for the first time. Write a paragraph describing one day's plans for exploring interesting areas of the city with your friend. Tell where you will take him or her and what you will see and do in the morning, in the afternoon, and in the evening. Start your paragraph with an appropriate main idea.

b. Some people try to make their city a better place in which to live, and others don't. Write a paragraph describing things you, your friends, shopkeepers, and others in your neighborhood do to have a cleaner, more pleasant environment. Include some details about people who don't try to do these things. Use the following items to guide you: cover trash, sweep sidewalks, walk a dog, throw papers, plant flowers.

c. Write a paragraph predicting your own future. Tell what you will do, where you will be, and so on ten years from now. Write a main idea sentence and give several details about your future life.

CHAPTER THREE B

HUMAN AND ARTIFICIAL INTELLIGENCE

PREREADING

Class Discussion.   What do these symbols mean? Where do we usually see them? Can you think of other symbols we use? Discuss why we use symbols instead of words for certain things.

New Words.   Try to understand the meanings of these words as they are used in the reading passage. Use a dictionary when necessary.

artificial	invent	symbol
unique	solution	conclusion
communicate	development	perform
experience		

READING

People and Computers: A Working Relationship

[1]   Can machines be as intelligent as human beings? There is a lot of discussion these days about artificial-intelligence machines and their relation to human intelligence.

[2]   Human beings are a unique species. They have larger brains than any other beings. They have the gift of speech and can communicate their thoughts, ideas, and feelings. Human beings are interested in the past and can learn from past experiences. They study their present problems carefully and decide what to do about them. They look to the future and plan their next activities. They invent tools and machines to help them in their work.

[3]   Some computer scientists are developing artificial-intelligence machines that they say will think like people. According to these scientists, the computer machines will understand written and spoken words and the ideas related to them. They will be able to correct their own mistakes. They will look at a problem in more than one way and choose the best solution. Computers will also use information to plan for the future. They might even program, or teach, other computers to be their helpers.

[4]   Recently, the *New York Times* reported the development of an extraordinary computer program called FRUMP. It seems that FRUMP understands the real meanings of words. It can change the idea of a word into a symbol. For example, when FRUMP is given the word *fire,* it changes the word *fire* into a symbol. The symbol then informs FRUMP about such related ideas as flames, smoke, burning buildings, firemen arriving, loss of life, and so on. FRUMP learns from the information and comes to a conclusion about the event. It prints a summary of the information in perfect English sentences. It can translate summaries from English to Chinese and Spanish. It doesn't match words from one language to another; it matches ideas. FRUMP's inventor says that it is beginning to perform like a human being.

[5]   In the future artificial-intelligence computers like FRUMP will be useful to many different people. Doctors will use them to find out more about a person's illness. With the help of computers geologists will make new discoveries of oil, other minerals, and even fossils. Computers will be programmed to write summaries for news reporters. Lawyers will find better solutions for problems by using computer helpers. At present computer machines follow 240 million instructions a second, and soon they'll perform a billion instructions a second.

[6]   Artificial-intelligence machines are examples of the human ability to invent things that make life easier. These machines can do many things better and faster than people. They'll perform in even more extraordinary ways in the future. But they won't be more intelligent than the people who program them. People and computers will have a good working relationship.

Summary Completion.   Choose the correct word from the columns following the paragraph to fill in each blank space in the paragraph.

Human beings are very (1) _____ . They look

back into the (2) _____ and learn from experience.

They also plan (3) _____ the future. They invent
(4) _____ to help them in their work. One invention is a
computer that (5) _____ do extraordinary things
like change words into (6) _____ . Computer machines will be (7) _____ to many different people
because they work very (8) _____ . Computers will make life
(9) _____ . However, they won't be more intelligent than the
people who (10) _____ them.

(1) ancient, intelligent	(5) doesn't, can	(8) fast, hard
(2) past, present	(6) speech, ideas	(9) slower, easier
(3) from, for	(7) useful, proper	(10) learn, program
(4) machines, stories		

VOCABULARY

1. **Expanding Vocabulary.**   Circle the number of the item that explains the meaning of the italicized word.

   a. People *communicate* by telephone, telegram, and letters, as well as in person.
   When people *communicate,* they

   (1) use machinery.
   (2) exchange thoughts.
   (3) are lonely.

   b. Visitors to foreign countries like to tell their interesting *experiences* to friends.
   Experiences are

   (1) instructions.
   (2) behavior.
   (3) happenings.

   c. Chemists make different kinds of *artificial* material like plastic and nylon.
   Something *artificial* is always

   (1) man-made.
   (2) useful.
   (3) natural.

d. It is sometimes difficult to find a *solution* to a math problem.
   When you find a *solution,* you

   (1) look in a textbook.

   (2) discover an answer.

   (3) ask a question.

e. Some students don't *perform* well on exams.
   To *perform* well means

   (1) to come late.

   (2) to do a good job.

   (3) to write clearly.

f. Many scientists today are taking part in the *development* of better computer programs for air traffic safety.
   Development means

   (1) bringing to an advanced state.

   (2) flying in an airplane.

   (3) making a summary.

g. Human beings are *unique* among all the animals because of their greater intelligence.
   To be *unique* means

   (1) to be the same.

   (2) to have no equal.

   (3) to go far.

h. Children learn the math *symbols* $+$, $-$, $\times$, and $\div$ in their early school years.
   Symbols are

   (1) math problems.

   (2) signs for something else.

   (3) pictures for real things.

i. We can come to a *conclusion* about a news story after we read all the information.
   When people come to a *conclusion,* they

   (1) understand words.

   (2) begin a story.

   (3) make a judgment.

j. Human beings are different from animals because they are able to *invent* all kinds of useful tools.
To *invent* something means to

(1) find it on the street.
(2) make if from an original idea.
(3) sell it in a store.

2. Using Vocabulary. The words in parentheses are from the New Word list. But the letters are mixed up. Put the letters in correct order, and write the word in the blank space.

We always try to find the best _____ (ulosniot) for
(1)
a problem. Sometimes a problem isn't _____ (qin-
(2)
ueu). So we can learn from our own past and also from other people's

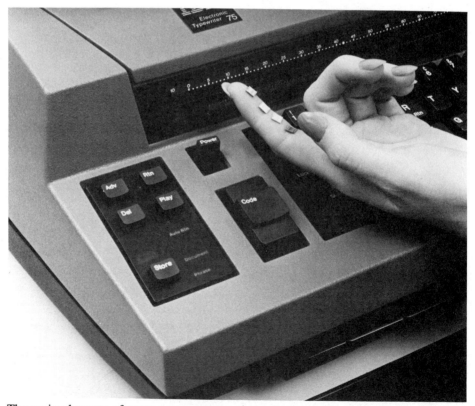

The main elements of some computers are tiny microprocessor chips like these on the woman's finger. They receive and interpret signals from this electronic typewriter.

_____ (epxreciene). We may feel sad or lonely, but
when we _____ (miccomutaen) with friends or relatives, we often feel better. Everyone has feelings. They are natural, not _____ (tiarfialic). Their _____ (tlovedmepen) starts at an early age. We can always come to a better _____ (clncounios) about a problem when we talk with others. Then we can _____ (epfmorr) better the next time a problem arises.

3. **Word Families.**   Some English nouns can be formed by adding the suffix *r*, *er*, or *or* to the verb. Sometimes the final consonant of a verb must be doubled before adding the suffix. This noun form means "one who" does something. Study the following lists.

Verb	Noun
speak	speaker
teach	teacher
write	writer
swim	swimmer
translate	translator
instruct	instructor
invent	inventor

Sentence Completion.   Fill in the blank space in the second sentence of each pair with a noun made from the verb in the first sentence. The first one is done for you.

a. It is difficult to *climb* mountains. A mountain *climber* _____ must be in very good health.

b. My friend *runs* in the park for twenty minutes every morning. She'll be one of the _____ in a race next week.

c. I *ride* the bus to school in the morning. Thousands of _____ use public transportation.

d. My aunt will *visit* New York in July. The Metropolitan Museum of Art is a wonderful place to take a _____ from out of town.

e. Many people *borrow* books from the library. A _____ must return books within a month.

f. The students will *begin* a course in English next semester. There are special textbooks for _____ .

g. Some American artists go to Paris to *paint*. Paris is an exciting city for a _____ .

h. It isn't difficult to *bake* bread. My mother is an excellent

_____ .

i. I'll *drive* to Mexico on my vacation. But I'll need another

_____ to help me.

READING COMPREHENSION

1. Understanding the Text.   Follow the directions for each item.

a. Mark *True* or *False* next to each statement. Underline the part of the passage where you find your answer.

(1) Human beings have larger brains than other beings. _____

(2) People are interested only in the present and future. _____

(3) FRUMP is an inventor of computer programs. _____

(4) FRUMP communicates information in speech. _____

(5) News reporters will find computers useful. _____

(6) Computers work faster than people. _____

b. Circle the letter of the correct answer.

(1) The main idea of Paragraph [2] is that human beings

a. have the gift of speech.

b. plan for the future.

c. are a unique species.

(2) The topic of Paragraph [3] is

a. why human beings are unique.

b. what computer machines will do.

c. how computer scientists work.

(3) In Paragraph [3], the last sentence, *They* refers to

a. computer scientists.

b. artificial-intelligence machines.

c. written and spoken words.

(4) FRUMP is able

    a. to change words into symbols.

    b. to send messages to China.

    c. to smell smoke.

(5) According to Paragraph [5], artificial-intelligence computers

    a. will cure illnesses.

    b. might write poems.

    c. can save people time.

(6) The first sentence in Paragraph [6] refers specifically to

    a. the first sentence in Paragraph [2].

    b. the second sentence in Paragraph [2].

    c. the last sentence in Paragraph [2].

(7) According to Paragraph [6], the development of artificial-intelligence machines

    a. will cause trouble for scientists.

    b. will bring out the best in human abilities.

    c. will make people less intelligent.

2. **Answering Information Questions.**   Write the answers to the following questions in complete sentences.

    a. What can human beings communicate through speech?

    b. Is FRUMP an extraordinary inventor or an extraordinary computer program?

    c. Does FRUMP print a summary in good English sentences or poor English sentences?

    d. Can FRUMP translate summaries from English to Spanish or to French?

    e. What will geologists do with the help of computers?

    f. How will lawyers find better solutions for problems?

    g. What kind of relationship will people and computers have?

3. **Identifying Specific Information.**   Specific information sentences give the details or facts in a paragraph. These sentences support the main idea of a paragraph. Details and facts explain the main idea sentence by answering the questions *why, when, where, how, what, who,* and *which* about the main idea. Specific information sentences can also give examples of something, or give a time order of when things happen.

a. In the following paragraph the main idea sentence is italicized. Read the specific information sentences carefully, and answer the questions at the end of the paragraph orally with your class.

> *In the future robot machines will take the place of human beings in difficult and dangerous jobs.* Robot machines will have arms to do all the unsafe work in factories. They will look for minerals deep underwater where no humans can go. Some robots will have special eyes to find people in burning buildings where firemen can't go. Robots with special fingers will work in hospitals helping doctors in delicate operations. Perhaps robots will work in space, on the moon, or on other planets.

(1) Do the specific information sentences give examples of something, or do they give a time order?

(2) Name all the things that answer the question *where,* and underline them in the paragraph.

(3) What kind of work will robots do in factories?

(4) What will robots look for deep underwater?

(5) How will robots help doctors?

(6) Do all the specific information sentences support the main idea?

b. Answer the following questions by referring back to the reading passage of this chapter. Write the number of the sentence on the line. The first one is done for you.

(1) In Paragraph [2] which sentence answers the question, *What* do human beings invent? *Sentence 7*

(2) In Paragraph [3] which sentence answers the question, *Who* is developing artificial-intelligence machines? _____

(3) In Paragraph [4] which sentence answers the question, *Which* newspaper reported the development of FRUMP? _____

(4) In Paragraph [5] which sentence answers the question, *How many* instructions a second do computers follow at present? _____

(5) In Paragraph [5] which sentence answers the question, *When* will computers perform a billion instructions a second? _____

c. The main idea sentence of Paragraph [2] is the first sentence. It states that human beings are a unique species. The sentences that follow give specific examples of their unique qualities. Number each sentence in Paragraph [2]. Then match the sentence number on the left with the specific example on the right by drawing a line.

Sentence 2	plan for the future
Sentence 3	decide about present problems
Sentence 4	communicate through speech
Sentence 5	invent useful things
Sentence 6	remember the past
Sentence 7	have large brains

WRITING EXERCISES

Future Tense with *Will* + Basic Form of Verbs

Will + the basic form of a verb is one way of expressing action that will be completed in the future. This form usually expresses a person's opinions, beliefs, or hopes about the future. It also expresses the idea of determination, promise, or inevitability.

I'm sure he will return. (belief)
The snow will melt when it gets warmer. (inevitability)
I will never forget you. (promise)

Intelligent human beings have invented many kinds of artificial-intelligence machines to help them in their work. Here air traffic controllers read radar screens at Kennedy Airport in New York City, where 3,200 flights daily are guided in and out of the area.

Study the following Future tense forms.

	Singular	**Plural**
First Person	I will use (I'll use)	My friend and I will use We will use (We'll use)
Second Person	You will use (You'll use)	You will use (You'll use)
Third Person	A reporter will use He/She/It will use (He'll/She'll/It'll use)	Reporters will use They will use (They'll use)

Notice that the auxiliary verb *will* never changes its form. Notice also that the main verb that follows *will* is always in its basic form. The negative form of the Future tense is *will not (won't)*.

1. **Recognizing Verb Forms.**   Read Paragraph [5] again. Underline each complete verb form of the Future tense.

    Can you tell why the first part of the sixth sentence uses the Simple Present tense? Which time expression signals the Simple Present tense? Can you find a prepositional phrase that signals the Future tense? Which other word in the paragraph signals the Future tense?

2. **Controlled Writing.**   Rewrite the following paragraph. Change the subject *secretaries* to *an artificial-intelligence computer*. Change the subject *they* to *it*. Change all the verbs to the Future tense. Your first sentence will be the following: *In offices of the future an artificial-intelligence computer will also be an important member of a company.*

    In offices everywhere secretaries are important members of a company. They understand everything about the boss's job. They know what to do when the boss wants a meeting. They arrange the proper time and place. They call people on the telephone. They make lists of things to talk about. They order coffee for the group. They take notes at the meeting and then type the reports. Secretaries don't have much free time. They are busy from 9 A.M. to 5 P.M.

3. **Scrambled Sentences.**   Rewrite the following mixed-up sentences so that they form correct English sentences. Remember to look for the complete verb first. Then look for the subject.

    a. summaries   reporters   .   write   for   will
       computers

    b. smarter   machines   be   won't   .   people   than

    c. dangerous   .   robots   and   do   difficult   jobs
will

    d. future   will   ?   the   work   computers   in
faster

    e. will   in   robots   .   someday   space   work

Simple Present Tense Negative Forms

The negative form of the Simple Present tense is the auxiliary verb *don't* + *base verb* for all persons, singular and plural, except the Third Person Singular. The Third Person Singular forms the negative by *doesn't* + *base verb*.

I (You, We, They) *don't communicate* **by telegram very often.**
A baby *doesn't understand* **many words.**
He (She, It) *doesn't write* **in correct English sentences.**

---

1. **Sentence Composing.**   Write the answers to the following questions in complete sentences. Use the Simple Present tense negative form of the verb in each question. The first one is done for you.

    a. Do robots look like human beings?

    Robots don't look like human beings.

    b. Does FRUMP communicate in speech?

    c. Does a reptile protect its babies?

    d. Do animals think about the past?

    e. Does a good translator make mistakes?

    f. Do artificial-intelligence machines work slowly?

    g. Does your instructor teach you French?

    h. Do your friends and you visit museums on weekdays?

    i. Does a car run without gas?

2. **Identifying Subjects and Verbs.**   Check your answers to the questions in Exercise 1. In the following chart put the subject of each sentence in the Subject column, the auxiliary verb in the Auxiliary column, the base verb in the Base Verb column. Check the last column if the subject and verb are Third Person Singular. The first one is done for you.

	Subject	Auxiliary	Base Verb	Third Person Singular
a	Robots	don't	look (like)	
b				
c				
d				
e				
f				
g				
h				
i				

3. **Sentence Completion.**   Fill in the blank space with the negative form of the same Simple Present tense verb in the first sentence of each pair. The first one is done for you.

   a. My friends and I *study* our lessons in the library. We *don't study* our lessons at home.

   b. My relatives *live* in Chicago. They _____ in New York.

   c. A geologist *has* a busy life. He or she _____ much free time.

   d. I *spend* two hours in the evening on my homework. I _____ much time watching television.

   e. An animal *uses* sounds to communicate. It _____ words.

   f. A computer scientist *studies* the human brain. He or she _____ fossil skeletons.

   g. Dr. Colbert *looks* for dinosaur bones. He _____ for oil or other minerals.

Linking Verbs + Adjectives

   Linking verbs are used to describe how a subject might *be, become, feel, seem, look,* or *appear.* A linking verb connects a subject with an adjective.

> I *am happy* in my new job.
> Sometimes people *feel sad*.
> Our future *seems exciting* with computers like FRUMP.
> The students *don't appear nervous* during an exam.

1. **Recognizing Linking Verbs + Adjectives.**   Listen carefully as your instructor reads the following paragraph. Underline the complete linking verb forms and their adjectives.

> Dr. Marvin Minsky has some interesting ideas about human and artificial intelligence. His ideas seem extraordinary at times. He thinks that the human brain will be different in the future. People will become more intelligent with the help of computers. Minsky's ideas are difficult to understand. They often seem unbelievable. Minsky is busy with ideas for artificial intelligence programs. His mind is active all the time. He feels hopeful about the future. The future looks exciting to him.

2. **Sentence Composing.**   Write a complete sentence following the directions for each item. Use a linking verb + adjective for each sentence. The following adjectives will help you write your sentences. The first one is done for you.

| careless | difficult | tired | messy | relaxed |
| friendly | blue | neat | nervous | careful |

a. Tell us how you feel on Sunday mornings?

   I feel tired on Sunday mornings.

b. Describe how the school cafeteria appears at lunchtime.

c. Tell how students seem during an exam.

d. Tell what color the sky appears to us.

e. Describe how you are when you meet a new person.

f. Tell how some drivers are on the road.

g. Tell how the exam seems when you don't know the answers.

Singular Possessives

> a person's illness (the illness of a person)
> Dr. Minsky's computer (the computer belonging to Dr. Minsky)
> Hawaii's people (the people of Hawaii)
> a dinosaur's behavior (the behavior of a dinosaur)

The *apostrophe* + *s* ('s) form is used to show that one person, place, or thing has or owns another noun.

1. **Dictation.**   Write the following sentences from your instructor's dictation. All the sentences have a singular possessive form.

    a. A baby's bones are very fragile.
    b. I always wait a long time in the dentist's office.
    c. A mother likes to hear about her child's work in school.
    d. A reporter's job is exciting.
    e. The teacher corrects the student's paper.

2. **Rewriting Sentences.**   Rewrite each sentence, changing the italicized expressions to singular possessives in the *apostrophe* + *s* form. The first one is done for you.

    a. *The ideas of Dr. Minsky* are difficult to understand.

    Dr. Minsky's ideas are difficult to understand.

    b. *The directions of the teacher* are clear.
    c. You have to be very active to do *the job of a geologist.*
    d. *The daughter of my friend* studies computer science.
    e. Sometimes I drive *the car belonging to my father.*
    f. There are a few good books about *the past of Hawaii.*
    g. On *the next trip of Dr. Colbert* to Texas, he'll look for dinosaur eggs.
    h. *The rays of the sun* are stronger in summer than in winter.

3. **Sentence Completion.**   Choose the correct word from the following list to fill in the blank space in each sentence. Change the noun before each blank space to the singular possessive form to show the correct relationship between the two nouns. The first one is done for you.

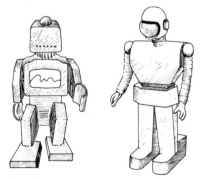

Robot machines may take the place of human beings in difficult and dangerous jobs.

museums	brain	house	desk
boss	wife	movements	problems

a. Dr. Colbert's *wife* _____ is an artist.

b. I'm going to my friend _____ for dinner.

c. My mother _____ is the president of the company.

d. It's funny to watch a robot _____ .

e. There is a typewriter on the secretary _____ .

f. Our city _____ are among the best in the United States.

g. A mother is interested in her child _____ .

h. A dinosaur _____ was very small.

Prepositional Phrases with *At*

1. *At* **with Phrases of Time.**   The preposition *at* is used with a point of time such as a specific hour of the day or with a general period of time.

> **I usually get up** *at seven o'clock.* **(specific time)**
> **We have a vacation** *at Christmas.* **(general period of time)**
> *At lunchtime* **the cafeteria is full of students. (general period of time)**

Note that we say *at night,* but *in the morning, in the afternoon, in the evening.*

Sentence Completion.   Fill in the blank spaces with *at, in,* or *on* to complete the prepositional phrase of time.

a. We always talk about the day's events _____ dinner time.

b. _____ weekends I usually go to bed _____ midnight.

c. _____ the beginning of the semester I'll buy my new textbooks.

d. I'll take a trip to Boston _____ Easter or _____ the summer.

e. My parents pay all their bills _____ the beginning of every month.

f. My friend from Colorado will visit me _____ July.

g. _____ Saturdays I usually go shopping _____ the afternoon.

h. Americans celebrate Independence Day _____ July 4.

i. I attend school _____ night because I work _____ the morning and afternoon.

j. I get home _____ 11 P.M. I'm very tired _____ the end of the day.

2. *At* **with Phrases of Place.**   The preposition *at* also refers to an area or place. It shows closeness of position or point of contact with a place.

> **He studies *at his desk* for long hours.**
> **She spends the summer *at the beach*.**

We also use *at* for arrival with the words *airport, station, terminal, someone's house, the theater, school,* and so on.

> **The train from Chicago will arrive *at the station* in an hour.**
> **We'll arrive *at the theater* in plenty of time.**

Another important use of *at* is with a specific street address.

> **I live *at 358 Morris Avenue*.**

Other useful phrases of place are *at work* and *at home*.

> **He doesn't stay *at work* late on Fridays.**
> **She never eats lunch *at home* during the week.**

Paragraph Completion.   Fill in the blank spaces in the following paragraph with *at* or *in* to complete the prepositional phrases of place.

My cousin works (1) _____ the computer science laboratory (2) _____ San Jose State College (3) _____ California. He lives (4) _____ a small apartment (5) _____ 24 Chirco Drive, a few

miles from the college. Before going to work, he meets his friends
(6) _____ a coffee shop for breakfast. They sit (7) _____
a table near the window and talk. After breakfast, they all wait
(8) _____ the bus stop together. They usually arrive (9) _____
the college before nine. My cousin has to be (10) _____ work by
nine o'clock. He's never late for work.

COMPOSING

1. **Developing a Paragraph.**

   a. *Outlining.*   Making an outline of a paragraph helps the reader understand
   the writer's main idea and how the idea is developed with specific information details. Outlining is also important for writing your own compositions. It helps you organize your thoughts before writing a paragraph.

   An outline begins with the complete main idea sentence. Then the
   specific information is written in brief note form.

   Look at Paragraph [5] of the reading passage. On the lines here fill
   in the main idea sentence of the paragraph. Then in the spaces following
   the main idea fill in the specific information in short note form. Two of
   the details are done for you.

   Main Idea: _____

   _____

   Details: *useful to doctors — help sick people* _____

   _____

   _____

   _____

   follow millions of instructions a second _____

   Now copy the main idea sentence from your outline on a separate sheet
   of paper. Without looking at Paragraph [5], use just your outline to complete a paragraph with your own sentences. You will have six sentences
   in your paragraph.

   b. Imagine that you will have a robot helper in the future. It will do wonderful
   things for you and your family. Think of all the jobs it will do. List the
   specific information in the following outline. List your notes in a time
   order: the things in the morning first, the afternoon next, and the evening
   jobs last. The main idea is given to you.

Main Idea: *My robot will do wonderful things for me and my family.*

Details: _____

_____

_____

_____

_____

_____

_____

c. Using some of the notes in the preceding outline, fill in the blank spaces in the following paragraph.

My robot will do wonderful things for me and my family. In the morning it _____ and _____ _____ . Then it will go _____ to buy _____ for the day. It will also _____ . At noon _____ _____ . Later in the afternoon _____ . At about 6 P.M. it will start _____ . During dinner _____ . After that, my robot _____ and _____ _____ .

2. Composing a Paragraph.

a. Think of some machines or household appliances such as refrigerators or air conditioners that have made your life easier. Write a paragraph describing a few of these items. Tell when you use them, where you use them, and how they help to make your life better. Begin your paragraph with an appropriate main idea.

b. What kind of job will you have in the future? Write a paragraph about the different things you will do on the job. Include information about the kind of place you will work in and the location of that place.

UNIT I REVIEW

1. **Sentence Completion.** Choose the correct item from the columns following the paragraph to fill in each blank space in the paragraph.

There (1) _____ extraordinary mountains on the earth called volcanoes. A volcano is (2) _____ mountain that erupts or blows up, leaving a large hole (3) _____ the top or on the side. From time to time, steam, ashes, and lava (4) _____ deep inside the earth blow out into the air. Active volcanoes can be very (5) _____ . Sometimes (6) _____ destroy whole cities. (7) _____ May 8, 1902, Mount Pelée, on the Caribbean island of Martinique, erupted (8) _____ killed thirty thousand people in the city of St. Pierre. Archeologists have discovered the (9) _____ city of Pompeii, which was buried under twenty feet of ashes two thousand years ago. Thousands of people died there, but we now (10) _____ a detailed record of their (11) _____ because the ashes preserved everything so well. People in Hawaii (12) _____ live near Mauna Loa volcano, so there isn't any (13) _____ when it (14) _____ . In fact, many people go to observe (15) _____ eruptions from a safe distance. Is there a way to predict volcanic eruptions (16) _____ In the future, geologists (17) _____ better ways to predict (18) _____ eruptions and so save lives.

(1) is/are/will be
(2) leave blank/an/a
(3) at/to/for
(4) on/of/from
(5) crowded/skillful/
    dangerous
(6) it/they/you
(7) On/In/At

(8) and/also/but
(9) roman/Rome/Roman
(10) has/have/will have
(11) live/lives/alive
(12) does/doesn't/don't
(13) danger/dangerous/
    dangerously
(14) informs/invents/erupts

(15) Mauna Loa's/Mauna
    Loas/Mauna Loa
(16) , / ? / .
(17) develop/development/
    will develop
(18) leave blank/an/a

2. Word Forms. Fill in the chart with the correct forms of the given words. (Some parts of speech may have more than one word.)

	Verb	Noun	Adjective	Adverb
1	protect			
2	produce			
3	X	intelligence		
4			special	
5	explore			X
6		observer		X
7		activities		
8	compare			
9	X		skillful	
10		behavior		

Word Form Completion. Fill in the blank space in each sentence with the correct form of the word from the same numbered item on the Word Form chart. Use verbs and nouns in their singular or plural form as necessary. For dictation with blanks, close your textbook.

1. Reptiles don't show _____ behavior toward their young ones.

2. Brazil _____ a great amount of coffee every year.

3. Scientists hope to find signs of _____ life in other parts of the universe.

4. My favorite restaurant _____ in northern Chinese cooking.

5. Christopher Columbus was an Italian _____ in the service of Spain.

6. Most babies are very _____ ; they notice everything around them.

7. I always take an _____ part in student organizations.

8. After class my friend and I study together and _____ notes.

9. Foreign students should read an American newspaper to improve their language _____ .

10. Your pet cat or dog will _____ well if you teach it properly.

3. Paragraph Composition. Write a paragraph that includes five to eight words from the Word Form chart. Select one of the following topics to write about or choose one of your own.

Office Workers
An Intelligent Pet
A Special Child

UNIT II

LANGUAGE

Writing in the Greek and Roman alphabets as well as Egyptian hieroglyphics adorns the Greek Temple of Abu Simbel, Egypt.

THE DEVELOPMENT OF LANGUAGE

PREREADING

Class Discussion. What are the people in the pictures communicating by their signs?

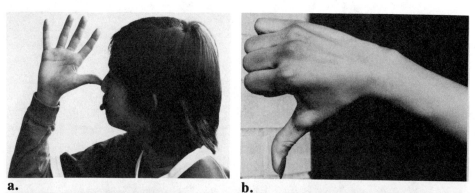

a.

b.

c.

What are some signs you would use to communicate the following information?

a. to show that you agree with someone

b. to show that you disagree with someone

c. to show anger

New Words.   Try to understand the meanings of these words as they are used in the reading passage. Use a dictionary when necessary.

communicate	emotion	invisible
probably	develop	invent
vocabulary	system	practical
	ancient	

READING

Communication: Signs, Pictures, and Letters

[1]   How did the first people on earth communicate with each other? They didn't talk to each other. They didn't use words at all. They probably used signs or pointed to things that they wanted. For example, perhaps they rubbed their stomachs to show that they were hungry. These early people had thoughts and ideas, but they didn't communicate them in words.

[2]   Nobody knows for certain when people first began to use words, but according to some scientists language may be about one million years old. What were the first words in the human vocabulary? They probably named things that were common and important. Perhaps the first words were short, simple sounds for things that humans saw or touched such as the sun, the moon, a tree, a stone, rain, or water. Words for basic human emotions such as love, dislike, fear, and pain were probably part of the earliest vocabulary.

[3]   Early human beings talked long before they developed a system of writing. The archeological evidence shows that writing is about eight thousand years old. The first kind of writing was "picture writing." People communicated their thoughts by drawing a picture of the thing they wanted to talk about. For example, in ancient Egypt the picture-writing "word" for *face* was . The ancient Chinese picture-writing "word" for *sun* was . A picture of a foot could mean the noun *foot* or the verb *walk*.

[4]   People communicated much better with picture writing. They did not need to see each other to communicate. But picture writing was sometimes difficult to understand. There was difficulty in using it for invisible things such as ideas or emotions. Picture writers needed many pictures to communicate their ideas.

[5]   About 3500 years ago a very important thing happened to language: The alphabet was invented. People changed pictures to letters. Each letter had one sound and people put the letters together to form words. An alphabet made writing easier. Writing with an alphabet was also practical because it took less time and less space than writing with pictures. Here is how the letter *A* developed from picture writing to alphabet writing:

Ancient Egyptian   Ancient Greek   Roman   Modern English

[6]   The invention of the alphabet made it easier to communicate information to a greater number of people. Ideas were carried from one land to another. The people of the ancient world had discovered a new tool for knowledge.

Guided Summary.   A summary communicates the main ideas of a reading passage. Complete the following sentences to make a summary. Write your new sentences in the form of a paragraph.

a. This passage tells about the development of . . .

b. The second paragraph tells about . . .

c. Paragraphs [3] and [4] inform us about . . .

d. The fifth paragraph tells us that . . .

e. The last paragraph states that the . . . made it easier to communicate . . .

VOCABULARY

1. Expanding Vocabulary.   Next to each word in Column A write the word(s) from Column B that means the same thing.

	A		**B**
a.	communicate	_____	most likely
b.	probably	*most likely*	very old
c.	system	*pattern*	created
d.	emotions	_____	exchange ideas
e.	vocabulary	_____	rarely
f.	developed	_____	feelings

g. ancient   _____   pattern

h. invisible   _____   made something grow

i. invented   _____   word list

j. practical   _____   not able to be seen

. pointed

not wasteful

2. **Using Vocabulary.**   Choose the correct word in parentheses to fill in the blank space in each sentence.

a. The archeological evidence shows that written words (rarely, probably) _____ developed about eight thousand years ago.

b. The first human (vocabulary, emotions) ___ *acbulary* ___ probably named common things such as the sun and the moon.

c. Picture writing is the most (practical, ancient) _____ form of writing.

d. The alphabet is a(n) (emotion, system) _____ of letters.

e. It is easier to (communicate, develop) _____ with an alphabet than with picture writing.

f. Picture writing is not as (invisible, practical) _____ as using an alphabet.

3. **Word Families.**   Study the following list of adjectives and their negative forms.

Adjectives	Negative Adjectives
correct	incorrect
visible	invisible
common	uncommon
important	unimportant
usual	unusual
related	unrelated
practical	impractical
possible	impossible

The prefix *in-, un-,* or *im-* often goes in front of a word to make it negative. Choose the correct word in parentheses to fill in the blank space in each sentence.

a. The sun and the moon are (common, uncommon) _____ to people all over the world.

b. The countries of South America are (related, unrelated) _____ by the same language, Spanish.

c. English is an (important, unimportant) _____ language in the United States, England, and Australia.

d. Students always try to give (correct, incorrect) _____ answers on exams.

e. Trees and stones are (visible, invisible) _____ things.

f. It is (usual, unusual) _____ for people today to use picture writing.

g. It was hard to talk about (visible, invisible) _____ things with picture writing.

h. It is (common, uncommon) _____ for one-year-old babies to talk.

i. Students learn to type because writing long reports by hand is (practical, impractical) _____.

READING COMPREHENSION

1. **Understanding the Text.**   Follow the directions for each item.

a. Mark the following sentences *True* or *False* according to the information in the reading passage. Underline the part of the passage where you find your information.

(1) The first people on earth communicated in picture writing. _____

(2) Early people didn't have thoughts and ideas. _____

(3) Human language may be about one million years old. _____

(4) Love and fear developed about eight thousand years ago. _____

(5) The alphabet was invented about 3500 years ago. _____

(6) Alphabet writing is easier than picture writing. _____

b. Circle the letter of the correct answer.

(1) The main topic of this reading passage is

    a. early human language.   **b.** what archeology shows us.

    c. picture writing.

(2) In the last sentence of Paragraph [2], the words *love, dislike, fear,* and *pain* are

    a. basic human emotions.

    b. common visible things.

    c. unrelated to human beings.

    d. signs.

(3) Picture writing developed

    a. long before people talked.

    b. long after people used signs for words.

    c. after alphabet writing.

(4) A picture of a foot could mean

    a. an action.   **b.** only a thing.   **c.** the noun *sun.*

(5) Picture writing

    a. didn't help people to communicate.

    b. was the only form of communication in the past.

    c. was a difficult form of communication.

(6) Alphabetic writing was practical because

    a. it was invented after picture writing.

    b. it saved time and space.

    c. it developed from picture writing.

c. Rewrite the following sentences in their correct time order according to the reading passage. The first thing that happened will be your first sentence.

(4) **(1)** Picture writing is about eight thousand years old.

(5) **(2)** Alphabet writing is about 3500 years old.

(2) **(3)** The earliest language used signs, not words.

(3) **(4)** The first words were simple sounds for common things.

(1) **(5)** Human language may be about one million years old.

2. Answering Information Questions.   Write the answers to the following questions in complete sentences.

a. What did the first people on earth use to communicate?

b. About how old is human language?

c. Is love an emotion or a visible thing?

d. About how old is picture writing?

e. What happened to language about 3500 years ago?

f. Did an alphabet make writing easier or harder?

g. Was writing with an alphabet practical or impractical?

3. **Linking Pronouns.**   Pronouns are words that take the place of nouns. Pronouns link, or tie, the writer's ideas together. The reader needs to know which words the pronouns are replacing.

Read the first paragraph of the reading passage again. The subject of the first sentence is *the first people*. The next four sentences do not use the subject *the first people*. These sentences use the pronoun *they*. *They* is a plural subject pronoun that takes the place of *the first people*. Pronouns must agree in number and form with the nouns they are replacing.

a. Circle the correct answer.

(1) The word *they* in the last sentence of Paragraph [1] takes the place of

a. words.   **b.** thoughts and ideas.   **c.** early people.

(2) The word *they* in the third sentence of Paragraph [2] takes the place of

a. human.   **b.** words.   **c.** years.

(3) The word *they* in the first sentence of Paragraph [3] replaces

a. early human beings.   **b.** writing.   **c.** time.

(4) The word *it* in the fourth sentence of Paragraph [4] replaces

a. people.   **b.** each other.   **c.** picture writing.

b. Fill in the blank spaces in the following sentences with the correct pronouns.

(1) Early human beings talked for a long time before _____ developed writing.

(2) In picture writing, people made a picture of the thing _____ wanted to talk about.

(3) Our earth is very ancient. _____ holds many secrets about the past.

(4) An atlas tells us about geography. _____ shows us maps of the world.

(5) I am studying English with my cousin. _____ always do _____ homework together.

WRITING EXERCISES

Simple Past Tense of *To Be*

The Simple Past tense is used to show that someone or something existed or that something happened or was finished in the past.

One million years ago language was simple. The vocabulary wasn't large.

Study the Simple Past tense forms of the verb *to be*.

	Singular	**Plural**
First Person	I was	A writer and I were We were
Second Person	You were	You were
Third Person	Writing was He/She/It was	Things were They were

Notice that only the First Person and Third Person Singular forms use *was*. The negative forms are *wasn't* and *weren't*.

1. **Sentence Completion.**   Fill in the blank space in each sentence with the correct form of the Simple Past tense of *to be*. Use negatives where you are asked to do so. The first one is done for you.

   a. (negative) Early people _____*weren't*_____ exactly like us.

   b. But they _____ the same as we are in some ways.

   c. Water _____ important to them, as it is to us.

   d. The sun _____ something they saw every day.

   e. Their basic emotions _____ probably similar to ours.

   f. (negative) The first people _____ able to talk.

    g. Early language ———————————— probably sign language.

    h. (negative) It ———————————— easy for early people to communicate.

    i. Simple sounds ———————————— probably the first words.

    j. Invisible things ———————————— probably hard to communicate.

    k. An idea ———————————— hard to talk about.

    l. (negative) Writing ———————————— invented until eight thousand years ago.

    m. Pictures ———————————— the first written words.

2. Scrambled Sentences.   Rewrite the following mixed-up sentences so that they form correct English sentences. Remember: Look for the verb first. Then look for the subject. The subject and verb must agree in number.

    a. early   important   were   .   trees   people   to

    b. at first   the   was   human   vocabulary   small   .

    c. things   to communicate   .   difficult   invisible   were

    d. wasn't   .   picture writing   understand   easy   to   always

    e. alphabet   the   ?   was   to invent   easy

3. Sentence Building.   Make a complete sentence using the words in each set. Do *not* change the form or the order of the words.

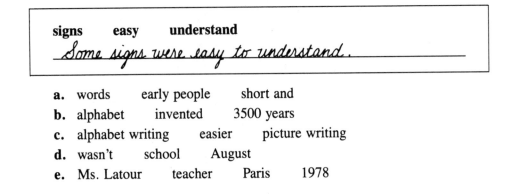

signs   easy   understand

Some signs were easy to understand.

    a. words   early people   short and

    b. alphabet   invented   3500 years

    c. alphabet writing   easier   picture writing

    d. wasn't   school   August

    e. Ms. Latour   teacher   Paris   1978

Simple Past Tense of Regular Verbs

The Simple Past tense of regular verbs adds *d* or *ed* to the base verb.

People *used* sign language before they *developed* picture writing.

---

1. **List Completion.**   Study the following list of regular verbs. Fill in the blank spaces with the correct forms.

Basic Verb	**Simple Past**
talk	talked
use	used
rub	rubbed
point	pointed
want	_____
_____	communicated
_____	showed
name	_____
touch	_____
_____	developed
need	_____
happen	_____
invent	_____
_____	changed

Note that the past tense of the verb *rub* is formed by doubling the final consonant before adding *ed*.

2. **Dictation.**   Write the following sentences from your instructor's dictation. These things all happened in the past. All the verbs will be in the Simple Past tense.

   a. The first people on earth used signs to communicate.
   b. They pointed to things such as rocks, trees, and animals.
   c. Picture writing developed about 8000 years ago.
   d. People in the Middle East invented the alphabet.
   e. The alphabet changed our way of writing.

3. **Recognizing Subjects and Verbs.** Check your dictation and correct your errors. In the following Subject column put the subject of each sentence. Mark it *S* for singular or *P* for plural. In the Verb column, put the verb of each sentence.

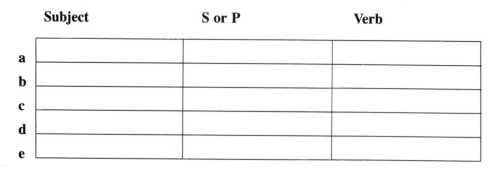

Subject	S or P	Verb
a		
b		
c		
d		
e		

Does the form of a verb in the Simple Past tense change for a singular or plural subject?

Simple Past Tense of Irregular Verbs

Many English verbs do not form the Simple Past tense in the regular way. Study the following verb forms.

Basic Verb	Change	Simple Past
begin	change vowel	began
do	change vowel add consonant	did
see	change vowels add consonant	saw
take	change vowel double vowel	took
have	change consonant	had
make	change consonant	made
speak	change vowels	spoke
put	no change	put
understand	change vowel	understood

You will find a list of commonly used irregular verbs in Appendix A.

1. **Sentence Completion.**   Fill in the blank spaces with the Simple Past tense of the verb in parentheses.

Two thousand years ago the Roman people (to speak) _____
(1)
Latin. Their vocabulary (to be) _____ large. The Romans
(2)
(to need) _____ numbers in addition to words. They (to
(3)
invent) _____ an interesting number system. They (to begin)
(4)
_____ with the number I. They (to make) _____
(5)   (6)
numbers 2 to 10 like this: II, III, IV, V, VI, VII, VIII, IX, and X. They
(to have) _____ numbers for 100 and 1000. The Roman
(7)
numbers (to be) _____ common all over the Western world.
(8)
But later the Western world (to take) _____ over the
(9)
number system of the Arabs. The Arabic number system (to be)
_____ easier to use.
(10)

2. **Sentence Composition.**   Answer the following questions in complete sentences. Note the use of time words for the Simple Past tense. Use these time words in your sentences. The first one is done for you.

   a.   Where did you do your homework last night?

   I did my homework in my room last night.   _____

   b.   What did you have for dinner last night?
   c.   When did you begin work yesterday?
   d.   What did you see on TV last night?
   e.   Where did you put your money yesterday?
   f.   What did you take to class this morning?

3. **Controlled Writing.**   Rewrite the following paragraph. Change the subject *children* to *I*. Change the pronouns to first person. Change the verbs from Simple Present to Simple Past tense.

   Your first sentence will be the following: *I didn't talk when I was very young.*

   Children don't talk when they are very young. But they communicate. They make sounds in their throats. They use a lot of sign language. They point to things that they want. Children soon develop ideas. Then they begin to talk. They make simple sounds. They take words from their parents. They name things and they invent words. That is how they learn to talk.

Simple Past Tense
Negative Forms

The negative form of the Simple Past tense is *didn't* + the basic verb. Study the examples.

The Romans *didn't use* **Arabic numbers.**
Writing *didn't develop* **quickly.**

---

1. **Sentence Composing.**   Use the following items to write complete sentences about what you did yesterday, last night, or this morning. Use time words, adjectives, and prepositional phrases to make your sentences more specific and interesting.

---

see a movie
I saw a good movie last night.

---

a. do my homework   **b.** begin a new book   **c.** make a drawing

d. use a pencil   **e.** need a dictionary   **f.** invent secret writing

g. be at home   **h.** change my mind   **i.** take a bus

2. **Rewriting Sentences.**   Now write your sentences in the negative.

I did my homework in my room. I didn't do my homework in my room.

The Definite Article

The word *the* has three important uses in English.

1. *The* refers to a person or thing that has just been talked about.

This chapter has a reading passage. *The passage* **is about language.**

---

2. *The* refers to someone or something that is the only one of its kind.

> *The sun* and *the moon* **were important to early human beings.**

3.   *The* refers to someone or something specific.

> **The Chinese people brought their system of writing to Japan.**
> (***Chinese people* are a specific group of people.**)

Article Completion.   Fill in the blank spaces with the word *the* where it is needed. Put an *X* in the blank spaces where *the* is not needed.

a.   Chinese writing developed about six thousand years ago. _the_ (1) ancient Chinese people never used an alphabet. They invented a form of ___X___ (2) picture writing. _the_ (3) picture-writing words were called _the_ (4) characters. _the_ (5) Chinese invented many thousands of characters. Many of _the_ (6) old characters are still used today.

b.   Ancient Egyptians knew how to make _the_ (1) ink. They used ink to write on _the_ (2) flat stones. They also used ink to write on

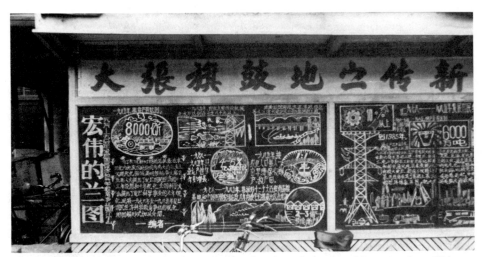

Chinese is the oldest continuously spoken and written language. Many modern Chinese characters are the same as those of ancient times.

_____ flat pieces of pottery. _____ flat stones and pottery
    (3)   (4)
pieces were not large. So _____ ancient Egyptians had to invent
                              (5)
a short form of _____ picture writing. They used _____ short
                   (6)   (7)
form of picture writing for _____ letters and _____ business
                               (8)   (9)
records.

Find some uses of the indefinite articles *a* or *an* in the preceding paragraphs.
Explain why these indefinite, not definite, articles are used.

Time Expressions

Study the following sentences that use expressions of time.

Language may be about *one million years old.*
            (number + time period + *old*)
Some people invented the alphabet *3500 years ago.*
            (number + time period + *ago*)

Sentence Composing.   Answer the following questions in complete sentences.
Use the appropriate time expression in your answer.

a. How old is your father?

b. Did you visit your cousin three days ago?

c. Did human beings see the sun a thousand years ago?

d. Is writing eight thousand or eighty years old?

e. Did people need water five thousand years ago?

f. How old is your best friend?

g. Did you speak to your friend a week ago?

h. Were you in school two weeks ago?

COMPOSING

1. **Developing a Paragraph.**   Answer the following questions in the form of a
    paragraph. Each answer will be a separate sentence. You may leave out some
    of the questions if you wish. Be careful of your punctuation and capitalization.
    Some helpful words to use in your sentences are given in parentheses.

a. Where did you live seven years ago? (in)

b. What language did you speak at home? (always; sometimes; usually)

c. What language did you use in school? (always; usually)

d. Did you learn to read in (your language)? (a little; very well)

e. Did you learn to write in (your language)? (a little; fairly well; very well)

f. Did you have a lot of homework in school? (a lot of; very little)

g. Did you begin English in school?

h. In what grade did you begin English?

i. Did you need an English dictionary? (always; sometimes; often)

j. Did you find English difficult to learn? (found)

2. Composing a Paragraph.

a. Write a paragraph that describes some signs or picture writing that are used in your native culture to communicate ideas. Here are two examples:

(1) In the United States, a red traffic light means stop.

(2) In India, people nod their heads from side to side to show disagreement.

Polynesian is an ancient tongue. Here an anthropologist records a native Polynesian speaker to preserve a sample of this disappearing language. The tape recorder is a useful instrument for communication. As a class, compose a paragraph that describes some of its uses.

Begin your paragraph with a main idea sentence.

b. The language of children is different from the language of adults. Write a paragraph that explains some of these differences. Think about the differences in pronunciation, grammar, length of sentences, size of vocabulary, and ability to read and write.

CHAPTER FOUR B

THE DEVELOPMENT OF AMERICAN ENGLISH

PREREADING

Class Discussion.   English spelling is difficult because the letters of words do not always show the pronunciation of the word. Pronounce each word after your instructor. Circle the letter(s) in each word that is not pronounced.

weather	cupboard
sign	night
island	east
column	love
would	knife

Do you spell words in your native language just the way they are pronounced? Or do some words in your language have extra letters? Give some examples to the class.

New Words.   Try to understand the meanings of these words as they are used in the reading passage. Use a dictionary when necessary.

borrow	angry	afraid
various	(un)popular	happen
insane	(un)known	alike

READING

English, American Style

[1]   People from the United States and England both speak the English language. They can understand each other's books, television programs, and movies.

But there are some interesting differences between American and British English because of the differences in the history of the two nations.

[2]   Most of the first immigrants to America came from England and spoke the English language. They discovered many new plants and animals on the North American continent for which they didn't have any English names. So they borrowed names for many of these things from the Native American languages.[1] For example, *skunk* and *tobacco* are not English words. They are words from Native American languages.

[3]   As the United States developed, the American vocabulary developed too. The various European and Asian immigrants who came to America brought their own vocabularies with them, and some of their words became English words. For instance, *boss* and *cookie* are Dutch words. *Canyon* and *cigar* are Spanish words. *Catsup (ketchup)* is a word of Chinese origin. In addition, Americans changed the meaning of some English words. For example, in England, the word *mad* meant insane, but in America the word *mad* also meant angry.

[4]   Noah Webster was a very important man in the development of American English. He began his work as a schoolteacher in a poor area of New York. Because his students were unable to buy many books, Webster wrote his first book for them. He called it *The American Spelling Book*. Webster wanted to make the spelling of American words easier. For example, he wanted to spell *weather* and *feather* as *wether* and *fether.* But his new spellings were very unpopular.

[5]   Noah Webster produced his first dictionary of American English in 1806. He put many of his unusual spellings in his dictionary. He also added over five thousand new American words that were unknown in England. Many people were unhappy with Webster's new spellings and new words so in his second dictionary of 1828 he changed many spellings to their old forms. In addition, he left out a lot of his new words from the earlier dictionary.

[6]   The American language changed a great deal in the early and middle 1800s. Americans moved west and south. They borrowed many more new words from the Native Americans and the Spanish. They gave new meanings to old words. They also invented many new words themselves. Their pronunciation became different from the pronunciation of the English people. Some Americans were afraid that American English would become a completely different language from British English. They were afraid that American and English people would not be able to understand each other. But that never happened. Today, American and British English are very much alike.

Guided Summary.   A summary tells us the most important ideas of an entire reading passage. It uses the main ideas from each paragraph. Complete the following sentences as a summary of this reading, and rewrite them in correct paragraph form.

---

[1]Native American is the preferred name for the peoples we commonly but incorrectly call American Indians.

a. This reading tells about . . .

b. The American vocabulary grew when . . .

c. Noah Webster was important to the development of American English because . . .

d. His dictionary . . .

e. The American language changed a lot when . . .

VOCABULARY

1. **Expanding Vocabulary.**   Circle the number of the words that are closest in meaning to the given word.

   a. borrow   **(1)** loan from   **(2)** give away to   **(3)** invent

   b. insane   **(1)** basic   **(2)** mentally ill   **(3)** natural

   c. angry   **(1)** numerous   **(2)** invisible   **(3)** in a rage

   d. various   **(1)** different   **(2)** important   **(3)** complete

   e. unpopular   **(1)** well liked   **(2)** not well liked   **(3)** happy

   f. unknown   **(1)** not correct   **(2)** not recognized   **(3)** not happy

   g. afraid   **(1)** new   **(2)** fearful   **(3)** dirty

   h. happen   **(1)** take place   **(2)** explore   **(3)** examine

   i. alike   **(1)** different   **(2)** splendid   **(3)** similar

2. **Using Vocabulary.**   Draw a line from each item in Column A to the related item in Column B. Then rewrite each complete item as a sentence.

	A		**B**
a.	I don't have a pen	a.	I look it up in a dictionary
b.	Our students are from *various* countries	b.	are very much *alike*
c.	When a word is *unknown* to me,	c.	because he gets *angry* easily
d.	The Spanish word *cigarro* and the English word *cigar*	d.	because I can't swim
e.	He is an *unpopular* person	e.	such as Haiti, China, and Mexico
f.	I am *afraid* of deep water	f.	if you drive carefully
g.	Nothing will *happen*	g.	so I must *borrow* yours

3. **Word Families.**   Study the following list of adjectives and their negative forms.

American pioneers moved west in Conestoga wagons such as the one pictured here. The name *Conestoga* comes from a tribe of Native Americans who lived in the area where the wagons were made.

Adjectives	Negative Adjectives
sane	insane
important	unimportant
able	unable
popular	unpopular
usual	unusual
known	unknown
happy	unhappy
afraid	unafraid
alike	unalike

Follow the directions for each item.

a. Put a check (√) next to the items that might make a teacher *unpopular.*

arrives late to class _____ knows students' names _____ marks homework carefully _____ never looks at homework _____ doesn't answer students' questions _____ helps students after class _____ gives many tests _____

b. In complete sentences, state two things that babies are *unable* to do.

> **Babies are unable to go to school.**

c. In complete sentences, state whether you are *afraid* or *unafraid* of each of the following things.

the dark   high places   airplanes   strange places
deep water   thunderstorms

d. Write one sentence telling what makes you *happy* and one sentence telling what makes you *unhappy.* Use one or both of the following patterns.

> **It makes me happy to see my friends.**
> **Smiling people make me happy.**

e. Complete the following sentence by telling one way in which you and another person are *alike:*
. . . and I are alike because . . .

> **My sister and I are alike because we both have green eyes.**

f. Put an *X* next to those items that are *unimportant* for learning a new language.

doing housework _____ using a dictionary _____

practicing new sounds _____ owning a dog _____ exploring

space _____ reading a newspaper every day _____

wearing new clothes _____

READING COMPREHENSION

1. **Understanding the Text.**   Follow the directions for each item.

   a. Mark *M.I.* (for Main Idea) next to each statement that tells a main idea of the reading passage.

   (1) American English borrowed many words from other languages.

   _____

   (2) *Cookie* is a Dutch word. _____

   (3) Noah Webster was a man. _____

   (4) Noah Webster was important in the development of American English.

   _____

   (5) American English changed a lot in the 1800s. _____

b. Circle the letter of the correct answer.

(1) According to Paragraph [2], the early Americans borrowed Native American words because

    a. the Native Americans had been kind to them.

    b. they needed new words for unknown things.

    c. they didn't like the English people.

(2) In Paragraph [3], the third sentence, the expression *for instance* means the same as

    a. for that reason. **b.** for example. **c.** in addition.

(3) Noah Webster wanted to change American spelling

    a. to make it easier. **b.** to make it more like Dutch.

    c. to sell his books.

(4) The new words and spellings in Webster's first dictionary

    a. were popular. **b.** were borrowed from Spanish. **c.** were not well liked.

(5) Webster produced his first dictionary in the nineteenth century. American English changed a lot in the nineteenth century. Check (√) the following dates that belong to the nineteenth century.

1624 _____ 1776 _____ 1806 _____ 1828 _____

1850 _____ 1909 _____ 1950 _____

(6) In Paragraph [6], the sentences that give specific details about how American English changed from British English are

    a. the first two sentences.

    b. the third, fourth, fifth, and sixth sentences.

    c. the last four sentences.

2. Answering Information Questions. Write the answers to the following questions in complete sentences.

    a. What language did most of the early American immigrants speak?

    b. From whom did the immigrants borrow the word *tobacco*?

    c. What did the word *mad* mean in England?

    d. Where did Noah Webster begin his work?

    e. Did Noah Webster write his spelling book or his dictionary first?

    f. How did Noah Webster want to spell the word *feather*?

    g. What did Webster change in his second dictionary?

h. When did the American language change a great deal?

3. **Linking Pronouns.**   Pronouns are words that take the place of nouns. Pronouns tie the writer's sentences together. They help the reader follow the writer's ideas.

Read the following paragraphs. All the pronouns are circled. Draw an arrow from each pronoun to the noun it is replacing. (The same noun may be used for more than one pronoun.) The first one is done for you.

a.   Most of the first immigrants to America came from England. (They) spoke the English language. But (they) discovered many new plants and animals in (their) new land. These things didn't have English names. But (they) had Native American names. The immigrants learned the Native American names. (They) borrowed (them) from the Native American languages.

b.   Noah Webster was a very important man in the development of the American language. (He) began (his) work as a schoolteacher in a poor area of New York. (His) students were unable to buy books because (they) were so expensive. So Webster wrote (his) first book for (them). (He) called (it) *The American Spelling Book.* (He) wanted to make spelling easier. But (his) new spellings were unpopular. No one liked (them).

WRITING EXERCISES

Simple Past Tense of *To Be*

The Simple Past tense of verbs is used to show that someone or something existed or that something happened or was finished in the past.

Noah Webster was a teacher and writer. His first book wasn't popular.

Study the Simple Past tense forms of the verb *to be*.

	Singular	**Plural**
First Person	I was	My family and I were We were

	Singular	**Plural**
Second Person	You were	You were
Third Person	Language was	People were
	He/She/It was	They were

Notice that only the First Person and Third Person Singular forms use *was*. The negative forms are *wasn't* and *weren't*.

1. **Sentence Building.**   Write a correct sentence by putting together a subject from Column A, a verb form from Column B, and one item to complete the sentence from Column C. Your sentences should contain true information from the text.

	A	**B**	**C**
a.	The first immigrants to America	was were	popular a new word to the first immigrants
b.	Noah Webster's first dictionary	wasn't weren't	from England
c.	Webster's students	were	some Dutch words
d.	What	was	an important American educator
e.	*Tobacco*		
f.	Webster		rich

2. **Recognizing Verb Forms.**   Listen carefully as your instructor reads the following paragraph. Then circle each Simple Past tense form of the verb *to be*. Draw an arrow from the verb to its subject. If the subject is singular, mark it *S*. If the subject is plural, mark it *P*. The first one is done for you.

         Anne Royall (was) an early American writer. She was born in Maryland in 1769. Very few schools were open in her area. So her father was her teacher. Words were always interesting to Anne Royall. Language was of interest to her even when she was young. When she was older, she studied the way people all over America talked. To Mrs. Royall the speech in Washington, D.C., was the best. In her opinion, speech in Philadelphia wasn't very good. Pronunciation in Philadelphia was poor. Southern words were the most interesting to Anne Royall. Southern and northern words weren't alike. Mrs. Royall's books were very interesting. Her writing was useful to early Americans.

3. **Writing Questions.**   Use the information in the paragraph about Anne Royall to make up five yes-no questions. Use the Simple Past tense of the verb *to be* in each question. Then ask your classmates to answer your questions in complete sentences.

Was Anne Royall an early American teacher?
No, she was an early American writer.

Simple Past Tense of Regular Verbs

The Simple Past tense of regular verbs adds *d* or *ed* to the base verb.

Webster *wanted* to make spelling easier, but no one *liked* the changes.

---

1. **List Completion.**   Study the following list of verbs. Fill in the blank spaces with the correct forms.

Basic Verb	Simple Past
discover	discovered
borrow	borrowed
develop	developed
change	_____
_____	immigrated
_____	called
receive	_____
produce	_____
_____	added
move	_____
_____	invented
happen	_____

2. **Dictation.** Write the following sentences from your instructor's dictation. These things all happened in the past. All the verbs will be in the Simple Past tense.

   a. The English people borrowed many Native American names.

   b. Americans changed the meanings of some English words.

   c. Noah Webster produced the first American spelling book.

   d. Many Americans moved west and south in the 1800s.

   e. Then their language changed a great deal.

3. **Recognizing Subjects and Verbs.** Check your dictation and correct your errors. In the following Subject column put the subject of each sentence. Mark it *S* for singular or *P* for plural. In the Verb column put the verb from each sentence.

	Subject	S or P	Verb
a			
b			
c			
d			
e			

Do verbs in the Simple Past tense change their forms for a singular or plural subject?

Simple Past Tense of Irregular Verbs

Many English verbs do not form the Simple Past tense in the regular way. Study the following verb forms.

Basic Verb	Change	Simple Past
come	change vowel	came
speak	change vowel	spoke
become	change vowel	became
begin	change vowel	began
write	change vowel	wrote
have	change consonant	had
mean	add consonant	meant

bring	change vowel and change consonant	brought
put	no change	put

1. **Sentence Completion.**   Fill in the blank spaces with the Simple Past tense of each verb in parentheses.

William McGuffey had an important place in American education. He (to be) _____ (1) born in western Pennsylvania in 1800. Then his parents (to move) _____ (2) further west to Ohio. His area (to have) _____ (3) very few schools. So McGuffey (to be) _____ (4) his own teacher. He (to begin) _____ (5) to teach school himself when he (to become) _____ (6) thirteen years old. But he (to want) _____ (7) to go to college. So he (to use) _____ (8) his free time to study. After eight years of part-time study, he (to receive) _____ (9) his degree. McGuffey (to become) _____ (10) very interested in the public schools. He (to write) _____ (11) many reading books for young children. McGuffey (to mean) _____ (12) to teach children good behavior in his books. So he (to put) _____ (13) in many little stories about how children should behave. McGuffey's readers (to become) _____ (14) the most popular schoolbooks in America.

2. **Scrambled Sentences.**   Rewrite the following mixed-up sentences so that they form correct English sentences. Remember to look for the verb first. Then look for its subject.

   a. England   insane   in   .   meant   word   *mad*   the

   b. students   poor   .   Webster's   very   were   first

   c. for them   Webster   .   his   book   wrote   first

   d. language   .   the   a lot   changed   the 1800s   American   in

3. **Sentence Composing.**   Write the answers to the following questions in complete sentences. Use the Simple Past tense of the main verb in each sentence. The first one is done for you.

A page from *McGuffey's First Eclectic Reader.* Make up a story about the people in this picture that would be interesting for a child to read.

   a. When did you begin English classes?

      I began English classes in 1979.

   b. What language did you speak first?

   c. Did you write yesterday's homework in pen or pencil?

   d. What did the word *mad* mean in England?

   e. How many books did you bring with you this morning?

   f. At what time did you come to school today?

   g. Where did you put your dictionary yesterday?

Simple Past Tense
Negative Forms

The negative form of the Simple Past tense is *didn't* + the basic verb.

> **I *didn't borrow* money to buy textbooks.**
> **Early in the term most students *didn't speak* clearly.**

1. **Sentence Composing.**   Use the following items to write sentences about what you did yesterday, last night, or this morning. Use time words, adjectives, and prepositional phrases to make your sentences more specific and interesting.

---

discover a store
I discovered a new department store on Main Street.

---

   a. be very tired   **b.** borrow a dollar   **c.** begin a lesson
   d. come to class late   **e.** speak to my instructor   **f.** take home books
   g. receive a letter   **h.** have an exam

2. **Rewriting Sentences.**   Now write your sentences in the negative.

I borrowed a dollar from my friend. I didn't borrow a dollar from my friend.

The Definite Article

The word *the* has three important uses in English.

   1. *The* refers to a person or thing that has just been talked about.

This chapter has a reading passage. *The passage* is about American English.

---

   2. *The* refers to someone or something that is the only one of its kind.

Noah Webster produced *the first American dictionary*.
(only one dictionary can be the first dictionary)

---

   3. *The* refers to someone or something specific.

> *The* earliest European settlers in North America were English.
> (*earliest European settlers* are a specific group of people)

Article Completion.   Fill in the blank spaces with the word *the* where it is needed. Put an *X* in the spaces where *the* is not needed.

a.   (1) _____ English language developed from an old German language. (2) _____ French language added many new words to English. Latin, (3) _____ language of the Roman people, also added many words to English. (4) _____ Spanish, Dutch, and Italian words are also part of our English vocabulary. When (5) _____ first immigrants came to America, they learned (6) _____ new Native American words. For example, (7) _____ word *tobacco* is a Native American word.

b.   (1) _____ British and American languages are not exactly alike. (2) _____ spelling of some words is different. For example, (3) _____ British word *tyre* is spelled *tire* in (4) _____ United States. A *truck* in (5) _____ United States is called a *lorry* in (6) _____ England. But (7) _____ biggest difference between British and American language is in pronunciation. Many Americans have (8) _____ difficulty understanding British speech.

Find some uses of the indefinite article *a* or *an* in these paragraphs. With your class, talk about why these indefinite, not definite, articles are used.

Time Expressions

1. Study the following sentence that uses an expression of time.

> **Noah Webster produced his first dictionary *in 1806*.**

Sentence Composing.   Use the time expression *in* + a specific year, month, or week in a complete sentence to answer the following questions.

a. In what year were you born?

b. In what month were you born?

c. When did you begin to study English?

d. Is Christmas in the first week or the last week of December?

e. In what month did you begin this school term.

2. Study the following list of dates and time expressions.

Date	Time Expression
1769	in the middle 1700s
1806	in the early 1800s
1828	in the early 1800s
1880–1889	in the late 1800s
1913	in the early 1900s
1958	in the 1950s
1981	in the 1980s

Rewriting Sentences.   Rewrite the following sentences using a time expression similar to those in the list. Replace the italicized dates in the sentence with your new time expression.

> **Many pioneers went to California *around 1848*.**
> **Many pioneers went to California *in the middle 1800s*.**

a. The first English immigrants came to America *around 1620*.

b. Anne Royall was born *in 1769*.

c. Noah Webster's first dictionary came out *in 1806*.

d. *From 1830–1870* many Americans moved west.

e. Many European immigrants came to America *from 1870–1890*.

f. Many scientific words were added to English *from 1920–1960*.

g. A new Webster's dictionary came out *around 1976*.

COMPOSING

1. **Developing a Paragraph.**

a. Read the following sentences about the development of the English language. Put *M.I.* (for Main Idea) next to the main idea sentence. Then number the other sentences in the correct order to form a logical paragraph. Look for time expressions, pronouns, and other words to help you. Rewrite the complete paragraph.

(1) Many of the English words we use in science, education, and government have a Latin origin. _____

(2) The English language has also borrowed words from Greek, Hindi, Arabic, and many other languages. _____

(3) From about 1200 to 1500, Latin words also entered the English language. _____

(4) First of all, English has a Germanic origin. _____

(5) The English language owes its development to many different languages. _____

(6) Many basic English words are similar to German words. _____

(7) Then in the late 1100s, a French king conquered England. _____

(8) And finally, English has created many new words for new inventions. _____

(9) French words became very common in English. _____

b. The following list gives you some ways that you can practice your English. Think about which of these things you did yesterday. Choose five or more items to use in a paragraph about how you practiced English yesterday. You may add items of your own. Begin your paragraph with a main idea sentence. Write complete sentences using your chosen items in paragraph form. Make your sentences specific and interesting by using adjectives and prepositional phrases. Use the Simple Past tense of verbs.

> **Yesterday I practiced English with my friends. We listened to the English news in the morning.**

(1) watch TV program(s)
(2) listen to the radio
(3) read a newspaper, book, and so on
(4) learn a new word(s)
(5) use a dictionary
(6) speak with friends, classmates, and so on
(7) have a class

(**8**) use a tape recorder or phonograph record

(**9**) play a game

(**10**) write a letter, paragraph, and so on

2. **Composing a Paragraph.**

   a. Noah Webster and William McGuffey were good teachers who helped their students a great deal. Write a paragraph about one of your teachers who helped you in your education.

   b. When people travel to new places, they usually see new and interesting things. Sometimes they see things they never saw before. Write a paragraph in which you tell about some new place you have traveled to, and some of the interesting sights you saw there.

CHAPTER FIVE A

INTERNATIONAL LANGUAGES TODAY

PREREADING

Alphabetizing. In some countries different groups of people speak different languages. The following lists show you the different languages that people speak in certain countries. Rewrite these lists in alphabetical order.

Israel	Indonesia	India
English	Madurese	Gujerati
Arabic	Sundanese	Assamese
French	Chinese	English
Judeo-Spanish	Balinese	Hindi
Aramaic	Javanese	Tamil (common)
Hebrew	Batak	Bengali
	English	Oriya
	Bugi	Tamil (high)
	Indonesian	Sanskrit
	Minangkabau	Marathi
		Kannada
		Malayalam
		Telugu
		Prakrits
		Kashmiri

Do people speak one, or more than one, language in your native country? Tell about the different languages spoken in your country.

New Words. Try to understand the meanings of these words as they are used in the reading passage. Use a dictionary when necessary.

native
oral
pronunciation
immigrant =

international =
currently =
official =
literate ≠ *illiterate*

primarily =
generally = *usually*

READING

Communicating Across Cultures

[1]   English is the native language of over 250 million people. This term you are learning English. You are reading English passages and answering questions in English. Probably you are studying English grammar too. Your instructor gives you directions and homework assignments in English. Perhaps you are practicing oral English with your friends or using a tape recorder to learn English pronunciation. Many foreign students and immigrants in the United States, in England, and in Australia are studying English as a second language just as you are. The reason for all this English language study is that English is an international language.

[2]   Only a few of the world's languages are used for international communication. Currently, the United Nations is using six official languages for international communication. English is one of these. The five other international languages of the United Nations are Arabic, French, Mandarin Chinese, Russian, and Spanish. English and French are the two basic languages at the United Nations. Most of the world's scientific and technical writing is produced in English. A small amount is also produced in French and Russian.

[3]   Mandarin Chinese is only one of many oral languages in China. But there is only one official written language. This written language uses characters that all literate Chinese can read. Look at the photograph of the Chinese man writing Chinese characters. He is not using a pen or a pencil. He is using a brush. He is holding the brush the way an artist does. He is forming the characters very carefully. Some of them have many separate strokes and are very difficult to write. Currently, the Chinese are trying to make their characters easier. Then more Chinese people will be able to read and write their language.

[4]   French is another international language. It is a native language for over 50 million people. French is used primarily in France, but people in Haiti and in some parts of Africa also speak French. French is also studied in high schools and colleges all over the world. Look at the photograph of the young African girls. They speak their own African language at home, but they are learning French as a second language in school. They are reading French words in a book. One of the girls is carrying a baby on her back as she studies.

[5]   Russian is another international language. Over 120 million people natively speak Russian. But Russian is generally spoken only in the Soviet Union and

some countries in Eastern Europe. Spanish and Arabic are international languages that are used in many different countries. Spanish, for example, is used all over Central and South America, in Spain, and in many parts of the United States. Nearly 150 million people are native Spanish speakers. Currently, many high school and college students are studying Spanish. There are many other languages such as Hindi, which millions of people also speak. But these languages are not officially used as international languages at the United Nations.

Oral Cloze.   Number a column in your notebook from 1 to 10. Your instructor will read Paragraph [4] aloud to you twice. Listen very carefully. Then your instructor will read the paragraph aloud again, but he or she will leave out some words. Your instructor will say "blank" where these words are left out. Next to each number on your paper write the word that correctly fills the blank space. Your instructor will read the paragraph with blanks to you several times. Now close your books.

French is another international language. It is a native blank for over 50 million blank. French is used primarily in France, but people in Haiti and in some parts blank Africa also speak French. French is also studied in high schools and blank all over the world. Look at the photograph blank the young African girls. They speak their own blank language at home, but they are blank French as a second language in school. They are blank French words in a book. Blank of the girls is carrying a baby on her back as blank studies.

VOCABULARY

1. **Expanding Vocabulary.**   Choose the item that explains the meaning of the italicized word.

    a. There are about 120 million *native* speakers of Russian.

        (1) belonging to a place by birth
        (2) brought to a place from somewhere else
        (3) learned in school

    b. I need a lot of *oral* practice in French.

        (1) speaking practice
        (2) reading practice
        (3) writing practice

    c. The *pronunciation* of Spanish is not difficult.

        (1) sound system   (2) vocabulary   (3) writing

d. Many *immigrants* to the United States study English.

(1) people who come to live in a new country
(2) people who come to study in a new country
(3) people who remain in their own country

e. English is an *international* language.

(1) used in only one country
(2) used in many different countries
(3) used only by women

f. You are *currently* studying English.

(1) in the past   (2) always   (3) at this time

g. French is an *official* language at the United Nations.

(1) according to the laws
(2) difficult to use
(3) not useful

h. It is useful to be *literate* in two languages.

(1) able to sing   (2) able to read and write   (3) able to speak

i. French is spoken *primarily* in France.

(1) most importantly   (2) rarely   (3) probably

j. North Americans *generally* speak only English.

(1) usually   (2) never   (3) easily

2. **Using Vocabulary.**   The words in parentheses are from the New Word list. But all the letters are mixed up. Put the letters in correct order, and write the word in the blank space.

_____ (strmimgnai) who come to the United States
      (1)

_____ (lylneagre) find English difficult. They may never
      (2)

learn _____ (raol) English like a ___native___
                (3)   (4)

(tevnai) speaker of English. But if they study, they will become

___literate___ (itlreaet) in English. Then they will be able to
      (5)

read English books and newspapers. ___currently___ (rrucnteyl),
                                              (6)

many people all over the world are studying English.

3. **Word Families.**   Adjectives describe nouns or pronouns.

English is an *international* language. (What kind of language? *international* language)

Adverbs of manner tell how (in what manner) verb action is done.

Business people use English *internationally*. (*How* is English used? It is used *internationally*.)

Most adverbs are formed by adding *ly* to adjectives.
Study the following list of adjectives and adverbs.

Adjectives	Adverbs
international	internationally
native	natively
current	currently
official	officially
technical	technically
oral	orally
careful	carefully
usual	usually
general	generally
Note spelling changes of these:	
primary	primarily
easy	easily
scientific	scientifically

In the blank space write the correct form of the words in parentheses.

a. English, French, and Russian are used for (scientific, scientifically) _____ writing.

b. I practice French (oral, orally) _____ with a tape recorder.

c. Now I can speak French (easy, easily) _____ .

d. What is the (primary, primarily) _____ language in your (native, natively) _____ country?

e. Hindi is the (official, officially) _____ language in India. But Indian people (general, generally) _____ speak more than one language.

f. The man in the photograph is (careful, carefully) _____ forming Chinese characters. Then the characters will be (easy, easily) _____ to read.

g. The United Nations (usual, usually) _____ gives tours in French and Spanish as well as English.

READING COMPREHENSION

1. **Understanding the Text.**   Choose the correct answer.

   a. Which sentence uses the word *passage* with the same meaning that it has in the third sentence of Paragraph [1]?

   (1) The old house had many secret doors and passages.
   (2) There are many interesting passages in my history book.
   (3) We made two passages to France by ship last year.

   b. Which sentence uses the word *directions* with the same meaning that it has in the fifth sentence of Paragraph [1]?

   (1) The children ran off in different directions.
   (2) The four main directions are north, south, east, and west.
   (3) Please give me directions for going to your house.

   c. Which pronoun correctly fits the blank space in the following sentence? Perhaps you are speaking English with _____ friends.

   (1) his   (2) their   (3) your

   d. Which of the following sentences means the same thing as the next to the last sentence in Paragraph [2]?

   (1) Very little scientific and technical writing is produced in Russian.
   (2) English is the primary language for scientific and technical writing.
   (3) English, French, and Russian are official languages at the United Nations.

   e. In the second sentence of Paragraph [4], *it* refers to

   (1) France   (2) language   (3) French

   f.   Why do you think one of the girls in the photograph is carrying a baby?

   (1) She is helping her mother to take care of the baby.

   (2) She wants the baby to study French with her.

   (3) She wants the baby to play games with her.

   g.   Which of the following sentences is true according to the last paragraph?

   (1) More people natively speak Spanish than Russian.

   (2) Russian is spoken all over Central and South America.

   (3) Hindi is an official language at the United Nations.

2.   **Answering Information Questions.**   Write your answers to the following questions in complete sentences.

   a.   What language are you learning this term? *English* .

   b.   Name three countries where foreign students and immigrants are studying English.

   c.   How many languages are officially used at the United Nations for international communication?

   d.   What is the Chinese man in the photograph doing?

   e.   What is he holding in his hand?

   f.   What language are the young African girls learning in school?

   g.   Name two areas of the world where Spanish is used.

   h.   Is Hindi or French an official language at the United Nations?

3.   **Scanning for Specific Information.**   *To scan* means to read a passage quickly to find specific facts. In order to scan for the answer to a question, you must first pick out the main words in the question.

   Answer the following questions by scanning the reading passage for facts. The main question words are italicized for you. Write the number of the paragraph and the number of the sentence where you find your answer. The first one is done for you.

   a.   *How many* people *natively* speak *English*?

   250 million   _Para. 1_   _first sentence_

   b.   *How many official languages* are used at the *United Nations*?

   ___6___   ___2___   ___2___

   c.   In *what language* is *most* of the *scientific and technical writing* produced?

   ___En___   ___2___   ___6___

d. *How many official written languages* are there *in China?*

_____ 3 _____ 2. _____

e. *How many* people *natively* speak *Russian?*

_____ 120 _____ 5. _____ 1, _____

f. Name *one country* where *Spanish* is spoken.

_____ 5 . _____ 5 _____

g. *How many* people are *native Spanish* speakers?

_____ 150, _____ 5 _____ 6. _____

h. Is *Hindi* an *official language* at the *United Nations?*

_____ No _____ 5 _____ 9 _____

WRITING EXERCISES

Present Continuous Tense

The Present Continuous tense of verbs is used for actions that are currently taking place. It tells about activity that is going on now or in the present period of time. The Present Continuous tense is formed by *am, is,* or *are* + the *ing* ending of the main verb.

I am studying English this semester.
Now we are learning the Present Continuous tense.

Study the Present Continuous tense of the verb *hold*.

	Singular	**Plural**
First Person	I am holding	A friend and I are holding
		We are holding
Second Person	You are holding	You are holding
Third Person	The man is holding	The girls are holding
	He/She/It is holding	They are holding

The negative forms are *am not (I'm not), is not (isn't),* and *are not (aren't)* + the *ing* form of the verb.

1. **Sentence Building.**   Write complete sentences by matching the subjects in Column A with the related Present Continuous verb phrase in Column B. The subjects must agree in number with their verbs. Use the information from the reading passage as a basis for your answers.

    A   **B**

    a. You   *f* is carrying a baby.
    b. The Chinese man   *e* are studying English in England.
    c. He   *i* are studying Spanish.
    d. The Chinese people   *b* is holding a brush.
    e. The young African girls   *a* are learning English this term.
    f. One of the African girls   *e* are learning French as a second language.
    g. The baby   *c* isn't using a pencil.
    h. Many foreign students   *d* are making their written characters easier.
    i. Many high school students   *g* isn't studying French.

2. **Controlled Writing.**   Look at the photograph of the United Nations tour guide. Rewrite the paragraph underneath it using plurals. Change the subject *a tour guide* to *tour guides*. Change *a tourist* to *tourists*. Make all the necessary verb, pronoun, and article changes from singular to plural. Your first sentence will be the following: *Tour guides are leading tourists around the United Nations.*

3. **Sentence Completion.**   Complete the following sentences by putting the verb in parentheses in the Present Continuous tense. Note that verbs that end in *e* drop the *e* before adding *ing*: *use* becomes *using*.

    a. You and your classmates (communicate) *are communicating* in English.

    b. Perhaps you (use) *are using* a tape recorder for pronunciation.

    c. The African girls in the photograph (negative: study) *aren't studying* Spanish as a second language.

    d. The Chinese man (write) *is writing* Chinese characters with a brush.

    e. He (form) *is forming* the characters very carefully.

A tour guide is leading a tourist around the United Nations. The tourist is from Colombia. She is listening to the tour guide. The tour guide is speaking Spanish to the tourist. The tour guide is pointing out some of the splendid objects at the United Nations. Today this Colombian tourist is discovering many interesting things about the United Nations. Later this afternoon the tour guide is giving another tour in French.

f. He (negative: write) _isn't writing_ an alphabetic language.

g. Currently, many high school and college students (learn) _are learning_ Spanish.

h. We hope that you (look) _are looking_ up new words in your dictionary.

Compound Sentence Parts with *And*

The word *and* connects sentence parts that add information. These sentence parts must be related in meaning, and they must have the same form.

French and *Spanish* are international languages.
(noun)   (noun)

The man *is holding* a brush and *forming* characters.
   (verb: Present Continuous)   (verb: Present Continuous)

Java has a *hot* and *wet* climate.
      (adjective) (adjective)

---

1. **Rewriting Sentences.** Study the following sentences that have compound sentence parts with *and*. Rewrite each sentence using the words in parentheses to replace the italicized compound parts. Name the type of compound parts you use in each sentence.

   a. *French and English* are two international languages. (Spanish, Arabic)
   b. We *are studying and learning* English. (reading, writing)
   c. Many foreign students *in the United States and in England* are studying English. (Canada, Australia)
   d. A lot of *scientific and technical* writing is produced in English. (beautiful, interesting)
   e. The man is forming Chinese characters *slowly and carefully.* (correctly, easily)

2. **Paragraph Building.** Make two columns on a separate sheet of paper. Read the following paragraph. Underline each set of compound sentence parts. Write the first item of the set in your left-hand column. Write the second item in your right-hand column. The first one is done for you.

<table>
<tr><td>French</td><td>Spanish</td></tr>
</table>

   French and Spanish are similar to each other. French and Spanish both come from Latin. They have many similar nouns and verbs. In French and in Spanish the verbs have many different endings and spellings. For that reason, French and Spanish verbs are difficult for some people to learn. It takes time to speak and write these languages easily and correctly.

   Read the paragraph several times. Then close your textbook. Using only your columns of compound parts, rebuild the paragraph sentence by sentence. Make it as similar to the original paragraph as you can.

3. **Sentence Completion.** Follow the directions in parentheses to complete each sentence. In some sets, one item is done for you.

   a. There are many different ways to study and ___*learn*___ a
       (compound verbs)
       new language.
   b. ___*Colleges*___ and ___*Universities*___ give classes in dif-
       (compound noun subjects)
       ferent languages.
   c. You can practice oral language with a phonograph and a _____ .
       (compound nouns)
   d. Television is a (an) ___*interesting*___ and _____ way
       (compound adjectives)
       to improve your listening skills.

e. For oral practice you should also speak the language with _____*family*_____
    <u>(compound nouns)</u>
    and classmates.

f. For reading practice, start with simple things such as advertisements and

    _____ .
    <u>(compound nouns)</u>

g. Then you can go on to read books and __*news paper*__ .
    <u>(compound nouns)</u>

h. Practice your new language at home and __*at work*__ .
    <u>(compound prepositional phrases)</u>

i. Soon you will produce your new language __*correctly*__ and
    <u>(compound adverbs)</u>
    __*early*__ .

j. Knowing English will help you to __*understand*__ and __*communicate*__
    <u>(compound verb phrases: basic form)</u>

Sentence Patterns with *Because*

We answer questions that ask *why* with the connecting word *because*. The word
because joins together two thoughts. One thought tells what happens, that is, the
result. The other thought gives a reason why.

Many people are learning English because it is an international language. (result)   (reason)

---

1. **Sentence Combining.** In each of the following items one sentence tells us
    the result, and the other sentence explains the reason. Combine the two sen-
    tences into one complete sentence using the connecting word *because*. Replace
    nouns with pronouns where necessary. Rewrite each new sentence with correct
    punctuation and capitalization.

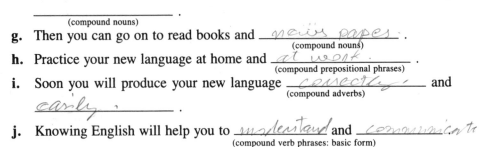

(1) **Java has a lot of vegetation.**
(2) **Java has a hot, wet climate.**

Java has a lot of vegetation because it has a hot, wet climate.

Note that in this sentence pattern the result always comes first.

a. (1) I want to have better English pronunciation.
    (2) I listen to English TV programs.

b. **(1)** My sister is studying French and English.

   (2) My sister wants to become a United Nations tour guide.

c. **(1)** It takes a long time to learn Chinese writing.

   (2) Chinese characters are very difficult to form.

d. **(1)** Spanish is a useful second language.

   (2) Spanish is spoken in many parts of the world.

e. **(1)** There are many factories near the river.

   (2) The river is very polluted.

f. **(1)** Most scientific writing is produced in English.

   (2) Scientists should study English.

2. **Sentence Expansion.**   Complete the following result clauses by adding a reason that explains why. Join the two sentence parts by the word *because*. Complete your new sentences in the space provided.

   a. The air in my city is very dirty _because there are many_ .

   b. Paris is an important city _____ .

   c. Very little vegetation grows in the desert _because it has hot & dry climate._ .

   d. It would be difficult to live on the moon _because it hasn't a_ .

   e. I am studying English _because I life in united_ .

   f. It is interesting to go to college _because_ .

   g. It is useful to speak two languages _because it_ .

Plural Possessives

You have already learned how to form singular possessives in the apostrophe + *s* form. Study the following model. It shows you how to write plural possessives in the *s* + apostrophe form.

Singular	Singular Possessive	Plural	Plural Possessive
a girl	a girl's teacher (teacher of a girl)	girls	girls' teachers (teachers of the girls)

With your instructor, talk about how the plural possessive is formed with an *s* + apostrophe. We mainly use this form of the plural possessive for human beings.

1. **List Completion.**   Fill in the missing forms on the following list. The first one is done for you.

   a. a friend *a friend's* tape recorder   friends *friends'* tape recorders

   b. _____ an immigrant's difficulty   immigrants _____ difficulties

   c. a man   a man's brush   _____   _____ brushes

   d. a student   _____ work   _____   _____ work

   e. _____   a scientist's interest   scientists   _____ interests

   f. a parent   _____ love   parents   _____ love

2. **Rewriting Sentences.**   Rewrite each sentence, changing the italicized expressions to plural possessives in the *s* + apostrophe form.

   > The *notebooks of the students* were filled with exercises.
   > *The students' notebooks were filled with exercises.*

   a. The *basic languages of the United Nations* are French and English.

   b. The *problems of the immigrants* were not easily solved.

   c. The *children of my neighbors* are literate in two languages.

   d. The *teacher of the African girls* speaks French.

   e. The *native language of Guatemalan Indians* is Quetzal.

   f. The *assignments of my instructors* are usually clear.

   Identify the subject of each new sentence. Draw a line from the subject to the verb. Do they agree in number?

COMPOSING

1. **Developing a Paragraph.**

   a. In the following paragraph an American student is describing a humorous confusion in vocabulary. Choose the correct item to complete each of the sentences that make up the paragraph. Rewrite the complete new paragraph.

   (1) A funny confusion in vocabulary happened when I was in Mexico. I was studying Spanish, but

   a. I didn't know too many words.

   b. I knew a lot of words.

Over 120 million people natively speak Russian. But Russian is generally spoken only in the Soviet Union and some Eastern European countries. Write three sentences about this photograph using compound nouns, verbs, or adjectives.

(2) I was at a restaurant in Mexico City, and

    a. I was enjoying the city.

    b. I wanted to eat some seafood.

(3) I told the waiter I wanted to order *camiones*.

    a. I thought the restaurant was closing.

    b. I thought that was the Spanish word for shrimps.

(4) The waiter looked surprised because

    a. *camiones* means trucks in Spanish.

    b. *camiones* are delicious.

(5) Then he smiled. "Oh," he said, "you mean *camarones*."

    a. "*Camarones* means shrimps."

    b. "*Camarones* means trucks."

(6) I laughed. The two Spanish words are very similar.

    a. That's why shrimps are expensive.

    b. That's why I had confused the two words.

b. The following paragraph describes the actions of a group of people in a college cafeteria at lunchtime. It begins with a main idea sentence that tells where the action is taking place. It also gives a general feeling or impression about the place. The sentences that tell how people *look, seem,* or *are* are in the Simple Present tense. The sentences that tell what people are doing are in the Present Continuous tense.

Read the paragraph carefully. In the blank spaces provided, write a sentence using the words in parentheses. You may change the form and the order of these words.

It is 1:00 P.M. and the college cafeteria is very busy. Lots of students are eating lunch. An older woman is sitting alone. She is reading a thick book. She is writing in her notebook. She looks serious. (perhaps, study, exam) _____

_____ .

Three young men are talking loudly. They are waving their arms around. They seem excited about something. (maybe, talk, problems)

_____ .

In one corner a young man and a young woman are holding hands. They seem quite happy. (smile, each other) _____

_____ .

They are speaking in low voices. Many students are reading newspapers. (They, smoke, drink coffee) _____

_____ .

They seem very relaxed.

2. **Composing a Paragraph.**

   a. Choose some public place such as a restaurant, library, or train. Look at the different people closely. Write a paragraph about what some of the people are doing. Try to use some adjectives to tell how they look. Begin with a main idea sentence that gives us a general idea about the place.

   b. Think about an incident when people were confused because you did not know a language well. Describe the difficulty this caused and how you finally solved the problem.

CHAPTER FIVE B

A MODERN DICTIONARY

PREREADING

Dictionary Use.   Study the following entries from the *Webster's New World Dictionary*. What order do the entries follow? What does the dictionary tell you about the entry word? What do the abbreviations mean?

   a. ex·pert (ek′-spērt, ik-spŭrt′), *adj.* [see experience], very skillful. *n.* (ek′-spērt), one who is very skillful or well-informed in some special field. — expert′ly, *adv.* — ex·pert′ness, *n.*

   b. pre·pare (pri-pâr′), *v.t.* [-pared, -paring], [<L.*prae,* before + *parare,* get ready], 1. to make ready. 2. to equip or furnish. 3. to put together; as *prepare* dinner. *v.i.* 1. to make things ready. 2. to make oneself ready.

New Words.   Try to understand the meanings of these words as they are used in the reading passage. Use a dictionary when necessary.

valuable	prepare	omit	appear
require	modern	individual (adjective)	controversy
expert	decide		

READING

A Dictionary: A Friend and Teacher

   [1]   Dictionaries give you valuable information about words. They give you the spelling and pronunciation of words quickly and easily. They tell you the most important meanings of words. They also tell you the part of speech. Are you using your dictionary every day? You should be. It will become your friend and teacher.

[2]   Look at the photograph of the young woman who is working in the library. Her instructors' assignments often require her to use a dictionary. Right now she is using the complete *Webster's New International Dictionary*. She is reviewing her assignment in biology. She is studying various definitions of the word *skeleton*. She isn't copying all of the information for that entry. She is only taking notes on the most important information. Later she will use her notes to help her study for a biology exam.

[3]   The complete *Webster's New International Dictionary* is the largest dictionary of American English. Language experts are working on this dictionary all the time. They are preparing new dictionaries for the future. These experts read modern books and articles every day to find new words. They may decide to omit some words from earlier dictionaries. They also prepare abbreviated, or shorter, Webster's dictionaries for home and individual use.

[4]   When the *Webster's Third New International Dictionary* appeared in 1961, there was a big controversy about it. It was unpopular with many language experts. The dictionary borrowed words from street English, or slang, such as the expression *wise up*. Many of the definitions were wrong or not clearly explained. The dictionary omitted much of the information about well-known people.

[5]   English is changing all the time. Modern developments in science add

new words to the dictionary. War and politics add new words and expressions to our language. Young people create new words and expressions that pass into common use. We are not speaking exactly the same English language that our parents and grandparents spoke. Dictionaries can help us to keep up with the changes in our language.

Oral Cloze.   Number a column in your notebook from 1 to 10. Your instructor will read Paragraph [2] aloud to you twice. Listen very carefully. Then your instructor will read the paragraph aloud again, but he or she will leave out some words. Your instructor will say "blank" where these words are left out. Next to each number on your paper write the word that correctly fills the blank space. Your instructor will read the paragraph with blanks to you several times. Now close your books.

Look at the photograph of the young woman who blank working in the library. Her instructors' assignments blank require her to use a dictionary. Right blank she is using the complete *Webster's New International Dictionary.* Blank is reviewing her assignment in biology. She is blank various definitions of the word *skeleton.* She blank copying all of the information for blank entry. She is only taking notes on blank most important information. Later she will blank her notes to help her study for blank biology exam.

VOCABULARY

1. **Expanding Vocabulary.**   Choose the best word from the New Word list to fill in the blank space in each sentence. Use the correct form of nouns and verbs.

    a. Your English instructor should _____ you to use a dictionary daily.

    b. Words _____ in the dictionary in alphabetical order.

    c. Dictionaries give you _____ information about word use.

    d. Language _____ discover new words in _____ books and articles.

    e. Is there a big _____ about language in your culture or native country?

    f. Dictionaries will _____ a word if it is never used any longer.

g. For _____ use, you should carry a pocket dictionary.

h. You may use a larger dictionary to _____ your homework assignments.

i. When you _____ to study a new language, you must get a dictionary.

2. **Using Vocabulary.** Each of the following sentences includes a word from the New Word list. Circle the number of the sentence that would correctly follow the given sentence.

   a. Dictionary writers *are preparing* a new dictionary.

   (1) It appeared last year.
   (2) It will appear very soon.
   (3) The new dictionary was unpopular.

   b. Dictionary writers read *modern* books and articles to find new words.

   (1) These writings contain interesting old words.
   (2) These books reveal how language is used today.
   (3) These books use spellings from the 1800s.

   c. Learning language *requires* the use of a good dictionary.

   (1) Students should always carry one.
   (2) Students rarely need one.
   (3) Students may use one if they want to.

   d. My dictionary contains *valuable* information about words.

   (1) It is difficult to learn new words.
   (2) Some words have a British and an American spelling.
   (3) It gives the spelling, pronunciation, and meaning of words.

   e. Even language *experts* need to refer to dictionaries.

   (1) They know nothing about words.
   (2) Some special words may be unknown to them.
   (3) Dictionaries include pictures of some words.

   f. *Omit* the word *the* in your first sentence.

   (1) It's correct.
   (2) It isn't necessary.
   (3) It sounds good there.

g. There is a big *controversy* about whether apes can learn language.

   (1) Everyone agrees that they cannot.

   (2) It isn't necessary to study the subject.

   (3) Not all scientists think alike on that subject.

h. Some people learn a language best with *individual* instruction.

   (1) They feel happy in a large class.

   (2) They feel happy practicing with only one person.

   (3) They feel happy using interesting books.

3. Word Families.   Adjectives describe nouns or pronouns.

We get *individual* assignments. (What kind of assignments? *individual* assignments)

Adverbs of manner tell how (in what manner) verb action is done.

We do our assignments *individually*. (How do we do our assignments? We do them *individually*.)

Most adverbs are formed by adding *ly* to adjectives.
   Study the following list of adjectives and adverbs.

Adjectives	**Adverbs**
quick	quickly
complete	completely
individual	individually
different	differently
active	actively
strange	strangely
careful	carefully
general	generally
correct	correctly
Note spelling changes of these:	
specific	specifically
easy	easily

a. Add one adverb from the list to each of the following sentences. The adverb will tell us *how,* or in what manner, the verb action is done.

(1) After much practice, you will speak English.

(2) Two experts may think about language.

(3) Geologists climb high rocks.

(4) Geologists put dinosaur bones together.

(5) Most children like to play.

(6) The dictionary will be finished in 1984.

b. Add one adjective from the list to each of the following sentences. The adjective should tell us something about the italicized noun.

(1) The model of a *dinosaur* was set up in the museum.

(2) Are you afraid of *places*?

(3) This is a *textbook* for reading and writing.

(4) Using a dictionary is like having *instruction.*

(5) Choose the *answer* to the problem.

(6) Language experts sometimes have *opinions* about word usage.

READING COMPREHENSION

1. **Understanding the Text.**   Choose the correct answer.

a. Dictionaries are friends and teachers because

(1) they are not expensive.

(2) they help you use language better.

(3) they come in different sizes.

b. According to Paragraph [2], dictionaries

(1) are valuable only for English assignments.

(2) are probably helpful in different subjects.

(3) are used only in libraries.

c. Which is not true of dictionary writers?

(1) They work on new dictionaries all the time.

(2) They study modern writing to find new words.

(3) They use every English word ever written.

(4) They prepare short dictionaries for home use.

d. Which of the following sentences is the main idea of Paragraph [4]?

   (1) *Wise up* is a slang expression.

   (2) The *Webster's Third New International Dictionary* appeared in 1961.

   (3) Language experts have different opinions about the *Webster's Third New International Dictionary*.

e. According to Paragraph [5], we speak and write differently from our parents and grandparents because

   (1) our parents and grandparents weren't educated.

   (2) science, war, and politics are increasing our vocabulary.

   (3) dictionaries are better than they used to be.

2. Answering Information Questions.   Write your answers to the following questions in complete sentences.

   a. Name three things dictionaries tell you about a word.

   b. Where is the young woman in the photograph working?

   c. What subject is she studying?

   d. Which dictionary is she using?

   e. What kind of dictionaries do language experts write for home use?

   f. When did the *Webster's Third New International Dictionary* appear?

   g. What is happening to English all the time?

3. Scanning for Specific Information.   *Scanning* means reading quickly to find specific facts or items. To scan passages for the facts that will answer a question, you must first pick out the key words in the questions.

   Read the following paragraph. Then answer the questions in short note form by scanning the paragraph for the specific information you need. The key words in the questions are underlined for you.

   Noah Webster wrote his famous *American Spelling* in 1783. With the money he earned, he was able to spend the next twenty years in the preparation of his first *American Dictionary*. This book appeared in two volumes in 1828. It contained 70,000 words and was very popular for its completeness, clearness, and correctness of definitions. In 1840 a larger edition of the *American Dictionary* appeared. When Webster died in 1847, G. & C. Merriam Company bought the rights to the *American Dictionary*. In 1847 this new company printed the *American Dictionary* in one volume. In 1859 G. & C. Merriam Company printed the *American Dictionary* with pictures for the first time. Two more editions of the *American*

Dictionary were printed in 1864 and 1890. By 1890, the vocabulary had reached 175,000 words. The *New International Dictionary* of 1909 had a vocabulary of 400,000 words.

1. When did Webster write his first *American Dictionary?*

   _____

2. Name two qualities that made the first *American Dictionary* popular.

   _____

3. When did the G. & C. Merriam Company buy the rights to Webster's *American Dictionary?*

   _____

4. What was special about the Merriam *American Dictionary* of 1859?

   _____

5. How many editions of the *American Dictionary* were put out by the Merriam Company between 1847 and 1909?

   _____

6. Did the vocabulary of Webster's *American Dictionary* increase or decrease by 1909? Complete the chart to support your answer.

   _____

   1828   20,000   words

   _____   _____words

   _____   _____words

WRITING EXERCISES

Present Continuous Tense

The Present Continuous tense of verbs is used for actions that are taking place now. It tells about activity that is going on in this period of time. The Present Continuous tense is formed by *am, is,* or *are* + the *ing* ending of the main verb.

I am taking four courses this semester.
Some students are studying in the library right now.

Study the Present Continuous tense of the verb *prepare.*

	Singular	**Plural**
First Person	I am preparing	A writer and I are preparing
		We are preparing
Second Person	You are preparing	You are preparing
Third Person	The writer is preparing	The writers are preparing
	He/She/It is preparing	They are preparing

The negative forms are *am not (I'm not), is not (isn't),* and *are not (aren't)* + the *ing* form of the verb.

1. **Recognizing Verb Forms.**   Listen carefully as your instructor reads Paragraph [2] of the reading passage. Underline each complete verb form of the Present Continuous tense.

   Can you state why the second sentence uses the Simple Present, not the Present Continuous tense? Which time word signals the Simple Present? Can you explain why the last sentence uses the Future tense? Which time word signals the Future tense?

2. **Controlled Writing.**   Rewrite Paragraph [2] with a plural subject. Change the subject *the young woman* to *some young women.* Change all the necessary verbs and pronouns to their plural forms. Your first sentence will be the following: *Look at the photograph of some young women who are working in the library.*

3. **Sentence Building.**   Use the words in each set in the same order to make a complete sentence. Change the verbs to the Present Continuous tense. Add as many words as you like to make your new sentences complete.

---

a lot	people	do	universities

A lot of people are doing interesting work in modern universities.

---

  a. geologists   look at   bones   laboratory

  b. they   study   put together   fragments   past

  c. popular anthropologist   teach   cultures   Asia

  d. students   waste (negative)   time

  e. they   read   write   languages

  f. they   listen to   take dictation from   tape recorder

  g. students   professors   use   library   8:00 A.M.   8:00 P.M.

  h. people   gain knowledge

Compound Sentence Parts with *And*

The word *and* connects sentence parts that add information. These sentence parts must be related in meaning, and they must have the same form.

A dictionary tells you the *spelling* and *meaning* of words.
         (noun)   (noun)

Dictionaries are *valuable* and *necessary* to students.
            (adjective)   (adjective)

We hope you *are checking* spelling and *looking up* synonyms in your
      (verb: Present Continuous)   (verb: Present Continuous)

dictionaries.

---

1. **Sentence Building.**   Complete the items in Column A by adding the related phrase from Column B. Each sentence will need the connecting word *and* to join its compound parts. Rewrite each complete new sentence. Remember that the sentence parts connected by *and* must be related in meaning and must have the same form.

A	B
a. *Webster's Third New International Dictionary* is the biggest	women wrote the newest *Webster's Dictionary*
b. Two early editions appeared in 1806	most complete dictionary of American English
c. Thomas A. Knott	preparing future dictionaries carefully
d. More than 250 men	Paul W. Carhart were the main writers of the 1934 edition
e. Today, writers are finding new words	an individual teacher
f. Dictionary writers work slowly	in 1828
g. Your dictionary is a pocket-sized friend	

2. **Paragraph Building.**   Make two columns on a separate sheet of paper. Read the following paragraph. Underline each set of compound sentence parts. Write the first item of the set in your left-hand column. Write the second item in your right-hand column. The first one is done for you.

interesting | valuable

   The big *Webster's Dictionary* tells you many interesting and valuable things about language. It has sections on history and biography. It gives you the meanings of abbreviations and signs. It tells you synonyms and antonyms of words. *Webster's Dictionary* helps both foreign students and native speakers to improve their English.

Read the paragraph several times. Then close your textbook. Using only your columns of compound parts, rebuild the paragraph sentence by sentence. Make it as similar to the original paragraph as you can.

3. **Sentence Combining.**   Make *one* new sentence from each set of sentences by combining the compound parts with *and*. Add new pronouns, and omit unnecessary words in your new sentences. Rewrite each complete new sentence in the space provided.

---

   a. Thomas A. Knott worked on the 1934 edition of *Webster's Dictionary*.
   b. Paul W. Carhart worked on the 1934 edition of *Webster's Dictionary*.

   Thomas A. Knott and Paul W. Carhart worked on the 1934 edition of Webster's Dictionary.

---

a. **(1)** I carry a pocket dictionary for school.
    (2) I have a big dictionary at home.

   _____

b. **(1)** Some students study in the cafeteria.
    (2) These students eat their lunch at the same time.

   _____

c. **(1)** A dictionary tells you the spelling of words.
    (2) A dictionary tells you the meaning of words.

   _____

d. **(1)** I look up new words in my dictionary.
    (2) Then I write the new words in a notebook.

   _____

e. **(1)** When I am reading a newspaper, I use a dictionary.

   (2) When I am preparing my homework, I use a dictionary.

_____

f. **(1)** The big _Webster's Dictionary_ has fifty-nine lines about language.

   (2) The big _Webster's Dictionary_ has forty lines about speech.

_____

Sentence Patterns with _Because_

We answer questions that ask _why_ with the connecting word _because_. The word _because_ joins together two thoughts. One thought tells us what happened, that is, the result. The second thought gives us a reason why.

> **Dictionaries are useful because they tell us many things about**
> (result)   (reason)
> **language.**

1. **Sentence Building.**   In Column A you are given results. In Column B you are given causes, or reasons. Build correct sentences by joining an item in Column A to its related item in Column B. Use the word _because_ as a connector of the result and the reason.

A	**B**
a. Geologists wear heavy boots	many Americans are immigrants
b. Geologists dig up dinosaur bones carefully	his pronunciation is different
c. Many different languages are spoken in the United States	language is changing all the time
d. An Englishman does not sound like an American	they climb in rocky places
e. Dictionaries list words alphabetically	they are easier to find that way
f. New dictionaries add new words	these old bones are fragile

2. Sentence Expansion.   Complete the following result clauses by adding a reason that explains why. Join the two sentence parts with the word *because*. Complete your new sentences in the space provided.

a. There is very little space in cities _____

_____

b. Museums are interesting places _____

_____

c. Architects are designing new cities for the future _____

_____

d. Many immigrants come to the United States _____

_____

e. Language changes _____

_____

Plural Possessives

You have already learned how to form singular possessives in the apostrophe + *s* form. Study the following model. It shows you how to write plural possessives in the *s* + apostrophe form.

Singular	Singular Possessive	Plural	Plural Possessive
a writer	a writer's decision (decision of a writer)	writers	writers' decisions (decisions of the writers)

With your instructor, talk about how the plural possessive is formed with an *s* + apostrophe. We mainly use this form of the plural possessive for human beings.

1. Rewriting Sentences.   Rewrite each sentence, changing the italicized expressions to plural possessives in the *s* + apostrophe form.

The teacher corrected all the *compositions of the students.*

The teacher corrected all the students' compositions.

---

a. The *children of the immigrants* learned English quickly.

b. At first, the *paragraphs of the students* were quite short.

c. The *first job of the geologists* was to find fossils.

d. The American Constitution protects the *rights of the citizens*.

e. I heard many different *opinions of teachers* about that book.

f. The *conditions of the workers* in the early 1900s were very bad.

Now identify the subject of each new sentence. Draw an arrow from the subject to its main verb. Do they agree in number?

2. **Proofreading.**   Some of the following sentences have errors in the formation of the possessive. Some sentences are correct. In the space provided, correct any error in the possessive. If the sentence is correct, write *C* in the space.

a. Dictionaries are writers' friends. _____

b. A writers' opinion can help you choose a good TV program.

_____

c. Childrens games often use special vocabularies. _____

d. It is difficult to understand architects plans. _____

e. English teachers must listen carefully to their students pronunciation.

_____

f. Anthropologist's dictionaries of Native American languages are very valuable to us. _____

g. A geologist's work requires a lot of climbing. _____

h. Babies first words are learned in their parents' homes. _____

i. A baby dinosaur's bones were very fragile. _____

COMPOSING

1. **Developing a Paragraph.**   In the following paragraph a student describes an occasion when he or she had to make a speech. Use the guide to corrections following the paragraph to improve this piece of writing.

[1] In Chinese culture for special occasions we have a banquet. [2] Everyone meets at a restaurant and has a meal. [3] Then someone gives a speech. [4] One time my family chose me to make the speech. [5] I prepare a speech. [6] It was a good speech. [7] I practiced it many time in front of the glass. [8] But I couldn't eat dinner. [9] I was so nervous about my

speech. [10] We had delicious soups and fish. [11] I stood up to speech, but I forgot every word. [12] Then I remembered the first line. [13] After that it was easy for me to complete my speech.

a. Which sentences are the introduction? How do they make the paragraph more interesting?

b. Which sentence is the main idea sentence?

c. Sentence [1] would be improved by adding the adverb of frequency that means "most of the time." Sentence [3] would be improved by adding the adverb of frequency that means "a lot of the time." Where would you put these adverbs?

d. In Sentence [5], the verb is the wrong tense.

e. Try combining Sentences [5] and [6] into one new sentence. Is that an improvement?

f. In Sentence [7], one noun must be made plural. What is a better word for *glass* in that sentence?

g. Combine Sentences [8] and [9] by adding a connecting word of reason.

h. In Sentence [11], a word is in the wrong form.

i. Should any sentence in the paragraph be left out? Explain your answer.

2. Composing a Paragraph.

a. Look carefully at the photograph that shows some Puerto Rican men playing dominoes in a public park. Write a main idea sentence about the photograph. This sentence should give your reader information about the subject or topic of the photograph. It should also give the reader your general feeling or impression about the people in the photograph.

When you have written a main idea sentence, compose a paragraph that gives the reader specific details about the people in the photograph. Tell the reader what the people look like and what they are doing. The following list of words may help you in composing your paragraph.

Verbs	Adjectives	Prepositional Phrases	Nouns
to relax	older	on benches	game
to play (dominoes)	retired	at tables	benches
to enjoy	Hispanic	in a park	tables
to sit	friendly	with friends	park
to talk	serious	in the afternoon	town
to wear	public	on the weekend	relaxation
		in the fresh air	

b. Choose some public place such as a subway train, a classroom, or a restaurant in which to watch people carefully. Write a paragraph about the different people you observe. Tell what they look like and what they are doing. Begin your paragraph with a main idea sentence. This sentence should tell the reader about the place you are observing. It should also include a general feeling or impression about the place. Your specific details should support your feeling or impression.

c. Write about an ocassion when you had to make a speech in front of a class or some other group of people. How did you prepare for this? How did you feel about it? Was it a successful speech? Why or why not?

CHAPTER SIX A

LANGUAGE IN THE FUTURE

PREREADING

Class Discussion.   In each of the following sets there are two sentences. One sentence is in English. The other is in a language that was invented to be a world language. Which words in the two sentences seem similar? Which words seem different? Do you recognize any words in the invented language that are similar to words in your native language?

a. *English:* Our Father, who is in heaven, blessed be your name!
   Volapük: O Fat obas, kel binol in süls, paisaludömoz nem ola!

b. *English:* The astronomer, by a special telescope, photographs the sun, the moon, and the planets.
   Esperanto: La astronomo, per speciala teleskopo fotografas la sunon, la lunon, ka la planedojn.

c. *English:* A professor of rocket science in Germany has invented a vehicle for exploring the moon.
   Interlingua: Un professor del rochetteria scientific in Germania ha adoptate un vehiculo al exploration del luna.

New Words.   Try to understand the meanings of these words as they are used in the reading passage. Use a dictionary when necessary.

trade	natural	symbol
universal	artificial	numerical
opinion	favor (verb)	advantage

READING

The Dream of a World Language

[1]   People have always dreamed of a world language. People from different nations want to communicate with each other. They would like to trade with other people all over the world. They want to understand each other and have peace

among all nations. A universal language would help communication among different peoples.

[2]   In the opinion of some people, the best universal language would be a natural language such as French, Spanish, or English. Millions of people in many parts of the world already speak these languages. There are already many teachers who could teach these languages and many textbooks that people could study on their own. Which natural language should we use for a universal language? Mario Pei, an American professor of languages, would choose Chinese. But he would change the Chinese characters into an alphabet.

[3]   Other people would not choose any natural language as a world language. They would prefer an artificial language such as Volapük, Esperanto, or Interlingua. These languages were invented by different people in Europe. They use some words from natural languages such as Italian, German, and Spanish. They also include completely new words made up by their inventors. These languages have simple grammars and small, basic vocabularies. People could learn them easily. Using an artificial world language would not favor any one country.

[4]   Another kind of world language would not use words at all. These languages would use symbols such as musical notes, numbers, or computer codes. For example, one person has invented a numerical language that uses numbers for words. In this language you would call a tree 31 and a man 10. Today some scientists are working on a universal computer language that would use mathematical signs for words. Would you want to learn one of these symbolic languages?

[5]   There are thousands of natural languages in the world today. There are also over six hundred artificial languages. Will one of these many languages ever become a universal language? There would be many advantages in having a world language. Think of a world where we could all communicate easily with each other, no matter which country we came from. At this time, however, a universal language is still a dream.

Guided Summary.   A summary tells the main ideas of a complete passage. Only the main ideas from each paragraph are in a summary. Write a summary paragraph of this reading by following the directions for each item.

  a. Begin your first sentence with the following words, and complete the sentence with the topic of the whole passage.
  This passage talks about people's need for . . .

  b. Begin your second sentence with the following words, and complete it with information from Paragraph [1].
  With a universal language people could . . . and . . . more easily.

  c. Begin your third sentence with the following words, and complete it with information from Paragraph [2].
  Some people would like to use a . . . language . . .

English is useful as a second language in various parts of the world. Here, a Nigerian man reads an English newspaper.

d. Begin your next sentence with the following words, and complete it with information from Paragraph [3].
Other people would prefer . . .

e. In your last sentence, state something important about artificial languages.

VOCABULARY

1. **Expanding Vocabulary.**   Replace the italicized words in each sentence with a word from the New Word list.

a. There would be many *benefits* in having a *world* language.

b. Traffic *signs* are already the same in many different countries.

c. Do you have a strong *point of view* about the use of a world language?

d. It is *normal* for all people to learn their native language.

e. Could people *do business* in a *man-made* language such as Esperanto?

f. Could we enjoy books written in a language *that uses numbers*?

g. Would you *prefer* learning English or French as a second language?

2. **Using Vocabulary.**   Follow the directions for each item.

a. Put a check next to each word that is related in meaning to the word *numerical*.

number ___✓___   nothing _____   numerous ___✓___

natural _____   numerically ___✓___   nation _____

b. Put an *N* next to items that are natural objects. Put an *A* next to items that are artificial.

plastic ___A___   the sun ___N___   computer codes ___A___

planets ___N___   nylon ___A___   rivers ___N___

cotton _____

c. Put an *O* next to the statements that are opinions. Put an *F* next to the statements that are facts.

(1) Esperanto should be our universal language. ___O___

(2) French is a beautiful language. ___O___

(3) Writing is about eight thousand years old. ___F___

(4) English is a working language at the United Nations. ___F___

(5) Chinese is more difficult to learn than French. ___O___

(6) The Chinese characters are not an alphabet. ___F___

(7) I favor newspapers over magazines for vocabulary practice. ___O___

d. Put a *C* next to each sentence in which the italicized word is used correctly. Put an *X* next to each sentence in which the italicized word is not used correctly.

(1) Studying English has a lot of *advantages*. ___C___

(2) Esperanto and Interlingua are *natural* languages. ___C___

(3) The American traffic *symbol* for "stop" is a red light. ___C___

(4) Love, hate, and happiness are common *opinions*. ___C___

(5) Do your friends speak the same *artificial* language that you do?

___C___

(6) Japan *trades* a great deal with the United States. ___C___

(7) Do you *favor* the library or the cafeteria for studying? ___C___

3. **Word Families.**   Many English adjectives are formed by adding *al* to the noun form of the word. Study the following list. Note the spelling changes that take place in some of the adjectives.

Noun	Adjective
universe	universal
music	musical
artifice	artificial
nature	natural
nation	national
number	numerical
mathematics	mathematical
office	official

Read the following paragraph. Then use the directions in the Key following the paragraph to give you the correct answers for the blank spaces.

Language is ___*universal*___ among human groups. Every
(1)
_____ has its own _____ language.
(2)   (3)
It may also have numerous other languages. It is _____
(4)
for children to learn the language of their parents. It is also becoming

common for people to learn a _____ of other languages
(5)
in school. Musicians learn _____ language. Mathe-
(6)
maticians learn _____ language. Perhaps in the future
(7)
we will all learn some _____ language.
(8)

Key

1. adjective form of *universe*
2. noun form of *national*
3. adjective form of *office*
4. adjective form of *nature*
5. noun form of *numerical*
6. adjective form of *music*
7. adjective form of *mathematics*
8. adjective form of *artifice*

READING COMPREHENSION

1. **Understanding the Text.**   Choose the correct answer.

   a. People have always dreamed of a universal language because

      (1) they would like to understand each other.

(2) their native languages are too difficult to learn.

(3) everyone has a different opinion.

b. In the first sentence of Paragraph [2], the expression *such as* tells us to expect

(1) difficult words.   (2) examples.   (3) negatives.

c. In the last sentence of Paragraph [2], the word *but* tells us that

(1) an exception follows.   (2) this is a negative sentence.

(3) the sentence is in the singular.

d. In the fifth sentence of Paragraph [3], the word *also* tells us that

(1) this sentence adds information to the sentence before it.

(2) this sentence states something opposite to the sentence before it.

(3) this sentence is not related to the sentence before it.

e. In Paragraph [4], musical language, numerical language, and computer language are

(1) examples of difficult languages.   (2) examples of natural languages.   (3) examples of symbolic languages.

f. In Paragraph [5], the expression *over six hundred artificial languages* means the same as

(1) fewer than six hundred artificial languages.   (2) more than six hundred artificial languages.   (3) exactly six hundred artificial languages.

g. In the last sentence of Paragraph [5], the word *however* means the same as

(1) and.   (2) or.   (3) but.

h. Paragraph [5] does not tell us the definition of a *natural* language. But from the way the word *natural* is used, it probably means a language

(1) that people already speak.

(2) that is invented by scientists.

(3) that is difficult to learn.

2. **Answering Information Questions.**   Write your answers to the following questions in complete sentences.

a. Name one natural language that some people would like to use for a world language.

b. What natural language would Mario Pei choose for a world language?

c. What kind of grammar do artificial languages have?

d. Do they have a small or a large vocabulary?

    e. What would you call a tree in numerical language?

    f. What would the computer language use for words?

    g. Would there be many or few advantages in having a world language?

3. Skimming for Main Ideas.   *To skim* means to read quickly for the main idea of a paragraph. Main idea sentences tell you the topic of the passage. They also tell you the writer's opinion about the topic. Main ideas do *not* tell you specific details or give you specific examples. Usually the main idea sentence is the first or second sentence in a paragraph. But sometimes it is the last or next to last sentence.

    Skim Paragraph [1]. The main idea sentence is the last sentence. It tells you the topic: universal language. It tells you what the writer thinks a universal language would do: It would help communication among different peoples.

    a. Skim Paragraph [2]. Which of the following sentences states the main idea?

        (1) In the past people wanted to make up a universal language.

        (2) Some people want a natural universal language.

        (3) French is a natural language.

    b. Skim Paragraph [3]. Which of the following sentences states the main idea?

        (1) An artificial language would have a simple grammar.

        (2) An artificial language might be the best universal language.

        (3) People could learn an artificial language easily.

    c. Skim Paragraph [4]. Which of the following sentences tells the main idea?

        (1) Some people want a universal language that uses symbols.

        (2) One person made up a musical language.

        (3) A computer language would use mathematical forms.

    d. Skim Paragraph [5]. Which of the following sentences tells the main idea?

        (1) A natural language might be the best world language.

        (2) A world language is still a dream of the future.

        (3) Many people are already studying English as a second language.

WRITING EXERCISES

Modals + Basic Form of Verbs

A modal is a helping part of a verb. Modals tell about certain conditions related to the main verb. The main verb following a modal is always in its basic form.

> We *may have* a world language in the future.

Study the following explanations and examples of some common modals. The frequently used negatives are in parentheses.

    a. *Can (can't)*: Present Possibility; Present Ability

> Some people *can learn* new languages easily.

    b. *Could (couldn't)*: Past Ability; Past Possibility

> Her daughter *could say* the alphabet at the age of two.

    c. *May*: Present or Future Possibility

> Our college *may offer* a course in Hindi next term.

    d. *Might*: Uncertain Possibility

> Esperanto *might become* a popular language in the future.

    e. *Must (mustn't)*: Necessity; Prohibition

> Children *must find* ways to communicate with their parents.
> You *mustn't touch* the paintings in a museum.

    f. *Should (shouldn't)*: Advisability; Obligation

> **Everybody *should study* a foreign language in school.**

g. *Will (won't)*: Future Certainty

> **Next term you *will read* more difficult texts in English.**

h. *Would (wouldn't)*: Future Probability; Conditional (if) statements with Simple Past tense

> **Most non-Chinese people *would need* a lifetime to master Chinese writing.**
> **If you reviewed your notes every night, you *would improve* your class work.**

1. **Identifying Modals.**   Read the following sentences. Underline the modal with its main verb in each sentence.

   a. People would like to trade all over the world.
   b. A universal language would help communication among nations.
   c. Mario Pei would choose Chinese for a universal language.
   d. But he would write Chinese with an alphabet.
   e. Other people might choose French or Spanish for a world language.
   f. An artificial language would use words from some natural languages.
   g. People everywhere could learn an artificial language easily.
   h. In my opinion, all children should learn a second language in school.
   i. Maybe English will be the future world language.
   j. A numerical language might be a good world language.

   Now circle the subject of each underlined modal-verb combination. Write an *S* for singular or a *P* for plural subjects. Does the modal change its form for a singular or plural subject?

2. **Scrambled Sentences.**   Rewrite the following mixed-up sentences so that they form correct English sentences. Remember to look for the modal and its main verb first. Then look for the subject.

a. child   learn   language   every   a   should   .
   second

b. people   could   an   language   learn   easily
   artificial   .

c. use   .   numbers   words   mathematical   for
   would   a   language

a mathematical
language
would use.
number for words.

d. wouldn't   Mario Pei   Greek   .   choose   language
   a   for   universal

e. French   you   will   third   study   language   a
   ?   as

3. **Sentence Composing.**   Write a complete sentence for each of the following items. Use modals in your answers.

   a. Name two things a dictionary can tell you about a word.
   b. Name two languages you would like to learn.
   c. Name two courses you might take next term.
   d. Name two things archeologists may discover in the ground.
   e. Name two cities where you might want to live in the future.

Verbs + Infinitives

An infinitive verb is formed by *to* + the basic form of the main verb. Some verbs such as *want, like, would like, hope, expect, learn,* and *begin* are often followed by infinitives.

> **Many people *want to have* a world language.**
> **We *learned to speak* our natural languages at home.**

Two verb phrases that include infinitives have special meanings. *Has* or *have to* + the base verb means *must. Used to* + the base verb means something that a person did in the past but doesn't do anymore.

> **I *have to write* to my parents.**
> **Europeans *used to speak* Latin.**

Schoolchildren dancing in the People's Republic of China.

1. **Identifying Verb + Infinitive Phrases.** Look at the photograph of the Chinese dance class. Your instructor will read the following sentences about the photograph. Underline the main verb + infinitive phrase in each sentence.

    a. These girls and boys like to perform their dances.
    b. They used to have difficulty with the steps.
    c. But then they began to practice every day.
    d. Now they are learning to move together to the music.
    e. They are planning to show the dance to their parents.

2. **Pair Dictation.** Dictate three of the sentences about the photograph to a partner. Then take dictation of three sentences from your partner. Correct your dictations together.

3. **Sentence Composing.** Write your answers to the following questions in complete sentences. Use verb + infinitive phrases in each answer.

    a. What language did you learn to speak at home?
    b. What languages would you like to speak in the future?
    c. What subject do you want to study next term?
    d. Name two games you used to play when you were young.
    e. When did you begin to study English? _I began._

    f. What do you hope to do when you finish school?

    g. Tell one thing students have to do every day.

Changing the Direction of a Thought: The Use of *But*

But is used to change the direction of a thought, or to present a contrasting idea. Study the following examples.

Some people want to use an artificial world language. *But* others want to use a natural language.

or

Some people want to use an artificial world language, *but* others want to use a natural language.

Note that when *but* is used in the middle of a sentence to separate clauses, a comma goes before it.

1. Sentence Rewriting.   Rewrite each of the following pairs of sentences using *But* or *, but*.

    a. **(1)** Human speech is probably about one million years old.

          (2) Writing is much newer.

    b. **(1)** The earliest writing was picture writing.

          (2) Today most languages use an alphabet.

    c. **(1)** There are thousands of languages in the world.

          (2) The United Nations uses only two official languages.

    d. **(1)** It is difficult to learn a second language.

          (2) Many people do.

    e. **(1)** Latin was a world language in the past.

          (2) Today very few people can speak it.

    f. **(1)** There is no world language today.

          (2) There may be one in the future.

2. Sentence Expansion.   Change the direction of the thought in each of the following sentences by adding *,but* + a new contrasting thought. You may want to use the words in parentheses in your new thought. Rewrite each new complete sentence.

Human beings live all over the earth. (moon)

Human beings live all over the earth, but they don't live on the moon.

---

   a. I would like to visit Egypt. (far away)

   b. English articles are simple. (verbs, difficult)

   c. I am not learning French. (studying, English)

   d. There are many planets in our solar system. (one sun)

   e. I would like to see a movie tonight. (must study)

3. **Sentence Completion.**   Read the following sentences carefully. Decide whether *and* or *but* is the correct connecting word to use in the blank space. Write in your answer using correct punctuation.

   a. Archeologists often find pottery in the earth _____ they don't usually find gold.

   b. Overpopulation is one serious problem _____ water pollution is another.

   c. There is only one moon circling the Earth _____ there are many moons around Jupiter.

   d. Chinese writing uses characters _____ English uses an alphabet.

   e. Millions of people speak Hindi _____ it is not an official language of the United Nations.

   f. Canadians speak English _____ Australians do too.

Punctuation: Series of Parallel Items

A series of parallel items is a group of three or more words that do the same kind of work in a sentence. A sentence may have a series of nouns, adjectives, verbs, or adverbs. Each item in a series is followed by a comma. The word *and* goes before the last item in the series. All the items in a series must have the same form.

French, *Spanish*, and *Chinese* are all natural languages.
(series of nouns)

It takes time to learn *musical, numerical,* and *mathematical* symbols.
(series of adjectives)

In class today we are *speaking, reading,* and *writing* English.
(series of verbs: Present Continuous)

---

1. **Sentence Combining.**   Combine each group of sentences into one complete sentence. Leave out unnecessary words. Add correct punctuation. The first one is done for you.

   a. **(1)** Archeologists find toys in the earth.

   (2) Archeologists find pots in the earth.

   (3) Archeologists find gold in the earth.

   Archeologists find toys, pots, and gold in the earth.

   b. **(1)** The sun is part of our universe.

   (2) The moon is part of our universe.

   (3) The planets are part of our universe.

   c. **(1)** A map shows us the location of rivers.

   (2) A map shows us the location of seas.

   (3) A map shows us the location of oceans.

   d. **(1)** Astronauts need special suits for space travel.

   (2) Astronauts need special shoes for space travel.

   (3) Astronauts need special food for space travel.

   e. **(1)** People in England speak English.

   (2) People in Australia speak English.

   (3) People in Canada speak English.

   f. **(1)** An artificial language would have a short vocabulary.

   (2) An artificial language would have a simple vocabulary.

   (3) An artificial language would have a useful vocabulary.

   g. **(1)** With a world language people could communicate easily.

   (2) With a world language people could trade easily.

   (3) With a world language people could travel easily.

2. **Sentence Composing.**   Follow the directions for each item.

   a. Use a series of adjectives to describe the characteristics of a friend or relative. (Use the verb *is*.)

   b. Use a series of verbs to tell what you usually do on weekends.

   c. Use a series of nouns to tell what subjects you would like to study in college.

   d. Use a series of nouns to tell what special foods people in your culture enjoy.

3. **Dictation.**   With your class and your instructor, choose five sentences from Exercise 2 for dictation.

COMPOSING

1. **Developing a Paragraph.**

   a. Read the following sentences. Put *M.I.* (for Main Idea) next to the main idea sentence. Then number the other sentences in the correct order to form a good paragraph. Look for pronouns and other words that suggest the correct order of the sentences. Rewrite the complete paragraph.

   (1) But many people in the western part of the world speak it. _____

   (2) Also, its spelling is very regular. _____

   (3) Spanish might be a useful world language. _____

Many Indian peoples in Latin America such as this Mexican potter speak Spanish in addition to their native language. Would the best universal language be a natural language such as Spanish?

(4) Its sounds are easy to pronounce. _____

(5) It is true that most people in Asia and Africa do not speak it. _____

(6) Spanish spelling indicates exactly how to pronounce a word. _____

b. Study the following lists. List A gives some reasons why a language might be a good universal language. List B gives some reasons why a language would not be a good universal language.

A	B
The grammar is simple.	The grammar is difficult.
There are few verb tenses.	There are many verb tenses.
There are few verb endings.	There are many verb endings.
The articles are easy.	The articles are difficult.
There are few rules for singular and plural.	There are many rules for singular and plural.
The spelling is regular.	The spelling is not regular.
The sounds are easy to pronounce.	The sounds are difficult to pronounce.
It uses a common alphabet.	It uses an uncommon alphabet.
Many people already speak it.	Few people speak it.
Many people are already studying it.	Few people are studying it.

Individually, as a class, or in small groups, write a paragraph that tells why English would or would not be a good universal language. Begin with a main idea sentence that tells us your opinion. Choose as many reasons as you want from List A or B to support your opinion. Do not use reasons that are opposite to the stated main idea. You may add reasons of your own. Put your reasons in good order. Review your finished paragraph for errors. Make your finished paragraph as correct as you can.

2. **Composing a Paragraph.**

   a. Write a paragraph that tells why your native language would or would not be a good universal language. In your first sentence mention the name of your language and clearly state your opinion about its use as a world language. State specific details about your language that support your opinion.

   b. Learning a new skill, like learning a new language, is usually difficult. Write a paragraph that tells about how you learned some special skill such as cooking, riding a bicycle, or driving a car. Describe your experience in learning this skill, and tell about the person(s) who helped you.

CHAPTER SIX B

EXPERIMENTS WITH LANGUAGE LEARNING

PREREADING

Class Discussion. All human beings are mammals, but not all mammals are human. Human beings and other mammals are alike in certain ways. For example, mammals give birth to their babies alive. Mammals take care of their young babies. They protect them by forming family units.

But human beings and other mammals are also different in certain ways. Talk about some ways in which human beings are different from other mammals. Your answers to the following questions will help you develop your ideas.

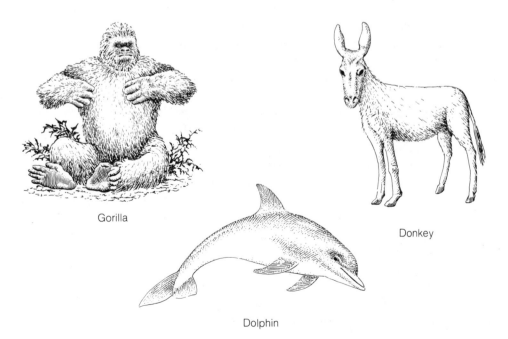

Gorilla

Dolphin

Donkey

a. How do human beings move around? How is this different from other mammals?

b. What are some ways that human beings protect themselves from cold, heat, and rain? How is this similar to or different from the way other mammals protect themselves?

c. How do human beings get some of their basic foods? Do other mammals get their food in the same way?

d. How do human beings communicate with each other? Name some things that other mammals do to communicate with each other?

New Words.   Try to understand the meanings of these words as they are used in the reading passage. Use a dictionary when necessary.

train (verb)	experiment (noun)	improve	create
ability	treat (verb)	visible	response
raise (verb)	patiently		

READING

Talking Apes: A Future Possibility?

[1]   In the past ten years several experts have tried to teach language to apes. One American psychologist trained his ape named Sarah to make sentences on a computer. Another American scientist trained an ape named Washoe to make signs for words. A third American scientist also trained an ape named Nim Chimpsky to use sign language. Nim learned over a hundred signs for different words. But can we say that these apes learned language?

[2]   Dr. Herbert Terrace of New York City is a psychologist. He wanted to study the language ability of apes. He decided that he would raise a young ape in his home. He would send this ape to school, and teachers would teach him sign language. Then Dr. Terrace would give different language tests to the ape. By this experiment he would discover if apes could learn language.

[3]   Dr. Terrace's ape, a chimpanzee named Nim Chimpsky, went to nursery school at Columbia University. There he had special teachers who taught him signs for English words. These teachers worked with Nim for five hours every day. They treated Nim lovingly and patiently. In four months Nim learned the signs for 125 words.

[4]   But during the next two years Nim's language did not improve very much. Nim still had a small vocabulary. Most of Nim's words were nouns for visible things such as *table* or *apple*. Nim learned a few active verbs such as *bite, jump,* and *hurry.* He also learned some basic colors such as *blue* and *red.* Nim

would often use two or three words together. He might make signs that said, "Nim   eat   apple." This seemed like an English sentence. But Nim would also use the signs meaning "eat   Nim   apple." This is not a correct English sentence.

[5]   Dr. Terrace decided that Nim could not really learn language as humans can. For example, Nim never created new words. He never added new information to his sentences. Nim couldn't even begin sentences. He would only give responses to his teachers' questions. Will future experiments show that apes can learn language? Dr. Terrace doesn't think so.

Summary Completion.   A summary gives the main ideas of a passage. It includes the most important supporting details of a passage. The following paragraph is a summary of this reading. But some of the sentences need to be completed by you. Choose the correct item from the columns following the paragraph to fill in each blank space in the paragraph.

In the past few years several scientists have done (1) _____ studies of the language abilities of apes. These scientists hope (2) _____ if apes (3) _____ language as humans do. After many experiments with his chimpanzee, Nim Chimpsky, Dr. Herbert Terrace believes that (4) _____ knows (5) _____ truth. Apes can learn some signs (6) _____ they cannot really learn (7) _____ language. The language of human children grows, improves (8) _____ becomes more creative. But Nim's language (9) _____ . Dr. Terrace's teachers (10) _____ very patient with Nim and (11) _____

Scientists have found some evidence that vervet monkeys use a kind of "language" to warn against danger. They have a variety of signals for such enemies as leopards, eagles, and snakes. Here, an American anthropologist studies vervet monkeys in their native East Africa.

treated him well. Nim learned signs for colors, visible nouns (12) _____

some action verbs. But he never really learned language (13) _____

he never created ideas or sentences. Many (14) _____ opinions are dif-

ferent from Dr. Terrace's. Some of these scientists are still (15) _____

experiments with the language ability of apes.

1. visible/
   valuable/
   angry/
   unknown
2. discover/
   to discover/
   discovered/
   is discovering
3. won't learn/
   must learn
   can learn/
   should learn
4. it/their/
   my/he

5. leave blank/
   a/an/the
6. and/then/
   ,/but
7. the/an/
   no/leave blank
8. ,/,and/but/
   leave blank
9. improves/
   always improved/
   never improved/
   doesn't improve
10. was/were/
    be/weren't

11. he/she/
    they/I
12. ,and/,/
    leave blank/
    also
13. because,/
    Because/
    because/
    because of
14. scientists/
    scientist's/
    scientists'/
    scientist
15. did/does/
    doing/do

VOCABULARY

1. Expanding Vocabulary. Replace the italicized word(s) in each sentence with a word from the New Word list.

   a. Dr. Terrace tried to *bring* Nim *up* like a child.

   b. He tried to *make* a warm feeling for Nim in his home.

   c. Nim learned some words for things *you can see,* and he used these words in his *answers* to his teachers' questions.

   d. Nim's teachers *handled* him *without irritation.*

   e. They *instructed* him to make signs for words.

   f. After two years, Nim's language didn't *get* much *better.*

   g. According to Dr. Terrace's *test,* apes don't have the mental *skill* to learn language.

2. Using Vocabulary. Follow the directions for each item.

   a. Each sentence in Column A uses the word *train* differently. In the blank space, write the letter of the correct meaning from Column B.

	A	**B**
(1)	_____ I tried to train my dog to shake hands.	**(a)** the long part of a dress that drags on the floor
(2)	_____ The train was several minutes early.	**(b)** practice
(3)	_____ Don't lose your train of thought when you're writing.	**(c)** connected ideas
(4)	_____ The bride's dress had a long silk train.	**(d)** a line of railroad cars
(5)	_____ Runners must train for many hours before each race.	**(e)** teach someone or something

b. Some English words keep the same form for the noun and the verb. You must look at the use of a word in a sentence to decide if a noun or a verb is being used. In the following sentences choose the correct set of words to complete the sentences. Be prepared to explain why you chose each set.

(1) (a raise, to raise) Since my work has improved, I will get

_____ .

(2) (a treat, to treat) Teachers should try _____ students

patiently.

(3) (an experiment, to experiment) Dr. Terrace did _____

on the language ability of apes.

(4) (a raise, to raise) It took a lot of patience _____

Nim Chimpsky like a child.

(5) (a train, to train) Nim's teachers wanted _____ Nim

in sign language.

c. Circle the things that human beings can *create*.
mountains   music   rice   paintings   a pleasant home
climate

d. Circle the things that are *visible*.
bananas   decisions   dictionaries   difficulty   dinosaur bones
patience

e. In complete sentences, tell three things that you have the ability to learn. Tell two things that snakes do not have the ability to do. Tell one thing that birds have the ability to do that human beings don't.

3. Word Families.   Study the following list of verbs and their related nouns. Note that *ion* and *ment* are common endings that change verb forms into nouns.

Verb	Noun
(1) protect	protection
(2) communicate	communication
(3) conclude	conclusion
(4) prepare	preparation
(5) omit	omission
(6) create	creation
(7) develop	development
(8) require	requirement
(9) treat	treatment
(10) improve	improvement

Your instructor will dictate ten sentences to you. Number each sentence 1 to 10 in sequence. In each sentence, when your instructor says "blank" for a missing word, draw a blank line. When the dictation is finished, fill in each blank space with either the verb or the noun from the corresponding item on the list. Now close your books.

1. Ape mothers _____ their babies from harm.

2. How do birds _____ with each other?

3. Dr. Terrace reached the _____ that apes don't learn language.

4. Your instructor can't _____ you for every new word.

5. There is an _____ of two words in that sentence.

6. In every language you can _____ new words.

7. A new _____ in science is interesting to read about.

8. Some instructors _____ two compositions each week.

9. Aspirin is a good _____ for a cold.

10. I hope to _____ my English this term.

READING COMPREHENSION

1. Understanding the Text.   Follow the directions for each item.

a. Mark *True* or *False* next to each statement. Be prepared to identify the part of the text where you find your answer.

(1) Human beings are mammals. _____

(2) Apes can learn signs for words. _____

(3) In four months Nim Chimpsky learned to speak English. _____

(4) Nim learned more nouns than verbs and adjectives. _____

(5) Nim always made correct English sentences. _____

(6) Dr. Terrace doesn't believe that apes have language ability. _____

b. Choose the correct answer.

(1) The writer's main purpose in this passage is to

    a. show similarities between apes and human beings.

    b. explain why Dr. Terrace is a good psychologist.

    c. describe the language ability of apes.

(2) In the first sentence of Paragraph [4], the word *But* tells us that

    a. this sentence presents a contrasting idea to the sentence before it.

    b. this sentence is not related to the sentence before it.

    c. this sentence isn't important.

(3) In Paragraph [4], the fifth sentence begins "He also learned . . ." The word *also* tells us that

    a. this sentence will be in contrast to the sentence before it.

    b. this sentence adds information to the sentence before it.

    c. this sentence will be in the negative.

(4) Which of the following sentences states the main idea of the entire reading passage?

    a. Apes can learn signs for nouns and verbs.

    b. Experiments with apes show that they don't have language ability.

    c. Nim Chimpsky was as smart as most human children.

c. Put a check [√] next to each sentence that shows that apes do not have real language ability.

(1) Nim Chimpsky learned the basic colors. _____

(2) Nim never learned how to make correct sentences. _____

(3) Nim didn't create new words. _____

(4) Nim went to nursery school. _____

(5) Nim learned over a hundred words in four months. _____

(6) Nim never added new information to sentences. _____

2. **Answering Information Questions.** Write the answers to the following questions in complete sentences.

   a. What did an American psychologist train Sarah to do?

   b. What did Dr. Herbert Terrace want to study?

   c. Where did Dr. Terrace raise Nim Chimpsky?

   d. How often did Nim's teachers work with him?

   e. How many signs did Nim Chimpsky learn?

   f. How many words could Nim use together?

   g. Did Nim or Nim's teachers always begin to talk first?

3. **Skimming for Main Ideas.** *To skim* means to read a passage quickly to get the main ideas. Each paragraph in a reading has its own main idea. A main idea tells you the subject of the passage and the writer's opinion about the subject. Sentences stating main ideas do not tell you specific details about the subject. Often the main idea sentence is the first or second sentence in a paragraph. But sometimes it is the last or next to last sentence.

   Skim the first paragraph of the Prereading. The main idea is in the second sentence. It tells you the subject: human beings and other mammals. It also gives you an opinion about the subject: Human beings and other mammals are alike.

   a. Skim Paragraph [1] of the reading passage. Which of its sentences expresses the main idea?

      (1) the first sentence   **(2)** the third sentence   **(3)** the last sentence

   b. The following sentences give us details about some of the things Dr. Terrace did with Nim Chimpsky. Skim Paragraphs [2] and [3] to find and underline the sentence that would be a good main idea for these details.

      (1) Dr. Terrace raised Nim in his home.

      (2) Dr. Terrace hired special teachers for Nim.

      (3) Dr. Terrace sent Nim to school.

      (4) Dr. Terrace's teachers taught Nim sign language.

      (5) Dr. Terrace tested Nim's vocabulary.

   c. Skim Paragraph [4]. The main idea is

      (1) the first sentence.   **(2)** the third sentence.   **(3)** the last sentence.

   d. Skim Paragraph [5] for its main idea. The main idea in this paragraph is not stated in one single sentence. In the space provided, write one sentence in your own words that explains the main idea of Paragraph [5].

   _____

WRITING EXERCISES

Modals + Basic Form of Verbs

A modal is a helping part of a verb. Modals tell about certain conditions related to the main verb. The main verb following a modal is always in its basic form.

Nim's teachers *would teach* him sign language.

Study the following explanations and examples of some common modals. The frequently used negatives are in parentheses.

  a. *Can (can't)*: Present Possibility; Present Ability

Many mammals *can learn* simple tricks.

---

  b. *Could (couldn't)*: Past Ability; Past Possibility

Nim *could make* signs after a few lessons.

---

  c. *May*: Present or Future Possibility

Dr. Terrace *may try* more experiments with apes.

---

  d. *Might*: Uncertain Possibility

Columbia University *might continue* to support Dr. Terrace's work.

---

  e. *Must (mustn't)*: Necessity; Prohibition

> Scientists *must perform* their experiments carefully.
> They *mustn't give* false information in their reports.

f. *Should (shouldn't)*: Advisability; Obligation

> Scientists *should communicate* with others in their profession.

g. *Will (won't)*: Future Certainty

> We *will learn* more about language in the next chapter.

h. *Would (wouldn't)*: Future Probability; Conditional (if) statements with Simple Past tense

> You *would need* a lot of patience to raise an ape in your home.
> If you studied apes closely, you *would learn* many interesting things.

1. **Identifying Modals.**   Read the following sentences. Underline the modal with its main verb in each sentence.

   a. Apes can learn to work computers.
   b. They can learn signs for words.
   c. But they will never learn language as human beings do.
   d. Nim could answer his teachers with signs.
   e. But he couldn't begin conversations with his teachers.
   f. Other mammals besides apes can understand human orders.
   g. The police might teach a dog to discover drugs.
   h. Many people think the police should use dogs in their work.
   i. Do you think we should train dogs for this purpose?

   Do any of the verbs that follow the modals end in *s, ed,* or *ing*? Use your answer to state a rule about the use of modals.

2. **Scrambled Sentences.**   Rewrite the following mixed-up sentences so that they form correct English sentences. Remember to look for the modal and its main verb first. Then look for the subject.

   a.   learn   apes   .   probably   language   can't   human

   b.   .   could   teachers   usually   Nim   his   understand
           school   in

   c.   scientists   in the future   try   experiments   .   may
           other   with apes

   d.   Dr. Terrace's   Nim   live   .   next year   won't   in
           home

   e.   would   to raise   ape   ?   an   like   at home   you

3. **Sentence Completion.**   Fill in a modal + a main verb in its basic form and whatever other words you need to create complete sentences from the items listed. Write your sentences in the space provided. The first one is done for you.

   a.   Tomorrow I . . . class . . .

   Tomorrow I can meet you after class.

   b.   When I was twelve years old, I . . .

   _____

   c.   I . . . $10.00 . . . to buy . . .

   _____

   d.   In the future people . . . moon . . .

   _____

   e.   Immigrants to the United States . . . English . . . job . . .

   _____

   f.   Students . . . for exams . . .

   _____

   g.   (negative) Nim Chimpsky . . . new words . . .

   _____

   h.   I . . . a letter . . .

   _____

Verbs + Infinitives

An infinitive verb is formed by *to* + the basic form of the main verb. Some verbs such as *want, like, would like, hope, expect, learn,* and *begin* are often followed by infinitives.

> **Dr. Terrace *wanted to study* the language ability of apes.**
> **The teachers *began to teach* Nim signs.**

Two verb phrases that include infinitives have special meanings. *Has* or *have to* + the base verb means *must*. *Used to* + the base verb means something that a person did in the past but doesn't do anymore.

> **Psychologists *have to* do their experiments carefully.**
> **Nim *used to* live in Dr. Terrace's apartment.**

---

1. **Answering Questions with Infinitives.**   Write your answers to the following information questions in complete sentences. Refer back to the reading passage for your information. Use an infinitive in each sentence.

    a. In the past ten years, what have some American experts tried to do?

    b. What did an American psychologist train Sarah to do?

    c. What did another scientist train Washoe to do?

    d. What did Dr. Terrace want to discover in his experiment?

    e. Where did Dr. Terrace decide to raise Nim?

    f. Does Dr. Terrace expect to train a talking ape in the future?

2. **Sentence Completion.**   Look at the photograph of the North African chiefs, and read the caption under it. Then complete the following sentences with details from the caption or with your own ideas. Use an infinitive in each of your sentences.

    a. These men are planning . . .

    b. They expect . . .

    c. They hope . . .

    d. They want . . .

    e. Their people want . . .

    f. After finishing this meeting, many of these men will begin . . .

These village chiefs from a rural area of North Africa are meeting to plan community development projects such as wells, schools, and roads.

3. **Sentence Composing.**   Write a complete sentence for each of the following items.

   a. What two courses do you want to take next term?

   b. Where would you like to go on vacation next summer?

   c. Why are you learning to speak English?

   d. Do you know how to run a computer?

   e. Name two things your parents used to do for you when you were a child?

   f. At what age did you begin to walk?

   g. What salary do you expect to earn on your first full-time job?

Changing the Direction of a Thought: The Use of *But*

But is used to change the direction of a thought, or to present a contrasting idea. Study the following examples.

> **Nim Chimpsky learned over a hundred signs. *But* he never really learned language.**
>
> **or**
>
> **Nim Chimpsky learned over a hundred signs, but he never really learned language.**

Note that when *but* is used in the middle of a sentence, a comma goes before it.

1. **Sentence Rewriting.** Rewrite each of the following pairs of sentences using *,but* or *But*.

    a. (1) Nim learned signs for words.
        (2) He never created new words himself.

    b. (1) Children's sentences grow longer all the time.
        (2) Nim's sentences had three words at the most.

    c. (1) The babies of mammals are born alive.
        (2) Bird babies are born from eggs.

    d. (1) Nim was not a human child.
        (2) He attended a nursery school with special teachers.

    e. (1) At first Dr. Terrace thought apes could learn language.
        (2) Then he discovered that they cannot.

    f. (1) Human beings walk on two legs.
        (2) Most other mammals walk on all four legs.

2. **Sentence Expansion.** Change the direction of the thought in each of the following sentences by adding *,but* + a new contrasting thought. Rewrite each new sentence. You may want to use the words in parentheses to guide you.

    > **Millions of people speak Chinese. (few, Welsh)**
    >
    > *Millions of people speak Chinese, but few speak Welsh.*

    a. American English writing is very similar to British English writing. (pronunciation, different)
    b. I would like to live in Paris. (expensive)
    c. A pocket dictionary doesn't have every word. (easy, school)
    d. Dogs can be trained to do many tricks. (rabbits)
    e. I would like to go bowling. (must study)

3. **Sentence Composing.** Respond to the following items in complete written sentences. Use *,but* in each sentence.

    a. Tell one kind of food you eat a lot of and one kind you rarely eat.
    b. Tell one sport you enjoy and one sport you don't like to play.
    c. Tell one language you can speak and one language you can't speak.

    d. Tell one pleasant thing about your native city and one unpleasant thing.

    e. Tell one interesting thing about studying English and one boring thing about it.

Punctuation: Series of Parallel Items

A series of parallel items is a group of three or more words that do the same kind of work in a sentence. A sentence may have a series of nouns, adjectives, verbs, or adverbs. Each item in a series is followed by a comma. The word *and* goes before the last item in the series. All the items in a series must have the same form.

Nim Chimpsky, Sarah, and Washoe all developed small vocabularies.
      (series of proper nouns)

Nim's teachers were *patient, able, and kind.*
      (series of adjectives)

Nim *slept, ate, and played* at Dr. Terrace's home.
    (series of verbs: Simple Past)

---

1. **Sentence Combining.** Combine each group of sentences into one complete sentence. Leave out unnecessary words. Add correct punctuation, and make whatever other small changes are needed. Rewrite each new sentence. The first one is done for you.

    a. **(1)** Nim was angry when he was left alone.

        (2) Nim was afraid when he was left alone.

        (3) Nim was unhappy when he was left alone.

        Nim was angry, afraid, and unhappy when he was left alone.

    b. **(1)** Immigrants brought their native cultures to the United States.

        (2) Immigrants brought their native customs to the United States.

        (3) Immigrants brought their native languages to the United States.

    c. **(1)** Some British words differ from American words in spelling.

        (2) Some British words differ from American words in pronunciation.

        (3) Some British words differ from American words in usage.

    d. **(1)** The big *Webster's Dictionary* would be an interesting gift for a friend.

        (2) The big *Webster's Dictionary* would be a valuable gift for a friend.

        (3) The big *Webster's Dictionary* would be a useful gift for a friend.

    e. **(1)** Nim Chimpsky liked to look at magazines.

       (2) Nim Chimpsky liked to play with pencils.

       (3) Nim Chimpsky liked to learn new signs.

    f. **(1)** Geologists climb mountains to discover fossils.

       (2) Geologists study rocks to discover fossils.

       (3) Geologists dig in the ground to discover fossils.

    g. **(1)** Future computers may teach school.

       (2) Future computers may put out fires.

       (3) Future computers may solve many problems.

2. **Sentence Composing.**   Follow the directions for each item.

    a. Use a series of parallel adjectives to tell how a main street in your native city is or looks.

    b. Use a series of verbs to state what you usually do after your English class.

    c. Use a series of nouns to name three sports or games you like to play.

    d. Use a series of proper nouns to tell what special holidays people in your native culture celebrate.

3. **Proofreading.**   There is one error in the use of parallel items in a series in each of the following sentences. On the line provided correct the error in each sentence.

    a. My friends enjoy swimming, running, and to play tennis in the summer.

       _____

    b. Maria, George, Pierre sit near me in English class. _____

    c. You can keep a pocket dictionary in your pocket your schoolbag, or your handbag. _____

    d. In our English class we listen to new sounds, learning new words, and write compositions. _____

    e. An intelligent and patient and kind teacher will try to answer students' questions about language. _____

COMPOSING

1. **Developing a Paragraph.**

    a. Put *M.I.* (for Main Idea) next to the sentence that states the main idea of the paragraph. Then number the other sentences in the correct order to form a good paragraph. Look for pronouns, time signals, and other words that will help you find the correct order. Rewrite the sentences in correct order as a paragraph.

(1) He sent him to nursery school with special teachers. _____

(2) The schoolroom was bright and colorful. _____

(3) Dr. Terrace created a very special environment for Nim Chimpsky.

_____

(4) When Nim learned a new sign, his teachers would give him a special treat. _____

(5) Here in school, Nim learned signs for words. _____

(6) It had a lot of pictures and magazines in it. _____

b. Study the following lists. Column A describes Ms. Jones's class in which children will develop language skills well. Column B describes Ms. Smith's class in which children may not develop language skills as well.

A (Ms. Jones's class)	**B (Ms. Smith's class)**
The classroom looks bright and cheerful.	The classroom looks dull and uninteresting.
The teacher reads stories to the children.	The teacher never reads stories to the children.
The teacher corrects mistakes patiently.	The teacher corrects mistakes impatiently.
There are many books and magazines.	There are few books and magazines.
The children sometimes create their own stories.	The children never create their own stories.
The children sometimes get a treat for good work.	The children rarely get a treat for good work.
The children often talk about their ideas and feelings.	The children rarely talk about their ideas and feelings.
The children sometimes work with each other.	The children always work alone.
There are some useful dictionaries in class.	There are no useful dictionaries in class.
The children experiment with new words.	The children never experiment with new words.

Write a paragraph that tells about Ms. Jones's or Ms. Smith's class. Begin with a main idea that states your topic: a class for language learning. The main idea should also tell your opinion about this class. Develop your paragraph by choosing statements from one of the columns to support your main idea. You may add reasons of your own. Arrange your sentences in good order. Review your finished paragraph for errors. Make it as correct as you can.

2. **Composing a Paragraph.**

   a. Have you ever trained an animal or instructed a child in some special skill? Write a paragraph in which you tell about this process. Describe the method and materials you used and the final result.

   b. Dr. Terrace raised Nim Chimpsky with kindness and gentleness. Some parents believe that children should be raised with strictness. Write a paragraph in which you discuss how you think children should be raised.

UNIT II REVIEW

1. **Sentence Completion.** Choose the correct item from the columns following the paragraph to fill in each blank space in the paragraph.

Since very (1) _____ times the different peoples of the world have spoken (2) _____ different languages. International communication has often been difficult (3) _____ people have not understood the languages of others. Many men (4) _____ women have developed systems for a universal language (5) _____ different language groups communicate. For example, (6) _____ French scientist Descartes thought that a symbolic language (7) _____ be useful. One hundred years ago a man named Sodre (8) _____ a musical language. He called (9) _____ Solresol because it (10) _____ musical notes such as *so, la,* (11) _____ *re.* These artificial languages have some (12) _____ : They have simple vocabularies and grammars. (13) _____ they have never developed large numbers of speakers. In fact, most of them have never gone further than their (14) _____ front doors. Yet currently, many people (15) _____ on a universal language.

1. numerical/
   ancient/
   literate/
   official
2. a/an/the/
   leave blank
3. and/but/
   because/then
4. but/and/
   ,/also
5. to helps/
   is helping/
   to help/help

6. the/a/an/
   leave blank
7. can/will/
   may/would
8. is inventing/
   invents/
   invented/
   inventor
9. her/him/
   their/it
10. uses/used/
    is using/to use

11. leave blank/
    ./,/and
12. opinions/
    emotions/
    immigrants/
    advantages
13. And/But/
    Because/
    Then
14. inventors/
    inventors'/
    inventor/
    inventor's

15. work/
    are working/
    worked/
    is working

2. **Word Forms.** Fill in the chart with the correct forms of the given words. (Some parts of speech may have more than one word.)

	Verb	Noun	Adjective	Adverb
a	communicate			X
b			various	
c	develop			
d	X		native	
e		immigrants		X
f	create			
g	prepare			X
h		symbols		
i	decide			
j	invent			

Word Form Completion. Fill in the blank space in each sentence with the correct form of the word from the same lettered item on the Word Form chart. Use verbs and nouns in their singular or plural form as necessary. For dictation with blanks, close your textbook.

a. There should be good _____ between parents and children.

b. We should study a _____ of subjects in college.

c. I would like to _____ my oral skills in French.

d. My grandfather was a _____ of Poland.

e. Many people _____ to the United States each year.

f. Artists, musicians, and sculptors are _____ people.

g. Men and women must have good _____ for their careers.

h. A red light _____ the word *stop*.

i. Have you reached a _____ about continuing your college education?

j. The ball-point pen is a very useful _____ .

3. **Paragraph Composition.** Write a paragraph that uses five to eight of the words from the Word Form chart. Select one of the following topics to write about or choose one of your own.

A Useful Invention
An Important Decision
A Beautiful Creation

UNIT III

WOMEN AND MEN

Permanence, respect, and cooperation in raising a family are the ideals of male-female relationships.

CHAPTER SEVEN A

WOMEN IN ANCIENT HISTORY

PREREADING

Strip Story. Listen to your instructor read the story "The Gift of the Goddess Athena." Then, as a class, or in groups, copy each of the following sentences onto a separate strip of paper. Put the strips in the proper order to tell the story of Athena. Use pronouns, time expressions, and other words as clues for sentence order. When the strips are correctly arranged, number them in sequence. Then read the story aloud from the strips.

Her uncle Poseidon was the powerful god of all the oceans and seas.

So they all went to the highest rock in the land to hold the contest.

They both wanted to rule Attica, an important area in ancient Greece.

When the contest was over, all the gods and goddesses voted.

They also decided that whoever gave the most useful gift to the people would be the winner.

After that, the people planted olive trees and called their capital city Athens to honor her.

At first, Poseidon wanted to fight with Athena for the rule.

Athena was a powerful goddess, protector of women and children.

Then they became rich from the olive oil trade.

First Poseidon struck the rock with his spear and a spring of salt water burst forth.

With some of the money they built a beautiful temple for Athena on the high rock in Athens.

But all the other gods and goddesses decided it would be better to have a peaceful contest between the two.

They chose Athena as the winner because her gift was more useful.

This is a myth about a contest between a god and a goddess of Greece.

Then Athena struck the rock with her spear and an olive tree grew out.

New Words.   Try to understand the meanings of these words as they are used in the reading passage. Use a dictionary when necessary.

ideal	respected	secluded	approach
modestly	responsible	ambitious	eventually
economical	recline	possessions	

READING

Two Ideals of Womanhood

[1]   People are expected to behave according to the rules of their society. From the writings of ancient historians, we know something about Roman and Etruscan society and how they expected their women to behave. We know something about the important differences between Roman and Etruscan ideals of womanhood.

[2]   Just outside of Rome, in an ancient cemetery, there is a tombstone of a woman named Claudia. On it is written: "You were a faithful and obedient wife;

The Athenian people built this temple for their goddess Athena on the high rock of Athens.

you were kind and gentle; you stayed in the house and worked wool; you dressed modestly, without calling attention to yourself; you kept a simple home and were economical; you cared for our family and you loved me." This was the message Claudia's husband put on her tombstone when she died over two thousand years ago. Claudia was the ideal Roman woman in ancient times.

[3]   Claudia was a highly respected member of Roman society. When she married, she became responsible for her husband's good name and for the wise management of their family. Although she had slaves, she raised her children by herself and educated them at home when they were young. She was strict with them even when they played games. Claudia didn't leave the house without her husband's permission. Most of the time she stayed home to do her household duties and be like a servant to her children. During meals she sat beside her husband while he reclined on a couch. Like many women of that time, Claudia generally spent her life among other females. While her husband was entertaining friends in the evening, she would spin wool with her older daughters and female slaves. Throughout early Roman history, women like Claudia were living a modest, secluded life. Archeologists have discovered many tombstones of such ideal women, showing them seated and working wool with a basket at their feet.

[4]   However, in another part of Italy north of Rome, women were leading a different kind of life. They were called Etruscans, and, unlike the Romans, these women were sharing much more in their husband's wealth, leisure time, and pleasures. The Etruscans liked comfort and had fine homes with beautiful furniture and splendid wall paintings. The women spent a good deal of time on their personal beauty and dress. They attracted attention by wearing expensive jewelry set with rare stones. In contrast to Roman women, respectable Etruscan wives weren't secluded. They often went out during the day and even sat beside their husbands at athletic games and contests. At dinner, the women reclined on the same couches

This portion of the ancient Roman monument called "The Altar of Peace" shows an ideal Roman family.

as their husbands, joining freely in the conversation with other couples. When the meal was over, the men as well as the women enjoyed themselves while musicians and dancers entertained them. Etruscan women seemed carefree and immodest, but they were only taking their place openly in a world of couples, not just men alone. Nevertheless, in the opinion of their Roman neighbors, Etruscan wives were not examples of ideal women.

[5]   All the Romans knew the story of Tanaquil, the restless and ambitious Etruscan woman, who had lived long before in a city north of Rome. She thought about the great advantages she and her husband Tarquin would have if they moved to another place. When she talked about moving to Rome, her husband listened. So they packed all their rich possessions and rode toward Rome. As they were approaching the city, Tanaquil stopped the carriage to observe an eagle flying overhead. From the movements of the bird, Tanaquil was able to predict her husband's future as king of Rome. When they arrived, they worked together, giving money and advice to the Roman people. Eventually, because of Tanaquil's ambition and ability, Tarquin ruled Rome. When Tarquin died, Tanaquil set up her son-in-law as the next king.

[6]   The Romans never forgot Tanaquil and the days of Etruscan rule. They never approved of the position of women in Etruscan society. When the Romans became more powerful, they destroyed the Etruscan power over Rome. Eventually, the Etruscan way of life changed. Etruscan women no longer shared equally in their husbands' life. Instead, they followed the Roman ideal of women like Claudia.

Guided Summary.   A summary tells us the most important ideas of a reading passage. Complete the following sentences to make a summary. Write your new sentences in the form of a paragraph.

    a.   This reading passage informs us about . . .

    b.   The second paragraph introduces us to . . .

    c.   The third paragraph describes Claudia as . . .

    d.   All the details of Paragraph [3] show that . . .

    e.   Paragraph [4] contrasts . . .

    f.   The details of Paragraph [4] show that . . .

    g.   Paragraph [5] gives an example of . . .

    h.   The sixth paragraph states that . . .

VOCABULARY

    1.   Expanding Vocabulary.   Replace the italicized word(s) in each sentence with a word from the New Word list.

        a.   Archeologists have found the household and personal *belongings* of the Etruscans in their tombs.

b. The statues of the Greek goddess Athena show her dressed *in a simple way,* just like Roman women.

c. The early Romans wanted to make a *perfect* home environment for raising children.

d. A *thrifty* person is a good household manager.

e. People in modern society don't *lean back* on a couch when they eat.

f. As you *come toward* Athens from the sea, you can observe the ancient temple of Athena on the high rock.

g. A Roman father was *accountable* for his son's education after the age of seven.

h. In a Roman house, there were special rooms for women *closed off* from the other rooms.

i. Many women in modern society are *eager for success* and are *looked at with honor* in their professions.

j. *In the course of time,* Etruscan women lost their equality with men.

2. **Using Vocabulary.**   Follow the directions for each item.

a. Draw a line from each item in Column A to the related item in Column B. Then rewrite each complete item as a sentence.

A	**B**
(1) Newly married people generally furnish their homes	**(a)** while I'm reading
(2) Parents are *responsible* for	**(b)** I'll be very proficient in English
(3) I like to *recline* in bed	**(c)** because it's more *economical*
(4) The spaceship *Voyager I* took splendid photographs	**(d)** *modestly* and inexpensively
(5) Some people prefer vegetable oil to olive oil	**(e)** the welfare of their children
(6) *Eventually*	**(f)** as it *approached* the planet Saturn

b. Check (✓) the sentences that use the italicized word from the New Word list correctly. Put an X next to the ones that don't.

(1) An *ideal* society would be one without war or poverty. _____✓_____

(2) Her many *possessions* made her free as a bird. _____✗_____

(3) He lived in a *secluded* area crowded with people. _____✗_____

(4) An *ambitious* student completes all assignments. _____✓_____

   c. Which sentence would be most likely to follow the given sentence? Mr. Finley is a *respected* professor of Greek and Roman history.

     (1) He invents interesting stories about Greek and Roman life.

     (2) He examines past events carefully and reports them fairly.

     (3) He gives his opinions about events without examining the facts.

3. Word Families.   Many of our words are formed from a common root or stem. These stems are usually formed from Greek or Latin words. We add prefixes and suffixes to the stem and change the form, but the meanings of all the words in a word family will have some relationship to each other. Recognizing the root or stem of a word will help you to increase your vocabulary. Study the following list.

Stem	Meaning	Example
duc	lead	e*duc*ate, con*duc*tor, intro*duc*e
clud, clus	close, shut	se*clude*, in*clude*, con*clus*ion
spect	look, watch	re*spect*, *spect*ator, in*spect*ion
scrib, script	write	de*scribe*, pre*script*ion
nat	born, birth	pre*nat*al, *nat*ural, *nat*ive
vis	see	*vis*ion, super*vis*or, in*vis*ible
mot	move	*mot*or, pro*mot*ion
dict	say, tell	pre*dict*, contra*dict*, *dict*ation

Choosing definitions.   Fill in the blank space with a word from the Example column that would make the sentence correct. The italicized words will help you make the correct choice.

a. If you can't *see* without glasses, you have very poor _____ .

b. The _____ of an orchestra is the one who *leads* all the musicians together as a group.

c. A _____ over*sees* the work of many people.

d. When a person *moves* up to a better job, we say that he or she receives a ___ *promotion* ___ .

e. To *say* the opposite of something that was stated before is to ___ con ___ the original statement.

f. When a doctor *writes* down symbols for your medicine, he or she is giving you a _____ .

g. At the *close* of a story we find out the author's _____ .

h. _____ care is important if babies are to be *born* healthy.

i. When you *look* into something closely, you make an _____ of it.

READING COMPREHENSION

1. **Understanding the Text.**   Follow the directions for each item.

   a. If the statement is true, write *T*. If the statement is false, write *F*. If the story does not give information about the sentence, write *N.I.* (no information). Underline the part of the passage where you find your true or false answers.

   (1) Claudia had great responsibilities at home. _____*T*_____

   (2) Claudia's slaves helped her raise her children. ____*F*____

   (3) Claudia never went out of the house. ____*F*____

   (4) Claudia's husband was a government official. ____*NI*____

   (5) In early Roman times there were many ideal women like Claudia.
   ____*T*____

   (6) Etruscan men shared their free time with their wives. ____*T*____

   (7) Sometimes Etruscan women worked at their wool. ____*NI*____

   (8) The Romans thought highly of Etruscan women. ____*F*____

   (9) Tanaquil's predictions came true. ____*T*____

   b. Circle the letter of the correct answer.

   (1) The message on Claudia's tombstone

      a. tells us when she died.

      b. shows that her husband thought little of her.

      c. describes the ideal Roman woman.

   (2) The second sentence of Paragraph [3] contains the clause "she became responsible for her husband's good name." This means that she

      a. had to act correctly to maintain his high position in society.

      b. could do anything she wanted without loss of his respect.

      c. had to give him a different name.

   (3) The third sentence of Paragraph [3] begins "Although she had slaves." This clause may also be written:

    a. She had slaves so

    b. She had slaves, but

    c. But she had slaves

(4) Claudia's relationship to her children was

    a. caring and easy-going.

    b. strict and harsh.

    c. kind but strict.

(5) Besides caring for her children, one of Claudia's main jobs was

    a. shopping for woolen cloth.

    b. spinning wool to make cloth.

    c. washing woolen cloth.

(6) According to the information in Paragraph [4], Etruscan women

    a. had more personal freedom than Roman women.

    b. were more economical than Roman women.

    c. lived a more secluded life than Roman women.

(7) In Paragraph [4], the next to the last sentence states that "Etruscan women seemed carefree and immodest." This clause means that

    a. they really were that way.

    b. they appeared that way compared to Roman women.

    c. they looked better than Roman women.

(8) The statement that Etruscan women "were only taking their place openly in a world of couples" means that

    a. it was immodest to share activities.

    b. it was correct behavior but only at home.

    c. it was natural to share activities publically and privately.

(9) The story of Tanaquil is a good example of an Etruscan woman

    a. working quietly in a city north of Rome.

    b. taking her place openly in a world of couples.

    c. living a secluded life.

(10) Eventually, Etruscan women followed the Roman ideal of womanhood because

    a. Roman women were happier.

    b. the Romans became more powerful.

    c. they wanted to be like Tanaquil.

2. **Answering Information Questions.**   Write the answers to the following questions in complete sentences.

   a. Where is Claudia's tombstone?

   b. When did Claudia die?

   c. Whose permission did Claudia need to leave the house?

   d. What would Claudia do in the evening?

   e. What kind of homes did the Etruscans have?

   f. What did Etruscan women often do during the day?

   g. What happened as Tanaquil and Tarquin were approaching Rome?

   h. Whom did Tanaquil set up as the next king when Tarquin died?

   i. Did the Romans approve or disapprove of Etruscan women?

3. **Signals of Contrast.**   When English writers want to contradict, or state something opposite to what they have just said, they usually use signal words of contrast. These words let the reader know that the writer is going to present two pieces of contradictory, contrasting, or opposite information. Study this list of signal words of contrast.

, but	in contrast,	although
however,	in contrast to _____ ,	unlike _____ ,
on the other hand,	nevertheless	

   a. Reread Paragraph [4] of the reading passage, and underline the signal words of contrast.

   b. Paragraph [4] describes Etruscan women in contrast to Roman women. However, the detailed information about Roman women is stated in Paragraphs [2] and [3]. Complete the following list of contrasting information by scanning Paragraphs [2], [3], and [4]. Write your answers in short note form. The first one is done for you.

Roman Women	Etruscan Women
(1) _kept a simple home_ _were economical_	had fine homes, furniture, paintings
(2) _____	spent time on beauty and dress
(3) didn't call attention to themselves	_____
(4) mostly stayed at home	_____
(5) _____	reclined with husband at meals
(6) _____	enjoyed entertainment after dinner

(7) did household duties   _____

(8) _____ took place openly as couples

(9) led a modest, secluded life   _____

c. Read the following paragraph and underline the signals of contrast.

> Another difference between the Romans and the Etruscans was in the use of names. Roman women were always called by the feminine form of their father's name. So Claudia was named after her father Claudius, and a girl born of a father Lucretius would be called Lucretia. In contrast, Etruscan women had their own names. A child of Etruscan parents had his or her own first name and both the father's and the mother's last name, although the father's name came first. Unlike Roman custom, a child born of a free mother and a slave father was a freeborn person and used only the mother's family name. In Roman society, however, a child with a free mother but a slave father would not have the rights of a freeborn person. Although the Etruscan way of life changed under Roman rule, the Etruscans continued to use their own way of naming their children.

Now complete the following exercise. Mark *T* if the statement is true. Mark *F* if it is false. Use the signal words of contrast to help you find your answers.

(1) Roman women didn't have their own names. ____T____

(2) Etruscan women had individual first names. ____T____

(3) An Etruscan had two last names, but the mother's came first.

____F____

(4) A Roman child of a slave father would have the same rights as an Etruscan child of a slave father. ____F____

(5) The Etruscans kept their custom of naming even when the Romans ruled. ____T____

WRITING EXERCISES

Past Continuous Tense

The Past Continuous tense of verbs is used for several purposes. It is used to show action that took place at one point of time in the past. It is also used to show ongoing, continuous action in the past. The main use of the Past Continuous tense is to show interrupted action in a sentence that also includes a clause in the Simple

Past tense. The Past Continuous tense is formed by *was* or *were* + the *ing* form of the main verb.

> **Last semester I was studying ancient history.**
> **I was studying last night when I heard the bad news on the radio.**

Study the Past Continuous tense of the verb *approach*.

	Singular	**Plural**
First Person	I was approaching	My friend and I were approaching We were approaching
Second Person	You were approaching	You were approaching
Third Person	Tanaquil was approaching He/She/It was approaching	Tanaquil and Tarquin were approaching They were approaching

The negative forms are *was not (wasn't)* and *were not (weren't)* + the *ing* form of the main verb.

1. **Identifying Past Continuous Tense.**   Listen carefully as your instructor reads the following paragraph to you. Underline each verb in the Past Continuous tense.

Etruscan husbands and wives spent a lot of time together. Here a tomb sculpture portrays a couple together as they were in life.

When Rome was a new small town, there weren't enough women in the population. Some of the men were beginning to feel lonely. They were constantly thinking about marriage and families. They tried to arrange marriages with the neighboring women, the Sabines, but they failed because the Sabine women were afraid of the Romans. The Roman men were getting restless, so they decided to steal the women away from their families. They held a great festival in Rome and invited all the Sabines. While the people were watching the activities, one of the Roman men gave a signal. Then they all began to carry off the young Sabine women. The women were screaming and crying while their parents watched helplessly. While the Roman men were running away with their prisoners, they thought about the wonderful wives they would soon have. The Sabine parents had to leave Rome without their daughters.

2. **Dictation.**   Your instructor will dictate five sentences from the paragraph that include Past Continuous verb forms. Pay special attention to verb forms.

3. **Paragraph Completion.**   The Past Continuous tense is frequently used in complex sentences with the Simple Past tense. In the following paragraph, which is a continuation of the story of the Sabine women, complete the blank spaces with the appropriate verb form as directed in the parentheses.

The Sabine women (live: Past Continuous) _____
                                                          (1)
peacefully as ideal wives of the Roman men. But the Sabine fathers

(forget: Simple Past; negative) _____ their daughters.
                                        (2)
They (plan: Past Continuous) ___were_____ a war against the
                                        (3)
Romans for the return of the women. When their army (be: Simple Past)

_____ ready, they (march: Simple Past) _____
          (4)   (5)
to Rome. Meanwhile, the Romans (prepare: Past Continuous) _____
                                                               (6)
for war against their fathers-in-law. When the Sabines (enter: Simple

Past) _____ Rome, every Roman male (stand: Past Con-
                (7)
tinuous) _____ ready. At first the Sabines (win: Past
                  (8)
Continuous) _____ the battle. They (destroy: Past Con-
                      (9)
tinuous) _____ the city while their daughters (watch:
                  (10)
Past Continuous) _____ helplessly. Then the Sabine
                          (11)
women (decide: Simple Past) _____ to throw them-
                                        (12)
selves between the two armies and beg for peace between their fathers

and their husbands. Thanks to the bravery of the women, the fighting

(stop: Simple Past) _____ and the Sabines and the
(13)
Romans (become: Simple Past) _____ one people, with
(14)
Rome as their capital.

Complex Sentences with
When and *While*

A clause is a sentence part that has a subject and a complete main verb. Complex sentences always include one dependent clause. A dependent clause is a clause that cannot stand by itself as a sentence. Dependent clauses must be joined to independent, or main, clauses.

When and *while* are time words that begin dependent clauses. Dependent clauses with *when* and *while* must join independent, or main, clauses to form a complete sentence.

When tells us about two kinds of time periods.

1. a long period of time during which many different actions take place

> **When Tarquin was king of Rome, he changed the system of government.**

2. a point of time when two actions take place together or immediately following each other (at that time)

> **When Tanaquil saw the eagle overhead, she predicted a bright future.**

While tells us about actions that take place during the same time period. *While* often introduces clauses using continuous tenses.

> **While Claudia was spinning wool, her husband entertained his friends.**

Identifying Dependent Clauses.   Reread Paragraph [3] of the reading passage. Copy the five sentences that contain *when* or *while* clauses. Then underline the complete dependent *when* or *while* clause in each sentence. Note that when the dependent clause comes before the independent clause, it is followed by a comma. Now discuss the following questions with your class.

a. Why does your first sentence have a comma after the word *married?*

b. Why isn't there a comma in your third sentence?

c. What is the difference between the position of the dependent clauses in your fourth and fifth sentences?

d. Why don't you have a comma in your fourth sentence?

e. Where does the comma appear in your fifth sentence?

Verb Tenses in Complex Sentences with *When* and *While*.   The two clauses in complex sentences with *when* and *while* must have the same or related verb tenses. Study the following examples of common pairs of verb tenses in *when* and *while* sentences.

Simple Present   **Simple Present and Future**

When a king or queen *enters* a room, everyone *stands* up.
When I *graduate* from college, I*'ll take* a trip to Rome.

Present Continuous   **Simple Present and Present Continuous**

While I*'m preparing* dinner, I always *listen* to the news on the radio.
She *is taking* courses in English while her husband *is working*.

Simple Past   **Simple Past**

When a Roman mother *became* ill, a female relative *took* care of her children.

Past Continuous   **Simple Past and Past Continuous**

While Roman girls *were spinning* wool, the boys *went* to meetings with their father.
The students *were studying* the reading passage, while the instructor *was checking* their homework.

Simple Past and Past Continuous   Could and Would

> **When a Roman boy *was* about seventeen, he *would spend* a year or two in the army.**
> **While he *was serving* in the army, a rich Roman boy *could have* a tutor to help him with his studies.**

1. **Sentence Combining.**   Combine each pair of sentences into one complete sentence with a dependent clause and an independent clause. Use *when* or *while* to combine them. Rewrite your complete new sentences.

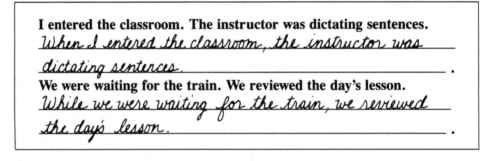

> **I entered the classroom. The instructor was dictating sentences.**
> *When I entered the classroom, the instructor was dictating sentences.*
> **We were waiting for the train. We reviewed the day's lesson.**
> *While we were waiting for the train, we reviewed the day's lesson.*

   a. Mr. Finley gives lectures on ancient Rome. Hundreds of students attend them.

   b. Dr. Larissa Bonfante returned from Italy last summer. She wrote an article about Etruscan women.

   c. The Etruscans lost their power. They couldn't keep all their old customs.

   d. Roman boys were riding horses and swimming. The girls stayed home with their mothers.

   e. I was studying my lessons. My little brother helped my mother with the dishes.

   f. Tanaquil's son-in-law became king of Rome. He built a great wall around the city to protect the people.

2. **Sentence Completion.**   Choose the clause that correctly completes the given clause. Write the new clause in the space provided.

   a. _____ when he lost the contest.

      (1) When Poseidon became very angry,   **(2)** Poseidon becomes very angry
      (3) Poseidon became very angry

b. People take on new responsibilities _____

    (1) while they got married.   **(2)** when they get married.

    (3) when they will get married.

c. While the men were fighting the battle, _____

    (1) the women are watching helplessly.

    (2) the women watch helplessly.

    (3) the women watched helplessly.

d. _____

    when she finishes her research next year.

    (1) Dr. Bonfante will write another article

    (2) Dr. Bonfante wrote another article

    (3) Dr. Bonfante writes another article

e. The archeologists would take careful notes _____

    (1) while they would dig.   **(2)** while they were digging.

    (3) while they are digging.

f. _____

    the students were listening closely.

    (1) While the instructor was dictating the sentences

    (2) While the instructor was dictating the sentences,

    (3) While the instructor is dictating the sentences,

g. When we examine the lives of the Romans and Etruscans, _____

    _____

    (1) we often learn a lot about ourselves.   **(2)** while we often learn a lot about ourselves.   **(3)** when we will learn a lot about ourselves.

3. Sentence Expansion.   Complete each sentence in the space provided. Make sure that the verbs in the new clauses are correctly related to the verbs in the given clauses.

a. When the weather gets warmer, *I will be able to swim* .

b. When I arrived at the station, *I meet my cousine* .

c. Someone *was watching me* while I was swimming at the beach last week.

d. The spectators *were excited .* when the players started the game.

e. When I don't understand a particular word in the reading passage, *I use a dictionary* .

f. While I was doing my homework, *I was listing to radio* .

g. I couldn't speak English very well *when I first came the USA*

Prepositions of Place

The following example contains some prepositions of place. These prepositions tell us where things are. They begin phrases that are called prepositional phrases of place.

> Tanaquil sat *next to* her husband as they traveled *along* the road to Rome. When they arrived just *outside* the city, she observed the eagle *over* her head.

Study this list of some common prepositions of place.

across	next to	along	on the side of
among	outside	beside	in the center of
within, inside	over, above	in, at the back of	by

1. **Identifying Prepositions of Place.**   Listen as your instructor reads the following paragraph. Underline the prepositions of place.

The entrance of a Roman town house was a simple doorway next to the shops on the street. Inside the doorway there was a small passageway that led to a courtyard. The roof of the courtyard had an opening in the center, and under the opening there was a basin on the ground to collect the rainwater. A little sunlight came through the opening, and it made the courtyard a pleasant place to sit. Along the sides there were usually a few small bedrooms. At the back of the courtyard was another room used for eating, studying, or sleeping. A large open garden area was located behind that room, and this was the best part of a Roman house. Here the Roman family would sit by the fish pool or among the fruit trees and enjoy their leisure time. Sometimes they ate in a dining room on the side of the garden. The kitchen was usually across the other side of the garden. The whole plan of the house was very simple, and it gave the family a lot of privacy.

2. Pair Dictation. Dictate the first three sentences to your partner. Then take dictation of the last three sentences from him or her.

a. There's a map of the world in the back of the book.

b. The library is across the street from my house.

c. I heard a loud noise outside the door.

d. On a rainy day I like to sit by the window and read.

e. A young couple lives in the apartment above me.

f. We had a difficult time driving through the snow.

Comparison of Adjectives

Read the following paragraph carefully. Pay special attention to the italicized adjectives.

Archeology has changed in the past 150 years. It is *more scientific* than it was in the nineteenth century. Archeologists use *better* tools and *more expensive* equipment. They are *more careful* in the way they dig, so *fewer* objects are lost or destroyed. But today government regulations are *stricter* than they were before. It is *harder* to get permission to dig, and it takes a *longer* time to wait for the government permit. In the past the governments of many countries were *friendlier* to foreign archeologists. Those archeologists became *more famous* than the ones today because they took many of the objects to *bigger* museums outside the country in which they were found. Now there are *stronger* international laws against doing this. Nevertheless, the men and women who work in archeology today are making *more important* contributions to our knowledge of the past than ever before.

Formation of Adjectives in the Comparative. The italicized adjectives in the paragraph are in the comparative form. The comparative form is used when *two* things or groups are being compared. Most adjectives in English form the comparative as follows.

One-Syllable Adjectives. Adjectives of one syllable add *er* or *r* to the base form: *short⟶shorter; large⟶larger.* In some cases the final consonant is doubled before adding *er: big⟶bigger; thin⟶thinner.*

Two-Syllable Adjectives Ending in y. Two-syllable adjectives that end in *y* drop the *y* and add *ier: dirty⟶dirtier; tasty⟶tastier.*

Most Other Two-Syllable and Three-Syllable Adjectives. Two-syllable adjectives that do not end in *y* (or in *ow* or *er*) and three-syllable adjectives keep their basic form, but take the comparative word *more* in front of them: *famous⟶more famous; careless⟶more careless; interesting⟶more interesting.*

1. **Answering Information Questions.** Write the answers to the following questions in complete sentences. Use the information from the paragraph on archeology. Each sentence will contain an adjective in the comparative form.

   a. Was archeology more scientific or less scientific in the nineteenth century?
   b. Do archeologists today use cheaper or more expensive equipment than in the past?
   c. Were more or fewer objects destroyed in the past?
   d. At present, is it easier or harder to get permission to dig?
   e. Does it take a longer or a shorter time to wait for a permit now?

2. **List Completion.** Complete the following list of adjectives in their basic and comparative forms.

Basic	Comparative
cheap	cheaper
clean	_____
_____	hotter
dirty	_____
few	_____
wealthy	_____
_____	simpler
serious	_____
careless	_____
_____	more suitable
big	_____
splendid	_____
ambitious	_____
_____	lazier

3. **Sentence Composition.** Look at the following pairs of subjects. Write sentences comparing the two subjects and using adjectives in the comparative form. Use the adjectives from Exercise 2 or the additional adjectives that follow the subjects. Remember to use the word *than*.

> The Etruscans were *wealthier* than the early Romans.
> My mother is *more emotional* than my father.

Subjects

my sister, I	women, men
ancient history, modern history	wool, cotton
gold, silver	English, my native language
my native country, the United States	Roman boys, Roman girls

Adjectives

free	thick	emotional	beautiful	independent
warm	shiny	expensive	crowded	interesting
easy	quiet	wealthy	hard	boring

Superlative Form of Adjectives

The superlative form of adjectives is used when three or more things are being compared. The patterns for the superlative are the same as for the comparative forms of adjectives, but

er is replaced by *est: shorter ⟶ shortest; rich ⟶ richest.*
ier is replaced by *iest; dirtier ⟶ dirtiest; easier ⟶ easiest.*
more is replaced by *most: more modest ⟶ most modest; more serious ⟶ most serious.*

1. **Paragraph Completion.**   Read over this paragraph once. Then fill in the blank spaces by using the directions in the Key following the paragraph. The first one is done for you.

Most Romans wore (1) *simple* clothing made of wool. But in (2) *later* Roman times, some people liked to wear clothing made of the (3) *most special* of all material, silk. Only the (4) *wealthier* people could afford it because it was far (5) *more expensive* than wool. Silk came from China over the (6) *longest* road in the ancient world. It was carried thousands of miles through the (7) _dried_ areas of Asia all the way to the Mediterranean Sea, and then brought by ship to Rome. However, we mustn't forget that it was the women of China who spent (8) _long_ hours spinning the silk thread. Working silk cloth was the (9) _most important_ job of Chinese females. Spinning silk is (10) _more difficult_ than spinning wool because the threads are (11) _finer_ . After they spun the cloth, the Chinese women beat it with sticks and then ironed it. The job was (12) _more tiring_ than other household duties they had to do. Some of the (13) _oldest_ examples of silk clothing have been found in Chinese tombs of (14) _famous_ women of long ago.

Key

1. basic form of *simpler*
2. comparative form of *late*
3. superlative form of *special*
4. superlative form of *wealthy*
5. comparative form of *expensive*
6. superlative form of *long*
7. superlative form of *dry*
8. basic form of *longer*
9. superlative form of *important*
10. comparative form of *difficult*
11. comparative form of *fine*
12. comparative form of *tiring*
13. superlative form of *ancient*
14. basic form of *more famous*

2. **Sentence Building.**   Write a complete English sentence using the words in each set. Add an adjective in the superlative form to describe the nouns in each sentence. The last part of each sentence will have a prepositional phrase with *in, at,* or *of.*

> Mary   person   all my friends
> *Mary is the happiest person of all my friends.*
> poverty   one of   problems   world
> *Poverty is one of the most serious problems in the world.*

a. Tokyo *is* city *of* Japan
b. gold *is* one of   metals   world
c. my friend Carlos   dancer   party
d. math   subject   all my courses
e. Tanaquil   one of   women   Etruscan history
f. North and South Poles   areas   earth
g. library   place   my neighborhood

COMPOSING

1. **Developing a Paragraph.**

   a. *Adding Signals of Contrast, Time, and Addition.*   Choose the appropriate signal of contrast, time, or addition from the columns following the paragraph for each blank space in the paragraph.

In modern society many women stay home (1) _____ *and* _____ take care of their small children. These mothers (2) _____ *also* _____ clean, do the laundry, shop, and cook for their family. They don't have paying jobs, (3) ___ *but* ___ they work long hours. Some mothers remain at home even (4) _____ *when* _____ their children are old enough to go to school. Other women, (5) _____ *However* _____ begin to work outside the home. (6) _____ *Unlike* _____ the housewife, a mother who works outside the home has greater responsibilities. (7) ___ *In addition* ___ to doing her job, she must arrange to take care of her home and children. She always has a lot of things to think about (8) _____ *while* _____ she is working. (9) _____ *Although* _____ it is difficult to be a working mother, many women enjoy learning new skills outside the home. Inside or outside the home, modern women are busy with their responsibilities.

(1) but/then/and
(2) also/in contrast/however,
(3) when/unlike/but
(4) leave blank/when/on the other hand
(5) however,/and/while
(6) Although/leave blank/Unlike
(7) But/In addition/Unlike
(8) leave blank/while/and
(9) When/Although/Then

b. The following paragraph about a mother's special place for sewing has been broken up into short, simple sentences. Combine the sentences into longer, more interesting statements. Use connectors and pronouns where necessary. Leave out all the unnecessary words, but do not omit any of the important ideas or details. Work right in the book for your first draft. Then write your complete new paragraph on a separate sheet of paper.

(1) My mother has a place.

(2) The place is special.

(3) The place is in the house.

(4) The place is where she sews.

In modern as in ancient times, some women set aside a special place in their homes for making cloth. Here a Greek farm woman weaves material on her family's loom.

(5) The place is a room.

(6) The room is small.

(7) The room is in the back of the house.

(8) There is a sewing machine.

(9) The sewing machine is electric.

(10) The sewing machine is near the window.

(11) My mother keeps some of her materials.

(12) The materials are in a box.

(13) The box is next to the sewing machine.

(14) There is a table.

(15) The table is long.

(16) The table is on the other side of the room.

(17) My mother keeps her patterns.

(18) The patterns are on the shelves.

(19) The shelves are above the table.

(20) Everything is neat.

(21) Everything is in this room.

(22) This room is secluded.

(23) My mother enjoys her time there.

2. **Composing a Paragraph.**

   a. Write a paragraph in which you compare the life-style of a married woman with the life-style of a single woman. Give specific examples of women you know. Use signals of contrast in your description. Try to use adjectives in the comparative form to contrast the two people. Begin your paragraph with a main idea that expresses your own opinion about these two life-styles.

   b. In modern homes and apartments, as in ancient Roman houses, there are separate areas for different activities. Describe a special place in your house where you enjoy spending time. Give reasons to explain your choice.

CHAPTER SEVEN B

WOMEN OF THE AMERICAN PAST

PREREADING

Strip Story.   Listen to your instructor read the story "Molly Pitcher, An American Patriot." Then as a class, or in groups, copy each of the following sentences onto a separate strip of paper. Put the strips in the proper order to tell the story of Molly Pitcher. Use pronouns, time expressions, and other words as clues for sentence order. When the strips are correctly arranged, number them in sequence. Then read the story aloud from the strips.

At camp she was useful in washing clothes, cooking, and keeping the camp clean and healthy.

Finally, the battle was over and the Americans had won.

Then, on June 28, 1778, the American army marched out to fight the British army in the Battle of Monmouth.

Much of the credit for this victory belongs to Molly Pitcher, a brave and quick-thinking American woman.

Molly dropped her pitcher and took over her husband's gun.

During the hard war years of 1777 and 1778, Mary joined her husband in the army camp at Valley Forge.

The heat was so great that day that the soldiers became terribly thirsty.

She fired round after round of shot at the British with it.

Suddenly, during the battle, Molly's husband fainted from heatstroke.

So Mary Ludwig followed the soldiers into battle with a pitcher of water for them to drink.

Molly Pitcher was a heroine of the Battle of Monmouth in the American Revolution.

Mary Ludwig was a heroine of the Battle of Monmouth in the American Revolutionary War.

That's why the soldiers gave her the nickname "Molly Pitcher."

She was married to John Hayes, who was a gunner in the American Revolutionary army.

Each time the pitcher was emptied, Mary would run back to a nearby stream to fill it.

New Words.   Try to understand the meanings of these words as they are used in the reading passage. Use a dictionary when necessary.

role	suffer	survive	honor (verb)
labor (verb)	loneliness	enrich	courageous
pioneer	spirit	immediately	

READING

Harriet Tubman: A Courageous Woman

[1]   In the development of the United States, many groups of women have played an important role. Native American women helped the earliest explorers to travel the long rivers and deep forests of our land. For over one hundred years,

black women from Africa labored as slaves in the fields and the homes of the American South. These women were not allowed to learn to read or write, but many of them became skillful healers and midwives. In the middle 1800s pioneer women moved west with their families. They suffered many hardships and much loneliness. They had to be very strong in body and spirit in order to survive. In the nineteenth and twentieth centuries many immigrant women made the long, difficult, and dangerous journey across the ocean to settle in America.

[2]   Some people think that women are the "weaker sex." They have the mistaken idea that women do not have the strength or ability of men. But American women of the past have shown that this is not true. The history books do not tell us the names of all the strong and skilled women who helped to build this country. But the stories of some of America's great women are told in books. The lives of these women instruct us and enrich our own lives today.

[3]   One such woman of strength and spirit was Harriet Tubman, a slave who escaped to freedom and helped many other slaves escape too. Harriet was born in 1820 to parents who were slaves. When she was only seven years old, she was taking care of a house and baby on a nearby plantation. Her mistress was harsh and cruel. Every hour that Harriet labored for this mean woman, she dreamed of freedom.

[4]   When Harriet was only a teenager, she was working in the fields under the hot sun all day long. While she worked, she continued to dream of freedom. She listened to stories of slaves who had escaped to freedom in the North. One day Harriet heard that she was going to be sold. When she heard this, she knew she had to escape immediately. She could not even say good-bye to her family because it was too dangerous. That night she walked off the plantation and followed the North Star to freedom in the North. She was hungry, lonely, and frightened, but she didn't stop until she got to the state of Pennsylvania.

[5]   When Harriet Tubman came to Pennsylvania, she was free. But she wanted other slaves to be free also. So she made many trips back to the South to lead other slaves to freedom. Several times she was nearly caught. But she had learned many tricks to outsmart the slave-catchers. In 1865, when the Civil War ended, the slaves gained their freedom. Then, Harriet Tubman's journeys were over. She had put her life in danger so that others could be free. People everywhere honored her for her courageous spirit and love of freedom.

Summary Completion.   Fill in each blank space with the appropriate word from the columns following the paragraph.

Woman have played an (1) _____ role in the development

(2) _____ the United States. Native American (3) _____ ,

slave women, pioneer women, (4) _____ immigrant women

have all (5) _____ to build this country. Harriet Tubman's

(6) _____ is an example of (7) _____

brave spirit of many (8) _____ women of the past.

(1) delicate/dangerous/
    important/unhappy
(2) from/of/to/with
(3) men/children/owners/
    women
(4) but/often/and/again

(5) decided/helped/brought/
    developed
(6) slavery/owner/life/
    cruelty
(7) a/leave blank/the/an
(8) America/the/United
    States/country/
    American

VOCABULARY

1. **Expanding Vocabulary.**   Fill in the blank space(s) in each sentence with the correct word(s) from the New Word list.

    a. Farm women often _____ in the fields with their husbands.

    b. Today women play an important _____ in the American work force.

    c. The closeness of grandparents can _____ a child's life.

    d. Immigrants sometimes _____ _____ because they don't know the language of their new country.

    e. It takes a brave _____ to make a life in a new country.

    f. Many _____ women were arrested for forming labor unions in the early 1900s.

    g. Some women go back to work _____ after having a child.

    h. A person can _____ without food, but not without water, for over a month.

    i. Most children are taught to _____ their parents' wishes.

    j. An American _____ family usually had to make its own clothes, grow its own food, and make its own soap.

2. **Using Vocabulary.**   Follow the directions for each item.

a.   Circle the words that are related in meaning to the word *honor.*
honest   homesick   only   honorable   honesty   horror
dishonored

b.   Check (√) the sentences that use the word *spirit* as it is used in the reading passage.

(1)   Wine and beer are mild *spirits.* _____

(2)   Sometimes wars are won because people keep up their fighting *spirit* against a much larger enemy. _____

(3)   We were in bad *spirits* because we lost the game. _____

(4)   The kidnappers *spirited* away the child in the middle of the night. _____

(5)   It takes a courageous *spirit* to speak out against injustice. _____

c.   Check (√) the sentences that use the italicized word from the New Word list correctly. Put an X next to the ones that don't.

(1)   The *role* of women in the American Civil War has not been fully recorded. _____

(2)   Her *loneliness* has made her many friends. _____

(3)   *Survival* would be difficult on the moon. _____

(4)   The students had one week to do their homework *immediately.* _____

d.   Circle the items that tell us where people *labor.*
in a movie   watching TV   on farms   swimming
in factories

e.   Circle the things you could *suffer* from.
a chair   a disease   boredom   happiness   loneliness
playing cards

f.   Which sentence would be most likely to follow the given sentence?
Mr. Pacheco's work enriches the lives of many people.

(1)   Two days a week he coaches neighborhood boys in baseball.

(2)   He usually relaxes by going to the movies.

(3)   His family sees very little of him on weekends.

3. **Word Families.**   The stem, or root, of a word is often found in other related words. The related words may have different forms, prefixes, or suffixes from the stem word. But the meanings of all the words in a word family will have some relationship to each other. Recognizing the root of a word in other words

will help you to increase your vocabulary. Study the word lists for each of the following paragraphs. Fill in the blank spaces in the paragraph with the correct word from the list.

a. verb: honor   **adjective:** honorable, honest, dishonorable, dishonest

    noun: honor, honesty,   **adverb:** honorably, honestly, dishonesty, dishonor   dishonorably, dishonestly

     Slavery was a (an) (1) _____ practice. Men and women who work deserve an (a) (2) _____ day's pay for their labor. Many Americans of the past (3) _____ wished to end slavery. They worked hard to erase the (4) _____ of slavery from the land. We (5) _____ such people as Harriet Tubman for their work against slavery.

b. verb: labor   **adjective:** laborious, laboring

    noun: labor, laborer,   **adverb:** laboriously
          laboriousness,
          laboratory
    related phrases: child labor, labor unions, slave labor

     (1) _____ men and women of the past had few rights and little protection. They (2) _____ many hours for very little money. There were no laws against (3) _____ , so children as young as seven often worked in mines and factories. But then (4) _____ in factories began to join together in (5) _____ _____ . They finally got better pay and working conditions.

READING COMPREHENSION

1. **Understanding the Text.**   Follow the directions for each item.

   a. If the sentence is true, write *T.* If it is false, write *F.* If the story does not give information about the sentence, write *N.I.* (no information).

     (1) Women did not play an important part in developing the United States.

     _____

(2) Women slaves were not allowed to educate themselves. _____

(3) Pioneer women often did not survive childbirth. _____

(4) Women are the weaker sex. _____

(5) Harriet Tubman was born a slave. _____

(6) No slaves ever escaped from Southern plantations. _____

(7) Harriet Tubman rode north to freedom by train. _____

(8) Harriet's husband was a free black man named John Tubman. _____

(9) Harriet Tubman's life shows that women do not have the strength of men. _____

b. Circle the number of the sentence that means the same thing as the given sentence. *Some people have the mistaken idea that women do not have the strength or ability of men.*

(1) Some people correctly think that women are weaker than men.

(2) Some people wrongly thing that women are less strong and able than men.

(3) Some people think that women make more mistakes than men.

c. The author writes that Harriet Tubman was *only* seven years old when she began to work as a housekeeper. The word *only* suggests that the author thinks

(1) seven years old is a good age to start working.

(2) seven years old is the usual age to start working.

(3) seven years old is too young to start working.

d. The story says that Harriet Tubman's first mistress was harsh and cruel. Check (√) the items that show this woman was harsh and cruel.

(1) She whipped Harriet often. _____

(2) She bought Harriet new dresses. _____

(3) She nearly starved Harriet. _____

(4) She paid Harriet only six cents a day. _____

e. In a complete sentence, tell why Harriet couldn't say anything to her family about her plans to escape from the plantation.

_____

_____

f. People honored Harriet Tubman because

    (1) she was a slave.   **(2)** she helped others escape slavery.

    (3) she escaped slavery.

g. The author uses Harriet Tubman's life mainly

    (1) as an example of a courageous American woman.

    (2) as a way of telling some of the history of the American South.

    (3) as a reason for having laws against child labor.

2. **Answering Information Questions.**   Write the answers to each of the following questions in a complete sentence.

    a. When pioneer women moved west, what did they suffer?

    b. Where do we learn about some of America's great women?

    c. Were Harriet Tubman's parents slaves or free people?

    d. What was Harriet doing when she was seven years old?

    e. Where was Harriet working when she was a teenager?

    f. What did Harriet dream about while she worked?

    g. When did Harriet stop walking north?

    h. What happened to the slaves at the end of the Civil War?

    i. Why were Harriet Tubman's journeys over in 1865?

3. **Signals of Contrast.**   When English writers want to contradict, or state something opposite to what they have just said, they usually use signal words of contrast. These words let the reader know that the writer is going to present two pieces of contradictory, contrasting, or opposite information.

    Study this list of signal words of contrast.

,but	in contrast,	although
however,	in contrast to _____ ,	unlike _____ ,
on the other hand,	nevertheless,	

Read the following paragraphs, and underline the signals of contrast in each.

a. Harriet Beecher Stowe was another woman named Harriet who fought against slavery. Unlike Harriet Tubman, however, Harriet Beecher Stowe was a free, white, well-educated woman from an old New England family. Harriet Tubman's relatives were poor slaves who could not help her in her work. But Harriet Beecher Stowe's family included a husband who was a professor and a brother who was a famous minister and writer. Harriet Tubman could not read or write; in contrast, Harriet Beecher Stowe was

These women astronomy students of one hundred years ago were very unusual. Most females in the past did not go on for higher education. Most Americans one hundred years ago did not have an education beyond grade school. Discuss the advantages of higher education today.

a professional writer. Her book against slavery, *Uncle Tom's Cabin,* awakened many people to the evils of slavery. These two Harriets had very different positions in life. Nevertheless, they both shared a powerful hatred of the system of slavery and the courage to fight against it.

Now make two lists of the different, contrasting qualities of Harriet Beecher Stowe and Harriet Tubman.

b.   In contrast to China, Egypt, and England, the United States has never had a female leader. The wives of some American presidents have been important and well known in their own right, but none has ever been elected to office herself. The United States has had a few women senators and representatives in Congress. No woman, however, has ever been a vice-president. Although the United States presidency has always been occupied by a male in the past, perhaps in the future we will see a woman occupying that position.

Mark *T* if the statement is true. Mark *F* if it is false.

a. China, Egypt, England, and the United States have all had female leaders.

_____

b. No American president's wife has ever been elected to office. _____

c. American women have been senators and members of Congress. _____

d. The president of the United States will always be a male. _____

WRITING EXERCISES

Past Continuous Tense

The Past Continuous tense of verbs is used for several purposes. It is used to show action that took place at one point of time in the past. It is also used to show ongoing, continuous action in the past. The main use of the Past Continuous tense is to show interrupted action in a sentence that also includes a clause in the Simple Past tense. The Past Continuous tense is formed by *was* or *were* + the *ing* form of the main verb.

> **Last week I was reading an interesting book about Harriet Tubman.**
> **While I was reading last night, the doorbell rang.**

Study the Past Continuous tense of the verb *move*.

	Singular	**Plural**
First Person	I was moving	My friend and I were moving We were moving
Second person	You were moving	You were moving
Third person	Harriet was moving He/She/It was moving	Harriet and her family were moving They were moving

The negative forms are *was not (wasn't)* and *were not (weren't)* + the *ing* form of the main verb.

1. **Recognizing Past Continuous Tense.**   Listen carefully as your instructor reads the following paragraph. Underline each verb in the Past Continuous tense. (The paragraph is part of a letter written by grandparents to their grandchildren about a winter hike through the mountains of northern California.)

> The snow was falling steadily. We knew we had to walk quickly to reach the road three miles away. Both of us were carrying heavy packs, which were soon wet with snow. Tree branches were hanging down over our path, and our progress was slow. Because the lake was frozen, we decided to walk on it instead of the narrow path. But as we were moving across the lake, we felt cracks and soft spots in the ice. The ice wasn't completely frozen near the edge. Also, the wind was blowing in our faces, and the snow was blinding us. So we returned to the path. After several hard, tiring hours, we finally reached the road.

2. **Dictation.**   Your instructor will dictate five sentences from the paragraph. Pay special attention to verb forms.

3. **Paragraph Completion.**   The Past Continuous tense is frequently used in complex sentences with the Simple Past tense. In the following paragraph, complete the blank spaces with the appropriate verb form as directed in the parentheses.

I (hurry: Past Continuous) _____(1)_____ down the street because I (want: Simple Past; negative) _____(2)_____ to be late for the meeting. When I (enter: Simple Past) _____(3)_____ , everyone (talk: Past Continuous) _____(4)_____ . They (wait: Past Continuous) _____(5)_____ for the guest speaker to arrive. The door suddenly (open: Simple Past) _____(6)_____ , and a famous congresswoman (walk: Simple Past) _____(7)_____ in. She (wear: Past Continuous) _____(8)_____ a very large hat, her trademark, and everyone (recognize: Simple Past) _____(9)_____ her at once. Reporters (follow: Past Continuous) _____(10)_____ her with notebooks and pencils, and photographers (take: Past Continuous) _____(11)_____ pictures of her. She (make: Simple Past) _____(12)_____ an exciting speech about women's rights. While she (speak: Past Continuous) _____(13)_____ , someone (present: Simple Past) _____(14)_____ her with a bouquet of red roses.

Complex Sentences with *When* and *While*

A clause is a sentence part that has a subject and a complete main verb. Complex sentences always include one dependent clause. A dependent clause is a clause that cannot stand by itself as a sentence. Dependent clauses must be joined to independent, or main, clauses.

When and *while* are time words that begin dependent clauses. Dependent clauses with *when* and *while* must join independent or main clauses to form a complete sentence.

When tells us about two kinds of time periods:

1. a long period of time during which many different actions take place

---

When Harriet Tubman was a slave, she was always dreaming of freedom.

---

2. a point of time when two actions take place together or immediately following each other (at that time)

When Harriet heard she was to be sold, she planned her escape.

While tells us about actions that take place during the same time period. *While* often introduces clauses using continuous tenses.

While Harriet was walking to freedom in the North, she thought sadly about her family.

Identifying Dependent Clauses.   Underline the dependent clause in each of the following sentences. Note that when the dependent clause begins the sentence, it is followed by a comma.

a. While I was studying last night, I heard some strange noises.
b. Immigrants often feel lonely when they first arrive in their new country.
c. College students may enjoy listening to music while they are studying.
d. I can't concentrate on my work when the television set is on.
e. When my daughter first read about Harriet Tubman, she became very interested in her.
f. Some students were rewriting their papers in class while others were doing grammar exercises.

Verb Tenses in Complex Sentences with *When* and *While*.   The two clauses in complex sentences with *when* or *while* must have the same or related verb tenses. Study the following examples of common pairs of verb tenses in *when* and *while* sentences.

Simple Present   **Simple Present and Future**

When students *enjoy* a certain history book, they often *recommend* it to others.
When we *finish* this chapter, we *will continue* with the next.

Present Continuous   **Simple Present and
                                       Present Continuous**

My sister *is working* while her children *attend* school.
Some students *are studying* English as a second language, while others *are learning* French.

Simple Past   **Simple Past**

When pioneer women *moved* west, they *suffered* many hardships.

Past Continuous   **Simple Past and Past Continuous**

While Harriet Tubman *was living* in Philadelphia, she *thought* a lot about her family.
Once, some slave-catchers were watching Harriet while she *was sitting* in a railway station.

Simple Past and Past Continuous   **Could and Would**

When Harriet *planned* her escape, she *couldn't tell* her family.
While pioneer families *were moving* west, their children *couldn't attend* school.

1. **Sentence Completion.**   Choose the clause that correctly completes the given clause. Write the new clause in the space provided.

   a. When I was a young girl, _____

   _____

(1) I want to be a teacher.   (2) I wanted to be a teacher.

(3) I can't be a teacher.

b. While Eleanor Roosevelt was President Roosevelt's wife, _____

_____

(1) she helped him in his work.   (2) she is helping him in his work.

(3) she won't help him in his work.

c. When Anne Royall's husband died, _____

_____

(1) she begins to travel and write.   (2) she isn't going to travel and write.

(3) she started to travel and write.

d. I understood more about courageous women of the past _____

_____

(1) when I will learn about Harriet Tubman.

(2) while I would learn about Harriet Tubman.

(3) when I learned about Harriet Tubman.

e. While men were soldiers in the American Civil War, _____

_____

(1) many women were working as nurses.

(2) many women are working as nurses.

(3) many women will be working as nurses.

f. Pioneer women suffered many hardships _____

_____

(1) when they are moving west.   (2) when they can move west.

(3) when they moved west.

2. **Sentence Expansion.**   Complete each sentence in the space provided. Make sure that the verbs in the new clauses are correctly related to the verbs in the given clauses.

a. When I studied for my test last week, _____

_____

b. When I lived in my native city, _____

_____

c. My friend wouldn't give me the answers when _____

_____

d. I usually _____ when it was raining last winter.

e. Last night, while I was reading, _____

_____

f. When I became 18, _____

_____

g. While the music was playing, _____

_____

h. Many students _____ while the instructor

_____

3. **Punctuation of Complex Sentences.**   Some of the following sentences are correctly punctuated. In others there are mistakes. Write a *C* in the blank space if the sentence is correct. If it is not correct, make whatever punctuation and capitalization changes are necessary.

a. Women's lives became easier, when electricity became common.

_____

b. Harriet Tubman risked her life for others when she led slaves to freedom.

_____

c. While Franklin Roosevelt was president of the United States. His wife Eleanor was a great help to him. _____

d. Eleanor Roosevelt was very shy when, she was a child. _____

e. When Harriet Beecher Stowe wrote *Uncle Tom's Cabin*. She sent a copy to President Abraham Lincoln. _____

f. When European explorers came to America, Native American women sometimes acted as their guides. _____

g. Women did not have the right to vote. When the United States was a young country. _____

h. Women had very little power while, they had no vote. _____

i. When immigrant women worked in the factories, they earned very low wages. _____

Prepositions of Place

The following example contains some prepositions of place. These prepositions tell us where things are. They begin phrases that are called prepositional phrases of place.

> **While Harriet Tubman was escaping *through* the woods and *across* the rivers of the South, she followed the North Star *above* her.**

Study this list of some common prepositions of place.

above, over	to the right (or left)	in the middle (or center)
on, on top of	around	behind, in back of
below, under, underneath	through	ahead of, in front of
against	between (two items)	near, next to

1. **Identifying Prepositions of Place.**   Listen as your instructor reads the following paragraph. Underline the prepositions of place.

> One time Harriet Tubman had a close escape from the slave-catchers. She was sitting inside the waiting room of a railroad station in Maryland. The door was straight ahead of her, and she could see everyone who came through it. Suddenly, a man walked through the door into the center of the room. He looked all around the room carefully. Harriet immediately knew that he was a slave-catcher. There was a book on the bench near her. She picked it up and held it on her lap as if she were reading it. When the slave-catcher looked at Harriet, he saw that she was reading. He knew that slaves were never allowed to learn to read, so he thought she could not be the escaped slave he was looking for. Harriet was safe once more.

2. **Sentence Composing.**   Describe your position in the classroom in a series of complete sentences. Tell who is sitting around you, in back of you, in front of you, and so on. Also describe the position of the teacher's desk, the blackboard, maps, pictures, and so on.

3. **Pair Dictation.**   Select three correct sentences from Exercise 2. Dictate these sentences to a partner. Then take dictation of three sentences from him or her.

Comparison of Adjectives

Read the following paragraph carefully. Pay special attention to the italicized adjectives.

Life was much *harder* for American women in 1880 than it is now. In the *earlier* period, there were *fewer* of the household appliances such as vacuum cleaners and refrigerators that make life *easier* today. The *newer, richer* houses of the 1880s had indoor plumbing, but the *older, poorer* homes did not. Some things were *cheaper* one hundred years ago, but men earned much *lower* salaries, and married women usually did not go out to work to earn extra money. In the 1880s, housewives were usually *busier* than they are today because families were *larger.* Today modern women have fewer children and *better* medical care than women had one hundred years ago. Modern women are *healthier* than their great-grandmothers were, and modern women live *longer* lives. Modern women have *wider* opportunities for education and careers than their great-grandmothers had. Do you think modern women are *happier* than women were one hundred years ago?

Formation of Adjectives in the Comparative.   The italicized adjectives in the paragraph are in the comparative form. The comparative form is used when *two* things are being compared. Most adjectives in English form the comparative as follows.

One-Syllable Adjectives.   Adjectives of one syllable add *er* or *r* to the base form: *old⟶older; large⟶larger.*

Two-Syllable Adjectives Ending in y.   Two-syllable adjectives that end in *y* drop the *y* and add *ier: easy⟶easier; busy⟶busier.*

Most Other Two-Syllable and Three-Syllable Adjectives.   Two-syllable adjectives that do not end in *y* (or in *ow* or *er*) and three-syllable adjectives keep their basic form, but take the comparative word *more* in front of them: *modern⟶more modern; fragile⟶more fragile.*

1. **Answering Information Questions.**   Write the answers to the following questions in complete sentences, using information from the paragraph. Each sentence will contain an adjective in the comparative form.

    a. Was life easier or harder for women one hundred years ago?

    b. Were there more or fewer household appliances one hundred years ago?

    c. Which kinds of houses had indoor plumbing one hundred years ago?

    d. Did men earn higher or lower wages one hundred years ago than they do today?

    e. Why were women of the 1880s busier than modern women are?

    f. Why are modern women healthier than women were in the 1880s?

2. **List Completion.**   Complete the following list of adjectives in their basic and comparative forms.

Men and women one hundred years ago had harder lives than they have today. There were few household appliances or farm machines to make life easier.

Basic	Comparative
early	earlier
long	longer
happy	_____
large	_____
_____	healthier
expensive	_____
_____	more popular
famous	_____
fragile	_____
_____	stranger
busy	_____
much	_____
_____	fewer

3. **Sentence Composing.**   Look at the list of different types of work. In the past these jobs were usually done by men, but today some women are doing these jobs. Compare these jobs by using the following adjectives in their comparative forms. Follow the sentence pattern in the example.

> **Construction work is more dangerous than dentistry.**

Types of Work

construction work	taxi driving	dentistry
police work	engineering	airplane piloting
truck driving	newspaper reporting	athletic coaching
accounting	television broadcasting	politics

Adjectives

boring	creative	easy	enjoyable	exciting	lonely
active	interesting	important	useful	noisy	difficult
dangerous	hard	well-paid	dull		

Superlative Form of Adjectives

The superlative form of adjectives is used when three or more things are being compared. The patterns for the superlative are the same as for the comparative forms of adjectives, but

er is replaced by *est: older——→oldest; poorer——→poorest*
ier is replaced by *iest: busier——→busiest; healthier——→healthiest.*
more is replaced by *most: more modern——→most modern; more expensive——→most expensive.*

1. **Paragraph Completion.**   Read this paragraph over once. Then fill in the blank spaces by using the directions in the Key following the paragraph. The first one is done for you.

Emily Dickinson (1830–1886) is one of America's (1) _most_

famous poets. As a child she was (2) _____ than most of her friends, but not very different from them. In school she was

(3) _____ in writing, but she also studied (4) _____

_____ subjects such as chemistry and physiology. When she was

about twenty-five, she had an (5) _____ love affair.
After this she became (6) _____ and (7) _____
_____ to people outside her own family than she had been before.
It was at this time that Dickinson wrote some of her (8) _____
_____ poetry. Although the language of her poetry appears
(9) _____ , her thoughts are (10) _____
to understand than they appear at first. Emily Dickinson is still one of
America's (11) _____ and (12) _____
poets one hundred years after her death.

Key

1. superlative form of *famous*
2. comparative form of *bright*
3. superlative form of *interested*
4. comparative form of *unusual*
5. basic form of adjective meaning "not happy"
6. comparative form of *shy*
7. comparative form of *unfriendly*
8. superlative form of *beautiful*
9. basic form of *simpler*
10. comparative form of *difficult*
11. superlative form of *respected*
12. superlative form of *popular*

2. **Sentence Composing.**   Make statements of description about different people using adjectives in the superlative form. Some useful phrases for descriptions with superlative adjectives are the following:

in our class (or family, group, crowd, apartment building)
at the party (or lecture, concert, dance)
of all my friends (or relatives, teachers)

My friend Joanna is the most intelligent of all my friends.
The boy in apartment 6B is the noisiest child in the building.

COMPOSING

1. **Developing a Paragraph.**

   a. *Adding Signals of Contrast, Time, and Addition.* From the numbered sets following the paragraph, choose the appropriate signal of contrast, time, or addition for the same numbered blank space in the paragraph.

   Emily Dickinson and Fay Chiang are different kinds of American poets. Dickinson lived (1) _____ wrote nearly one hundred years ago. (2) _____ _____ Fay Chiang is a modern poet, alive and writing today. Dickinson was a shy, solitary person. (3) _____ she was writing, she almost never left her house. Fay Chiang, (4) _____ is an activist who works in an Asian-American artists' community in New York's Chinatown. Chiang (5) _____ works with writers of other minority groups. (6) _____ Dickinson and Chiang are very different kinds of American women, they both express similarly powerful emotions through their poems.

   (1) but/and/then
   (2) Also/In contrast,/While
   (3) Leave blank/But/While
   (4) and/however,/in addition,
   (5) leave blank/on the other hand/also
   (6) When/Although/And

   b. Study the preceding paragraph carefully. Label all the sentences that tell about the *two* poets *A–B*. Label the sentences only about Emily Dickinson *A*. Label the sentences only about Fay Chiang *B*. Study how the paragraph develops the contrast between the two women by giving us details about one, then about the other, in alternating sentences.

2. **Composing a Paragraph.**

   a. Write a paragraph in which you contrast two different people whom you know well. Follow a pattern of alternating details as in the paragraph in Exercise 1a. Try to use adjectives in the comparative form about your two subjects. Begin with a main idea sentence that identifies your subjects.

   b. Write a paragraph in which you compare or contrast your native city and the city in which you are now living. Choose such points to talk about as the cleanliness; degree of noise, traffic, or crowdedness; number of parks or recreational areas; or safety. Begin with a main idea statement that introduces the topic and identifies the two cities you will be describing.

CHAPTER EIGHT A

BRIDES AND GROOMS

PREREADING

Class Discussion. The following poem was written in China over a thousand years ago by a young groom to his bride.

> A feast being spread in spring-time,
> With a cup of new wine and a joyous song.
> I repeat my salutation and offer my three wishes:
> First, may you have a long life;
> Second, may I have good health;
> Third, may we live as the swallows on the beam,
> Happily together all the year round.

What might the bride's wishes be? What would living happily together mean to you in today's world? Do you think that your own ideas of happiness might be different from those of the Chinese poet? If a couple you know were getting married, what kind of message would you compose for them?

New Words. Try to understand the meanings of these words as they are used in the reading passage. Use a dictionary when necessary.

unite	control	cooperation
personal	benefit (noun)	gradually
strengthen	loyalty	successful
reputation		

READING

Arranging a Marriage

[1]   Different cultures have different ideals of marriage. In the United States we think of marriage as a private arrangement between two people. Men and women are free to choose a marriage partner from their own social, economic,

or religious background or outside it. Although there may be strong ties with parents, sisters, or brothers, the strongest feelings are between the two people themselves. After the couple marries, they generally live apart from relatives and build a new, independent family environment. Ideally, this type of marriage arrangement unites two people who love each other and brings personal happiness to them and their children.

[2]   However, marriage isn't always a matter of personal need for love and happiness. In most societies of the world, marriage is an important way to strengthen the main family line by uniting it with another family of the same social, economic, or religious background. In these societies, there are many rules about whom a person can or cannot marry. Parents have a strong interest in seeing that their children continue the family's good reputation and position in society. They also want their children to have a good life. So sons and daughters are not free to choose their mates. By arranging marriages, parents can control the choice of a new member for the benefit of the children, the whole family, and the class to which they belong.

[3]   In India, for example, the ideal household includes the parents, the sons, and the sons' wives and children. In this type of arrangement, the strength of the family lies in the respect, loyalty, and cooperation among the children, and between the children and their parents. If a son is too interested in his wife, or if the wife is too independent or uncooperative, they may cause trouble by breaking the unity of respect and loyalty within the family. A good wife is one who is a good daughter-in-law. She is modest and obedient. She gradually breaks the ties with her own family and becomes completely interested in her husband's. In India many parents arrange a marriage for a son with the right kind of girl.

[4]   Romesh Roy is the son of a successful businessman in Bombay, India. He is a college graduate and thinks of himself as a modern young man. His parents are afraid that he is too independent and might choose his own bride. So while Romesh is busy with his career, Mr. and Mrs. Roy are both looking for a suitable girl for him to marry. They would like a girl whose family has a slightly lower position in society than their own so that the girl's family will treat the Roys with more respect. But they want a girl whose family will offer a good marriage gift. They prefer a pretty girl, and one who is not too tall for their son. She should be well educated, but home loving. Her parents must not expect to see too much of her once she is married. The ideal wife for Romesh will be the ideal daughter-in-law for the Roy family.

[5]   The Roys know many families with marriageable daughters. However, it isn't easy to arrange a good match. One of the girls is too plain. Another one is attractive, but she is taller than Romesh. Still another is too "forward" and "thinks too much of herself." Mr. Roy knows a suitable girl who is the daughter of a business partner. But the girl's parents don't want Romesh for a son-in-law; they are looking for a wealthier family than the Roys for their daughter. Mr. and

This bride and groom from the Indian subcontinent have an arranged marriage. Beautiful wedding jewelry adorns the bride.

Mrs. Roy may have to wait a few years before they can make the best arrangement for the benefit of everyone concerned.

[6]   Eventually Romesh will meet a girl of his parents' choice. He will see her at least once or twice before they marry. The families will exchange gifts of money or jewelry, and then there will be a great wedding ceremony. The couple will live together with Romesh's parents and younger sisters and brothers. The girl will be obedient and cooperative. Since Mr. and Mrs. Roy are kind people, the girl will be well treated and comfortable in her new environment. She will provide company for Mrs. Roy and help in the management of the household. When Mr. and Mrs. Roy are away on vacation, she will take care of her husband's little sisters and brothers. Someday she will have her own children. When her son is grown, she too will look for a suitable bride for him.

Paragraph Completion.   Fill in the blank spaces with a word that is correct in both form and meaning.

In India, for example, the ideal household includes the parents, the sons, and the sons' wives and children. In this type of arrangement, the (1) _The strength_ of the family lies in the (2) _in respect_ , loyalty, and cooperation among the children, (3) _and between_ between the children and their (4) _parents_ . If a son is too interested (5) _in_ his wife, or if the wife (6) _is_ _____ too independent or uncooperative, they may (7) _cause_ _____ trouble by breaking the unity (8) _of_ respect and loyalty within the (9) _____family_____ . A good wife is one who is (10) _____a_____ good daughter-in-law. She is (11) _____modest_____ and obedient. She gradually breaks the (12) _____ties_____ with her own family and becomes (13) _____completly_____ interested in her husband's. In India (14) _____many_____ parents arrange a marriage for a (15) _____son_____ with the right kind of girl.

VOCABULARY

1. **Choosing Synonyms.** In the blank space in Column A write the letter of the synonym from Column B.

A		B	
unite	d	a.	little by little
personal	e	b.	have authority over
strengthen	h	c.	a good or advantageous thing
reputation	g	d.	join together
control	b	e.	individual
benefit	c	f.	prosperous
loyalty	i	g.	favorable position or name
cooperation	j	h.	make stronger
gradually	a	i.	devotion
successful	f	j.	working together

2. **Using Vocabulary.** Follow the directions for each item.

   a. Circle the items that can only be done *gradually*.

   grow old   become proficient in English
   swallow a pill   run for the bus
   buy a newspaper   learn to walk (as a baby)

   b. Circle the words that are related to the word *unite*.
   untie   unity   disunited   until   united   unit   reunite

   c. The words *loyalty, disloyalty; personal, impersonal;* and *successful, unsuccessful* are antonyms. Fill in each blank space in the following paragraph with the word from the New Word list or its antonym.

Many marriages are (1) _____successful_____ because the partners work together for the good of the family. A man and woman can't have an (2) _____impersonal_____ relationship but must be deeply involved with each other in their daily problems. If one of the partners works against the other, it is considered an act of (3) _____disloyalty_____ The marriage will be (4) _____unsuccessful_____without a (5) _____ sense of (6) _____loyalty_____. and love.

d. Circle the items that you can *control*.

the movement of stars   the daily news
your grades in school   √ the amount of time you watch TV
√ your weight   the color of your eyes
the change of seasons

e. Circle the number of the sentence that would correctly follow the given sentence.
Cooperation is very important in planning a family vacation.

(1) Everyone should do what he or she wants.
(2) If you go to Europe, you'll have a good time.
(3) Parents and children should talk about the places they want to see together.

f. Circle the items that could be considered *benefits* of living in a large city.

bad air   √ museums   √ public transportation
lots of cars   small apartments   √ job opportunities
√ variety of schools   crowded streets

g. Complete the following sentence by circling the appropriate phrases.
You can *strengthen* your body by

√ playing tennis.   eating sweets.
smoking cigarettes.   going to the movies.
√ eating proper foods.   √ taking dance lessons.

h. Check (√) the sentences that use the word *reputation* correctly.

(1) An honest businessperson will earn a good reputation. _____
(2) To learn history you need a good reputation for names and dates.

_____

(3) I filled out two copies of a reputation for a driver's license. _____

(4) Some politicians have a reputation for dishonesty. _____

3. **Word Families.**   Nouns in English sometimes end in *ness*, *ty (ity)*, *ship*, *ence (ance)*, and *ment*. Study the following list of sample nouns with these endings.

kindness   loyalty   friendship   experience   arrangement
happiness   majority   partnership   importance   treatment

Follow the directions for each item. Write your answers in the space provided.

a.   The verbs *arrange* and *treat* add *ment* to become nouns. Make nouns of the following verbs in the same way.

manage _ment_____   develop _ment_____

govern _ment_____   agree _ment_____

b.   What nouns ending in *ness* are the opposite of

kindness _____

happiness ___ sadness _____

c.   What noun ending in *ness* can be formed from the adjective *lonely?*
___ loneliness _____ What noun ending in *ness* can be formed from the antonym of the adjective *messy?* ___ neatness _____

d.   What noun ending in *ty* or in *ity* means the opposite of *dishonesty?*
_____ impossibility? _____

e.   The noun *majority* means more than 50 percent of something. What is the noun ending in *ity* that means less than 50 percent of something?

_____

f.   The suffix *ship* means "the condition of being" or "the skill of." Write the noun forms ending in *ship* for each of the following conditions or skills.

the skill of a leader ___ ship _____

the condition of being a citizen ___ ship _____

the condition of being a member ___ ship _____

g.   _____ is the adjective form of the noun *intelligence*.

Independent is the adjective form of the noun _____ .

h. What noun ending in *ance* can be formed from the verb *to appear*?
_____ What noun ending in *ence* can be formed from
the verb *to prefer*? _____

READING COMPREHENSION

1. Understanding the Text.   Follow the directions for each item.

   a. Mark the following sentences *True* or *False* according to the information
   in the reading passage. Underline the part of the passage where you find
   your information.

   (1) In some societies sons and daughters are not free to choose their own

   marriage partners. ___T___

   (2) In India the ideal household includes married daughters. ___F___

   (3) An Indian father also takes part in arranging a marriage. ___T___

   (4) The marriage gift is one of the considerations in arranging a marriage.

   ___T___

   (5) Romesh Roy will not see his bride before he marries. ___T___

   b. Circle the letter of the correct answer.

   (1) Paragraphs [1] and [2]

      a. are both concerned with marriage in the United States.
      b. offer contrasting views of marriage.
      c. tell us that love is the most important thing in most marriages.

   (2) In most societies of the world

      a. marriage is a private arrangement between two people.
      b. married couples break the ties with their families.
      c. there are many rules about whom a person can or cannot marry.

   (3) The information in Paragraph [3]

      a. gives specific details for Paragraph [2].
      b. is an example for Paragraph [1].
      c. introduces a completely new topic to the reading passage.

   (4) The information in Paragraph [3] suggests that the main family line
   in India

    a. is broken by marriage.

    b. is continued through the males in the family.

    c. is controlled by the daughters-in-law.

(5) In Paragraph [4], the author suggests that the Roys want their son's marriage

    a. to be in the tradition of Indian culture.

    b. to be different from their own marriage.

    c. to be a real love match.

(6) Mr. and Mrs. Roy are looking for a daughter-in-law who is

    a. short, well educated, and independent.

    b. plain, tall, and obedient.

    c. pretty, home loving, and cooperative.

(7) In India, a girl's parents

    a. must accept any offer of a husband for their daughter.

    b. can reject a boy as unsuitable for their daughter.

    c. may prefer their daughter to remain unmarried.

(8) In Paragraph [6], which would be the best place for the following sentence: The groom will wear a business suit, but the bride will wear traditional Indian dress and jewelry.

    a. after the first sentence

    b. after the second sentence

    c. after the third sentence

(9) In Paragraph [6], the author suggests that

    a. Romesh's bride will be the ideal Indian daughter-in-law.

    b. Romesh will help in the management of the household.

    c. Romesh's parents will be away a lot of the time.

2. **Answering Information Questions.**   Write the answers to the following questions in complete sentences.

  a. Do married couples in the United States generally live with or apart from relatives?

  b. In most societies, how does marriage strengthen the main family line?

  c. Who are the members of the ideal Indian family?

  d. What can happen if an Indian wife is too independent or uncooperative?

  e. Does an Indian wife strengthen or break the ties with her own family?

  f. What are the Roys afraid Romesh might do?

g. What will the families do before Romesh's wedding ceremony?

h. Who will take care of Romesh's sisters and brothers when their parents are away?

i. What will Romesh's wife do when her son is grown?

3. **Paraphrasing.**   Writers may express the same ideas in different ways. A paraphrase is another, usually simpler, way of saying something. Follow the directions for each item.

a. The following sentences are paraphrases of some of the ideas in Paragraphs [1] and [2]. In the blank space next to each sentence, write the paragraph and sentence number of the original sentence. The first one is done for you.

(1) The love between a married couple is stronger than the ties they may have with their own relatives. _Para. 1_   _Sent. 4_

(2) Married couples live their own lives in new surroundings.
_P___1_   _S.___6_

(3) Parents feel strongly that their children should carry on the family's good name. ____2____   ____5____

(4) Young people in certain cultures aren't free to marry whomever they wish. ____2____   ____3____

(5) Arranged marriages offer advantages to family members and their social class. ____2____   ____8.____

b. Put a check (√) next to the two sentences that mean the same thing.

(1) a. An Indian wife will add to the wealth of her husband's family with gifts given by her parents when she marries. _____

b. In India the groom's family offers a small gift to the bride's family before the wedding ceremony. _____

c. Money and jewelry are common types of marriage gifts in India.
____√____

d. A bride's parents contribute money or jewelry to their daughter's new family unit as a marriage gift. ___√___

(2) a. The divorce rate is increasing around the world. _____

b. Some "love matches" end in divorce. ___√___

    c. Even if you marry for love, the marriage may not last. _____✓_____

    d. Love may grow deeply between a couple in an arranged marriage.

    _____

(3) **a.** The Roys think that their son's future bride should be clever and bright. _____

    b. The Roys are looking for an obedient, modest wife for their son.

    _____

    c. The Roys want their son's bride to have a nice appearance. _____✓_____

    d. The Roys are interested in the physical characteristics of a bride-to-be for their son. _____✓_____

(4) **a.** In the United States the majority of marriages are "love matches."

    _____

    b. In most societies "love matches" are rare. _____✓_____

    c. People in the United States generally marry at a later age than they did fifty years ago. _____

    d. "Love matches" are in the minority among the marriage customs of the world. _____✓_____

(5) **a.** Some Indian sons act independently and marry women of their own choosing. _____✓_____

    b. Some Indian sons leave their parents' home to find jobs in other countries. _____

    c. Not all Indian sons marry women chosen by their parents. _____✓_____

    d. Indian sons working in other countries often return home to get married. _____

WRITING EXERCISES

Pronoun Use

Pronouns may be used to replace subjects, objects, or possessives in a sentence. Pronouns must agree in number, person, form, and gender with the nouns they replace. Study the following pronoun chart and examples.

After American couples marry, they generally build a new life apart from relatives, based on love and personal happiness.

Subject	Object (of verb or preposition)	Possessive	Possessive Adjective (+ noun)	Reflexive
I	me	mine	my (job)	myself
you	you	yours	your (job)	yourself
he	him	his	his (job)	himself
she	her	hers	her (job)	herself
it	it	—	its (shape)	itself
we	us	ours	our (jobs)	ourselves
you	you	yours	your (jobs)	yourselves
they	them	theirs	their (jobs)	themselves

When families in India arrange marriages, *they* are very respectful toward each other.   (plural Third Person subject)

Romesh's little sister will marry a suitable man when *she* grows up.
(singular Third Person subject female)

Americans prefer to choose *their* own marriage partners.
(plural Third Person possessive adjective)

1. **Sentence Completion.**   Read the following paragraph about marriage gifts. Then fill in the blank spaces with the correct form of the pronoun in parentheses.

In the United States, couples usually receive gifts from (them, their, theirs) _____ relatives and friends when (we, you, they) _____

(1)   (2)
get married. Sometimes a bride will exchange a gift for something else if (he, she, her) _____ doesn't find (it, its, them) _____ useful.

(3)   (4)
(We, Our, Us) _____ give gifts to express our good wishes for the

(5)
marriage, but gifts aren't necessary for the marriage (yourself, itself, ourselves) _____ . However, in some societies gifts are very impor-

(6)
tant, and the marriage isn't legal without (themselves, it, them) _____ .

(7)
One type of gift is called bride service. A young husband must work for a period of time for (his, her, their) _____ wife's family. (She,

(8)
You, He) _____ may work for as long as fifteen years or until the

(9)
third child is born. Bride service may seem strange to (we, us, them)

_____ , but (it, he, she) _____ is necessary in societies where

(10)   (11)
people don't have money or material things to exchange at marriage.

2. **Pronoun Reference.**   Draw an arrow from each pronoun to the noun that it is replacing. The first one is done for you. (The precise nouns for the starred pronouns are not actually given in the text. Can you figure out what noun is meant?)

In Greece the dowry is a common kind of marriage gift. It started in ancient times as a contribution of money or land from a bride's parents to their son-in-law. At that time a wife didn't work outside the home, but she was expected to add to her husband's wealth and to take care of the home and children. But the government of Greece wants to do away with dowries. It says that they aren't necessary now because women work outside the home and can earn as much as men. Many unmarried Greek women think dowries are bad. They often have to wait many years before their family has enough money for a dowry. They say it is the same as "buying a husband." They also think that a man may marry a woman not for herself, but for the amount of money she may bring him. But one

Greek lawyer says the dowry should be continued as "one of those necessary evils we* should not worry too much about." What do you* think?

Now name each of the circled pronouns in the paragraph according to the headings on the pronoun chart.

3. **Sentence Completion.**   Fill in the blanks with the correct pronoun.

   a. When I got married, __My__ husband gave __me__ a beautiful ring that had belonged to __his__ mother. __It__ is gold set with rare stones. __I__ wear __it__ all the time.

   b. Aliki is a young Greek girl. __Her__ parents don't have enough money for a dowry, but __she__ is getting married without __it__ . __Her__ future husband says __he__ loves __her__ and doesn't care about money. Both of __them__ will work, so a dowry isn't necessary.

   c. I have a bicycle, but __My__ brother doesn't. So when __he__ wants to ride, __he__ borrows __my__ . __I__ always share __my__ possessions with each other.

   d. If you want __my__ children to help __you__ with the housework, __you__ have to teach __them__ to be cooperative. __Their__ cooperation will make __yours__ life easier.

Conditionals: Simple Present and Simple Past Tense

The word *if* is the sign of a conditional statement. An *if* clause tells us that certain conditions must be true, or must happen before something else takes place. The *if* clause states the condition. The other clause in the sentence states the result. The result clause contains a modal + a main verb.

> **Children will be helpful to you if you teach them to be cooperative.**
>   (result)   (condition)
>
> **If Romesh married a woman of his own choice, his parents would be hurt.**
>   (condition)   (result)

Note that when the *if* clause begins the sentence, it is followed by a comma. When the *if* clause is the second clause, there is no comma.

Present Conditionals.   When the main verb of an *if* clause is in the Present tense, the most common modals in the result clause are these: *can, may, must, should,* and *will*. This type of conditional expresses the idea of possibility.

> **If the Greek government *does* away with the dowry, women *can marry* at a younger age.**

1. **Sentence Completion.**   Complete each of the following conditional statements with a second clause containing a modal + a main verb. You may use negatives. Use pronouns carefully. Rewrite your complete new sentences.

   a.   If Mrs. Roy finds a suitable girl for Romesh, . . .
   b.   If Romesh's bride wants to be a good daughter-in-law, . . .
   c.   If children watch too much television, . . .
   d.   If you don't know the meaning of a word , . . .
   e.   If my friend from India visits me , . . .
   f.   If parents of small children want to go out in the evening , . . .

2. **Sentence Building.**   There are two items in each set. Make the first item into an *if* clause. Use the verb in the Simple Present tense. Make the second item into a result clause. Use an appropriate modal with the verb in the second clause. Add appropriate subjects and whatever other words are necessary to make a complete sentence. The first one is done for you.

   a.   have enough credits, graduate

   If I have enough credits, I will graduate next year.

   b.   study hard, pass courses
   c.   have money, visit Greece
   d.   don't feel well, stay
   e.   borrow books, return
   f.   eat too much, do exercises
   g.   don't cooperate, cause trouble

3. **Sentence Composing.**   Write a complete conditional sentence for each of the following items.

   a.   Tell what you will do if you get to school early.

   b. Tell what you should do if you see an accident.

   c. Tell one thing children can do if they want to help their parents.

   d. Tell one thing you may buy if you earn enough money.

   e. Tell what a person must have if he or she wants to drive a car.

   f. Tell how the instructor will feel if everyone passes the course.

Simple Past Conditionals.   When the main verb of an *if* clause is in the Simple Past tense, the most common modals in the result clause are these: *could, might,* and *would*. This type of conditional expresses the idea of improbability.

If we *had* clean air, we *would live* a healthier life.

---

1. **Sentence Completion.**   Circle the number of the result clause that best completes the given conditional clause.

   a. If I studied harder,

      (1) I can succeed.

      (2) I could succeed.

      (3) I will succeed.

   b. If I didn't know any English,

      (1) I wouldn't enjoy American movies.

      (2) I can't enjoy American movies.

      (3) I won't enjoy American movies.

   c. If I took a trip to India,

      (1) I find out more about the marriage customs.

      (2) I can find out more about the marriage customs.

      (3) I would find out more about the marriage customs.

   d. If Greek women didn't need a dowry,

      (1) they might get married at a younger age.

      (2) they shouldn't get married at a younger age.

      (3) they must get married at a younger age.

   e. If American parents wanted to arrange a marriage for a son,

      (1) the son can't cooperate.

      (2) the son might not cooperate.

      (3) the son shouldn't cooperate.

2. **Sentence Composing.**   Write a complete conditional sentence to answer each of the following questions.

  a. If your sister got married, what wedding gift would you give her?
  b. If you traveled to Europe, which languages would you find useful?
  c. If astronauts returned to the moon, what discovery might they make?
  d. If there were one world language, which one would you prefer people to speak?
  e. If scientists found life on another planet, would you go there to live?
  f. If governments didn't control the use of dangerous chemicals, what could happen to the environment?

3. **Sentence Completion.**   Fill in the blank space with either a conditional clause or a result clause to complete the following statements. Pay special attention to the tense sequence and modal use. The first one is done for you.

  a. _If I had children,_ _____ I would teach them to cooperate with each other.

  b. You can observe many stars _____ .

  c. If you want to see a lot of Roman art, _____ .

  d. _____ if I traveled a lot.

  e. _____ you shouldn't smoke.

  f. You could pass this course _____ .

Useful Expressions with *The*

When you want to talk about a part of a larger group, you may use the expression *one (two, some, many, most, all) of the* + a plural noun.

Many of the students in this class speak Spanish.

Note that the subject of the sentence is the word before the preposition *of.* In this example, the subject is *many.*

When you use the superlative form of an adjective, you put *the* before it.

The Ganges is *the longest* river in India.
Mrs. Indira Gandhi is one of *the most famous* women in India.

---

1. **Sentence Building.**   Write a complete sentence using the words in each set. Add as many words as you need to make a correct sentence. Do not change the form or the order of the words. The first one is done for you.

   a. many of   books   library   old

   Many of the books in the library are old.

   b. One   windows   classroom   open
   c. Most of   students   school   part-time
   d. All of   stores   neighborhood   closed   Sunday
   e. Three of   people   class   Chinese
   f. Some of   stars   universe   visible   night
   g. One   chairs   livingroom   broken
   h. Some of   exercises   book   difficult

2. **Answering Information Questions.**   Write the answers to each of the questions in complete sentences.

   a. What is the easiest way to get to school?
   b. Who is one of the most loyal friends you have?
   c. Who is the most cooperative member of your family?
   d. When is the best time of the year for you?
   e. Where are most of the students at lunchtime?
   f. What are some of the foods that you like?

3. **Article Completion.**   Fill in the blank spaces with the correct article: *a, an,* or *the*. If no article is needed, mark *X* in the space.

   There was (1) ＿＿＿＿＿ great ceremony in London for (2) ＿＿＿＿＿ wedding of (3) ＿＿＿＿＿ Prince Charles and Lady Diana. Many of (4) ＿＿＿＿＿ world's leaders attended it. All of (5) ＿＿＿＿＿ guests wore beautiful clothing suitable for such (6) ＿＿＿＿＿ grand occasion. But (7) ＿＿＿＿＿ best dressed woman was (8) ＿＿＿＿＿ bride in (9) ＿＿＿ splendid white gown. (10) ＿＿＿＿＿ groom looked very handsome in (11) ＿＿＿＿＿ military uniform. Prince Charles will be (12) ＿＿＿＿＿ next king of England, so his marriage was (13) ＿＿＿＿＿ important event. People all over (14) ＿＿＿＿＿ world wish them (15) ＿＿＿＿＿ long life, good health, and (16) ＿＿＿＿＿ happiness.

In any society married life has its problems. Here an Indonesian comedy makes fun of some marital difficulties. With a partner(s), write a dialogue or a story about this scene in the play.

COMPOSING

1. **Developing a Paragraph.**

   a. *Recognizing General Ideas and Specific Details.*   Next to each sentence in the following paragraphs there is a blank space. As your instructor reads each sentence aloud, mark *G* in the blank space if the sentence is a general idea or opinion. Mark *S* in the blank space if the sentence is a specific detail or example.

   (1)   In India traditional society is divided into groups called castes.

   _____ The different castes are related to certain occupations.

   _____ The Brahmins are priests and scholars. _____ The Kshatryas are soldiers. _____ The Vaisha are businessmen or merchants. _____ The Shudras are factory workers and craftsmen.

   _____ Traditionally, a person belongs to one of these castes by birth. _____ For example, a child born of a father who makes jewelry is a Shudra. _____ In the past, a person from one caste didn't marry someone from another. _____ A Brahmin never married a Vaisha, and a Shudra couldn't marry a Kshatrya. _____ However, under modern Indian law, all the groups are equal. _____ So the caste system has become weaker, and people sometimes marry outside their traditional group. _____

(2)   In many parts of the world there are rules about marrying a person from the same place, or outside that place. _____ In Kalaphur, India, a man must take a wife from outside his village. _____ All of the married women in Kalaphur come from many different villages in the area. _____Some people think that life is difficult in Kalaphur because the married women don't know each other. _____ In Mexican villages, however, women usually marry within the village. _____ In the village of Tepotzlan, over 90 percent of marriages take place within the village. _____ Over 40 percent of the women marry men from the same neighborhood. _____ Observers say that there is more unity in Mexican villages because most of the people know each other. _____

b. The following list includes some items that are considered important for a wedding ceremony.

location of the celebration	bridesmaids' dresses
time of day and the season	music and dancing
performance of the ceremony	flowers
wedding dress	wedding cake
groom's suit	

Think about a wedding that you have observed. Write a paragraph giving your ideas or opinions about it. For example, do you think it was well planned? Was it beautiful? Did it please the parents of the bride and groom? Did people enjoy themselves? Use the list of items to guide you.

2. **Composing a Paragraph.**

a. Imagine yourself as the parent of a grown son or daughter. Describe what kind of marriage partner you would want for him or her. Be specific about the qualities that person should have. Tell why that person would help make a successful marriage with your son or daughter.

b. It is traditional to give gifts to a newly married couple. These presents may be beautiful, interesting, or useful. Describe the kinds of marriage gifts that people in your culture traditionally give to a bride and groom. Begin your paragraph with an appropriate main idea.

CHAPTER EIGHT B

MEN'S AND WOMEN'S ROLES: A CHANGING VIEW

PREREADING

Class Discussion.   Men's and women's roles have been changing in modern American society. We can even see these changes in the letters to newspaper advice columns such as "Dear Abby." Read the following letter. Discuss your opinions about the question. After you have discussed the letter, your instructor may ask you to compose a response.

Dear Abby,

  I am a seventeen-year-old girl with a twin brother. Whenever my mother needs help with the housework, she always asks me. She never asks my brother because she says housework is women's work and it will be good training for me when I become a wife. I think that's an old-fashioned, unfair attitude. Whose side are you on?

Sincerely yours,
Jill H.

New Words.   Try to understand the meanings of these words as they are used in the reading passage. Use a dictionary when necessary.

economic	responsibility	leisure
goal	influence (noun)	occupation
typical	industrial	promotion
involve		pressure

READING

New Influences in American Life

[1]   Once it was possible to define male and female roles easily by the division of labor. Men worked outside the home and earned the income to support their families. Women cooked the meals and took care of the home and the children. These roles were firmly fixed for most people, and there was not much opportunity for men or women to exchange their roles. But by the middle of this century, men's and women's roles were becoming less firmly fixed.

[2]   In the 1950s, economic and social success was the goal of the typical American. But in the 1960s a new force developed called the counterculture. The people involved in this movement did not value the middle-class American goals. The counterculture presented men and women with new role choices. Men became more interested in child care. They began to share child-raising tasks with their wives. In fact, some young men and women moved to communal homes or farms where the economic and child care responsibilities were shared equally by both sexes. In addition, many Americans did not value the traditional male role of soldier. Some young men refused to be drafted as soldiers to fight in the war in Vietnam.

[3]   In terms of numbers, the counterculture was not a very large group of people. But its influence spread to many parts of American society. Working men of all classes began to change their economic and social patterns. Industrial workers and business executives alike cut down on "overtime" work so that they could spend more leisure time with their families. Some doctors, lawyers, and teachers turned away from high paying situations to practice their professions in poorer

Men have always been the professional chefs while women have cooked at home. But now women, like the student on the right, are pursuing this traditionally male career.

neighborhoods. Some young people joined the Peace Corps to share their skills with people in nonindustrialized countries around the world.

[4]   In the 1970s, the feminist movement, or women's liberation, produced additional economic and social changes. Women of all ages and at all levels of society were entering the work force in greater numbers. Most of them still took traditional women's jobs such as public school teaching, nursing, and secretarial work. But some women began to enter traditionally male occupations: police work, banking, dentistry, and construction work. Women were asking for equal pay for equal work, and equal opportunities for promotion. Women's groups were organizing more day-care centers for the children of working mothers.

[5]   Today the experts generally agree that important changes are taking place in the roles of men and women. Naturally, there are difficulties in adjusting to

Some women have begun to enter traditionally male occupations such as telephone repair work.

these changes. It is not easy for men and women to learn to share the labor of the workplace. It is not easy for women to meet the demands and pressures of work outside the home and still take care of a family. Not all men are willing to share home and child care responsibilities with their working wives. But perhaps more men are beginning to feel like Rafael Suarez, Jr., a New York City college student who looks forward to the new type of society. "Who needs the pressure of being a typical male?" asks Rafael. "It's more fun being a human being first."

Paragraph Completion.   Fill in the blank spaces with a word that is correct in both form and meaning.

In the 1970s, the feminist movement, (1) _____ wom-

en's liberation, produced additional economic and (2) _____

changes. Women of all ages (3) _____ at all levels of

society were entering (4) _____ work force in greater num-

bers. Most (5) _____ them still took traditional women's

jobs (6) _____ as public school teaching, nursing,

(7) _____ secretarial work. But some women began to

(8) _____ traditionally male occupations: police work,

banking, dentistry, and (9) _____ work. Women were ask-

ing for equal (10) _____ for equal work, and equal oppor-

tunities (11) _____ promotion. Women's groups were

organizing (12) _____ day-care centers for the children of

working mothers.

VOCABULARY

1. **Expanding Vocabulary.**   Circle the number of the correct answer.
    a. Working mothers don't have much *leisure. Leisure* means
       (1) happiness.   (2) free time.   (3) money.
    b. When a family's *economic* situation is not good, the children may have to work after school. *Economic* situation refers to the family's
       (1) religion.   (2) size.   (3) amount of money.
    c. Is your *goal* to graduate from college? A *goal* is
       (1) an expert.   (2) an education.   (3) an aim.

d. In a *typical* office, the secretary is female. *Typical* means

   (1) rare.   **(2)** usual.   **(3)** interesting.

e. Women's work usually *involves* child care. *Involves* means

   (1) improves.   **(2)** produces.   **(3)** includes.

f. It has been the man's *responsibility* to support his family. A *responsibility* is

   (1) a duty.   **(2)** a boring job.   **(3)** an invention.

g. The counterculture had an *influence* on American society. An *influence* is

   (1) an effect.   **(2)** a communication.   **(3)** damage.

h. *Industrial* workers in the United States are mostly male. *Industrial* refers to people who work in

   (1) offices.   **(2)** schools.   **(3)** manufacturing plants.

i. Typical female *occupations* are public school teaching and nursing. *Occupations* are

   (1) levels of schooling.   **(2)** types of paid work.

   (3) ways of spending leisure time.

j. Women workers ought to have the same possibilities for *promotion* as men. When a person gets a *promotion,* he or she

   (1) moves to a better job.   **(2)** goes to school at night.

   (3) changes his or her place of work.

k. People in certain occupations are under a lot of *pressure. Pressure* means

   (1) stress.   **(2)** temperature.   **(3)** comfort.

2. Using Vocabulary. The following list contains words or forms of words from the New Word list. Use each word correctly in one of the blank spaces in the paragraph.

involves	responsibilities	leisure	typical
influenced	industry	economic	goals
occupations	promotion	pressure	

   In a (1) _____ American business office, men's jobs and women's jobs are different from each other. Typing, filing, and other secretarial work usually (2) _____ women. A female typist may get a (3) _____ to a secretary's position, but

she will find it harder to move into management. In most firms men still
have the major (4) _____ and enjoy a higher (5) _____
level. But in these higher level (6) _____ there is more
(7) _____ and less (8) _____ time.
The women's movement has (9) _____ women to set
higher occupational (10) _____ for themselves. But
women who move up in (11) _____ or business often
find they have two full-time jobs: the one they are paid for and their
housework and child care at home.

3. **Word Families.**   Nouns in English often end in *age, ure, ment, ion,* or *hood.*
    Here are some examples of nouns with these endings.

advantage	leisure	involvement	tradition	parenthood
courage	culture	movement	situation	brotherhood

    Follow the directions for each item. Write your answers in the space provided.

    a. What noun ending in *age* is the opposite of *advantage*? _____

    b. What noun can be made by adding *en* to *courage* and adding one of the
    noun endings from the word family list? _____

    c. What noun ending in *ure* can be formed from the verb *to please*?

    _____

    What noun rhymes with this and means "to take the size of something"?

    _____

    d. What noun name ending in *ure* do we give to that part of our environment
    that includes plants, animals, and weather? _____

    e. The verbs *involve* and *move* add *ment* to become nouns. Make nouns of
    the following verbs in the same way.

    discourage _____ advance _____

    replace _____ disappoint _____

    f. What noun that ends in *ion* means an explanation for a word?

    _____

    g. What nouns ending in *ion* describe the four basic processes of arithmetic?

    _____ _____ _____

    _____

h. Write the noun forms ending in *hood* for each of the following conditions.

(1) when women think of themselves as sisters in a universal family

_____

(2) what Alaska and Hawaii gained when they became states of the United States _____

(3) the stage of a child's life up to the age of twelve _____

READING COMPREHENSION

1. **Understanding the Text.**   Circle the number of the correct answer.

a. Which sentence best expresses the main idea of Paragraph [1]?

(1) Men's and women's roles were usually quite separate in the past.
(2) Women usually worked outside the home for wages.
(3) Men's and women's roles were easily exchanged in the past.

b. Which sentence best expresses the main idea of Paragraph [2]?

(1) the first sentence   (2) the fourth sentence   (3) the last sentence

c. In Paragraphs [2] and [3], the author suggests that the counterculture

(1) destroyed the United States.   (2) changed some American values.
(3) was not important in the United States.

d. The main idea of Paragraph [4] is stated in

(1) the second sentence.   (2) the fifth sentence.   (3) the last sentence.

e. In Paragraph [4], which would be the best place for the following sentence: *They also became taxicab drivers, pilots, and college presidents.*

(1) after the first sentence   (2) after the fourth sentence
(3) after the last sentence

f. In Paragraph [5], the author suggests that

(1) men and women will never share the same goals.
(2) most men will be happy to take care of their children.
(3) some men may be willing to change their traditional male roles.

g. The quotation by Rafael Suarez, Jr., in Paragraph [5] suggests that

(1) he would not permit his wife to hold a job.
(2) he would share some of the household responsibilities with his wife.
(3) he wants a job with a lot of pressure.

2. **Answering Information Questions.**   Write the answers to each question in complete sentences.

   a. In the past, which sex took care of the home and children?
   b. In the past, which sex worked outside the home?
   c. Did the counterculture value or reject the goals of the 1950s?
   d. List two specific ways in which the values of the counterculture were different from traditional male values of the 1950s.
   e. Why did some men turn down "overtime" work in the 1960s?
   f. Why did some young people join the Peace Corps?
   g. What are some traditional female occupations?
   h. What did women's groups do for working mothers?
   i. Does the quotation by Rafael Suarez, Jr., show agreement or disagreement with women's liberation?

3. **Paraphrasing.**   Writers may express the same ideas in different ways. A paraphrase is another, usually simpler, way of saying something. Follow the directions for each item.

   a. The following sentences are paraphrases of some of the ideas in Paragraphs [2] and [3]. In the blank space next to each sentence, write the paragraph and sentence number of the original sentence. The first one is done for you.

   (1) The members of the counterculture didn't want the same things from life as did most middle-class Americans. *Para. 2*
       *Sent. 3*

   (2) Fathers took over more of the job of being a parent.
       _____   _____

   (3) On communes both men and women share the outside work and the child care. _____   _____

   (4) Some men wouldn't go into military service.
       _____   _____

   (5) Men wanted to work shorter hours so they could see their families more. _____   _____

b. Put a check (√) next to the two sentences that mean the same thing.

(1) a. More American households are headed by women than ever before. _____

  b. There has been an increase in the number of women who return to work after having children. _____

  c. Many American women leave their jobs when they have children. _____

  d. The number of American homes with no adult male member is increasing. _____

(2) a. In many colleges in the United States men and women live in the same dormitories. _____

  b. A number of all-male colleges are beginning to admit women students. _____

  c. Women are starting to enter some colleges that used to be only for men. _____

  d. Women in some colleges are taking part-time jobs that used to be held by men. _____

(3) a. Divorced mothers are returning to college in increasing numbers. _____

  b. More divorced men are asking to have their children live with them. _____

  c. Most children of divorced parents live with their mothers. _____

  d. The number of divorced men raising their children is growing. _____

(4) a. In the United States secretaries are usually women. _____

  b. In European and South American offices secretaries are frequently male. _____

  c. Male secretaries are quite common in the offices of Europe and South America. _____

  d. European offices are usually better run than American offices. _____

(5) **a.** Research shows that the more education a woman gets, the fewer children she usually has. _____

b. Research shows that many women now combine going to college with having children. _____

c. Research shows that educated women have high educational goals for their children. _____

d. Research shows an increase in the number of mothers going back for higher education. _____

WRITING EXERCISES

Pronoun Use

Pronouns may be used to replace subjects, objects, or possessives in a sentence. Pronouns must agree in number, person, form, and gender with the nouns they replace. Study the following pronoun chart and examples.

Subject	Object (of verb or preposition)	Possessive	Possessive Adjective (+ noun)	Reflexive
I	me	mine	my (book)	myself
you	you	yours	your (book)	yourself
he	him	his	his (book)	himself
she	her	hers	her (book)	herself
it	it	—	its (color)	itself
we	us	ours	our (books)	ourselves
you	you	yours	your (books)	yourselves
they	them	theirs	their (books)	themselves

When mothers work outside the home, *they* **still have child care responsibilities.**   (plural Third Person subject)

My brother worked part-time while *he* **attended college.**
(singular Third Person subject male)

Many fathers want to spend more time with *their* **families.**
(plural Third Person possessive adjective)

1. **Sentence Completion.**   A newspaper recently printed the following complaint. First read the paragraph. Then fill in the blank spaces with the correct form of the pronoun in parentheses. Finally, discuss with your class the roles of a grandmother or grandfather in your family or in other families you know.

    There are no grandmas any more. (You, Your, Yours) _____
    (1)
    won't find (they, their, them) _____ in the kitchen baking cakes or at
    (2)
    home knitting sweaters for (her, my, their) _____ grandchildren. There
    (3)
    are no more traditional grandmas; there are only grandmothers: young
    looking, athletic, and active. (Them, They, Theirs) _____ are jog-
    (4)
    ging, playing tennis, and driving (your, their, our) _____ cars all over
    (5)
    town. (We, Our, Us) _____ must say goodbye to grandma as
    (6)
    (ours, our, their) _____ babysitter because (her, she, they) _____
    (7)   (8)
    is usually out dancing (himself, themselves, herself) _____ .
    (9)
    I am going to put an ad in (mine, me, my) _____ local newspaper.
    (10)
    (Its, It, Itself) _____ will say: "Wanted, one old fashioned grand-
    (11)
    mother."

2. **Pronoun Reference.**   Draw an arrow from each pronoun to the noun that it is replacing. The first one is done for you. (The precise noun for the starred pronoun is not actually given in the text. Can you figure out what noun is meant?)

Here a grandmother and granddaughter pick vegetables together. Discuss the relationships between grandparents and grandchildren in your family. Write a paragraph about a pleasant experience with your grandparent(s).

John Gidman is sixteen years old. Earlier this year he joined the volleyball team at his high school. But he had to quit after only a few games. Why? It is a girl's team, which means it is for girls only. If a girl wants to play on a boy's team, she can. The choice is hers. But boys can't make the same choice. The coaches are afraid that the boys will be too competitive, and they will push the girls aside. John Gidman thinks that the rules that put him off the team are unfair. There is no boys' volleyball team for him to join. Should John get his chance on the girls' team? What's your* opinion?

Now name each of the circled pronouns in the paragraph according to the headings on the pronoun chart.

3. **Sentence Completion.**   Fill in the blanks with the correct pronoun.

   a. Aretha Franklin is a famous singer. _____ records are very popular and _____ has earned a good living from _____ .

   b. Eleanor and Franklin D. Roosevelt were a good political team. _____ worked very well together during President Roosevelt's term of office. If Franklin couldn't address a certain meeting, _____ wife often went to _____ in _____ place.

   c. My ten-year-old daughter prefers pants to skirts. _____ says that wearing jeans allows _____ to be more active.

   d. My two children are quite different in _____ interests. _____ daughter is interested in sports and nature, but _____ brother enjoys art and music.

   e. As American parents, we encourage _____ children to be independent of _____ . _____ want _____ to take responsibility for _____ own decisions. If _____ want extra money, _____ think that _____ should earn _____ with a part-time job.

Conditionals: Simple Present and Simple Past Tense

The word *if* is the sign of a conditional statement. An *if* clause tells us that certain conditions must be true or must happen before something else takes place. The *if* clause tells us the condition. The other clause in the sentence tells us the result. The result clause contains a modal + a main verb.

> **You will pass your courses if you study hard.**
>   (result)   (condition)
>
> **If more women completed their educations, they would find better jobs.**
>   (condition)   (result)

Note that when the *if* clause begins the sentence, it is followed by a comma. When the *if* clause is the second clause, there is no comma.

Present Conditionals.   When the main verb of an *if* clause is in the Present tense, the most common modals in the result clause are these: *can, may, must, should,* and *will.* This conditional expresses the idea of possibility.

> **If more mothers *go* out to work, more employers *may offer* day-care.**

1. **Sentence Completion.**   Complete each of the following conditional statements with a second clause containing a modal + a main verb. You may use negatives. Use pronouns carefully. Rewrite your complete new sentences.

   a. If a husband helps his wife with the housework . . .
   b. If girls and boys play the same sports . . .
   c. If young boys learn to cook . . .
   d. If women want to become fire fighters . . .
   e. If women want job promotions . . .
   f. If men want to spend more time with their families . . .

2. **Sentence Building.**   There are two items in each set. Make the first item into an *if* clause. Use the verb in the Simple Present tense. Make the second item into a *result* clause. Use an appropriate modal with the verb in the second clause. Add appropriate subjects and whatever other words are necessary to make a complete sentence. The first one is done for you.

   a. work long hours, feel tired

   If you work long hours, you may feel very tired at night.

   b. play active sports, wear clothing

   c. give a baseball, learn

   d. give dolls, play

   e. watch their mother, learn

   f. do well in school, continue education

   g. practice conversation, improve English

3. Sentence Composing. Write a complete conditional sentence for each of the following items.

   a. Tell what item you will wear or carry if it rains tomorrow.

   b. Tell one thing that may happen if we elect a woman president.

   c. Tell one thing you will do next summer if you have the money.

   d. Tell one thing you should do if you are preparing for an exam.

   e. Tell one thing you must do if you want to improve your English.

Simple Past Conditionals. When the main verb of an *if* clause is in the Simple Past tense, the most common modals in the result clause are these: *could, might,* and *would.* This conditional expresses the idea of improbability.

If my daughter *wanted* to become a scientist, I *would encourage* her.

---

1. Sentence Completion. Circle the number of the result clause that best completes the given conditional clause.

   a. If a man took a pilot's job,

      (1) he can't see his family very often.

      (2) he shouldn't see his family very often.

      (3) he couldn't see his family very often.

   b. If parents' jobs required them to travel,

      (1) they would need excellent child care.

      (2) they need excellent child care.

      (3) they must need excellent child care.

   c. If little girls shared more sports activities with little boys,

      (1) real friendships might develop.

      (2) real friendships will develop.

      (3) real friendships can't develop.

   d. If there were more good day-care centers,

     (1) more mothers may work.

     (2) more mothers will work.

     (3) more mothers would work.

   e. If I wanted to be a construction worker,

     (1) I need a lot of strength.

     (2) I would need a lot of strength.

     (3) I will need a lot of strength.

2. Sentence Composing.   Write a complete conditional sentence to answer each of the following questions.

   a. If you became mayor of your city, what would you do to improve public transportation?

   b. If you were the manager of a professional baseball team, would you hire a woman player?

   c. If you had a daughter, what gift might you give her for her seventh birthday?

   d. If your friend gave birth to a boy, what gift would you give the baby?

   e. If your mother needed help around the house, what chores might you do for her?

   f. If a person liked working with children, what job might he or she enjoy doing?

   g. If you called a wrong telephone number by mistake, what expression could you use?

   h. If you won one thousand dollars in the lottery, how would you spend it?

Useful Expressions with *The*

When you want to talk about a part of a larger group, you may use the expression *one (two, some, many, most, all) of the* + a plural noun.

> ***Some of the women*** **in my family hold full-time jobs.**

Note that the subject of the sentence is the word before the preposition *of*. In this example, the subject is *some*.

When you use the superlative form of an adjective, you put *the* before it.

> The President holds *the highest* position of any government official. Mrs. Shirley Patel is one of *the most active* members of our block association.

1. **Answering Information Questions.**   Write the answers to each of the following questions in complete sentences.

   a. Who are two of the tallest members of your family?
   b. What is one of the newspapers you read often?
   c. Who is one of the kindest people you know?
   d. Who are some of the most famous women in your native country?
   e. Who are some of the students who sit next to you?
   f. Who has the hardest job in your family?
   g. Who is the most studious person in your family?
   h. What are most of the students in your class doing now?
   i. What is the most interesting course you are taking this term?
   j. What is one of the most difficult features of English?
   k. Where are most of the stores in your neighborhood?
   l. What is the warmest article of clothing you own?

2. **Pair Dictation.**   Dictate three of your best sentences from Exercise 1 to your partner. Then take dictation from your partner.

3. **Article Completion.**   Fill in the blank spaces with the correct article: *a, an,* or *the*. If no article is needed, mark *X* in the space.

   At Rutgers University (1) _____ last year there was (2) _____ conference of some of (3) _____ most famous creative women in (4) _____ world. Most of (5) _____ speakers were older women writers and artists who had achieved (6) _____ success in their fields many years ago. They spoke about some of (7) _____ greatest difficulties they had faced as (8) _____ creative, independent women. One of (9) _____ best-known American writers there was Lillian Hellman. She has written (10) _____ excellent novels and plays about (11) _____ modern American life. Emily Hahn, (12) _____ magazine writer who has written (13) _____ lot about China, was also there. These women told (14) _____ audience what it felt like to be (15) _____ woman in (16) _____ man's world fifty years ago.

COMPOSING

1. **Developing a Paragraph.**

   a. *Recognizing General Ideas and Specific Details.*   Next to each sentence in the following paragraphs there is a blank. As your instructor reads each sentence aloud, mark *G* in the blank if the sentence is a general idea or opinion. Mark *S* in the blank if the sentence is a specific detail or example.

      (1)   Change has come to the world of women's marathon running. _____ Women are running the twenty-six mile races faster each year. _____ In 1971 Australian Adrienne Beams ran the marathon in two hours, forty-six minutes, and thirty seconds. _____ In 1975 Jacqueline Hanson of the United States ran it in under two hours and forty minutes. _____ These top women runners are training longer and harder than before. _____ For example, Grete Waitz, the three-time winner of the New York Marathon, runs about ninety hours every week. _____

      (2)   Changes in the American life-style have affected the American family. _____ The number of households headed by women keeps increasing. _____ In 1970 about 5.6 million American homes were headed by women. _____ In 1979 that number had increased to 8.5 million. _____ There are several reasons for this. _____ First, many young working women are living alone in their own apartments. _____ Also, divorce has increased the number of households where the female is the sole parent. _____

   b. The following lists include some of the household activities typically done by men and women in the United States. Write a paragraph about your own family, or another family you know well, and tell about some of the different household jobs done by each sex. Use some of the items in the

Today many women participate in sports for health and fun. This women's four-mile race in New York City's Central Park is an example. What sports do women enjoy in your culture?

lists. You may add others of your own. Remember that a good paragraph has some general ideas or opinions and some specific details or examples that explain or support the general ideas. Use the paragraphs in Exercise 1 as a model if you wish.

Women	Men
wash dishes	move heavy furniture
iron	wash windows
vacuum	repair broken items
do laundry	take care of the car
take children to the doctor	put out the trash
cook dinner	hang pictures
shop for food	do carpentry
shop for clothes for the family	

c. Read the following information about the requirements for two types of jobs. The first is secretarial work, usually done by women. The second is parcel post delivery work, usually done by men.

Secretarial Work	**Parcel Post Delivery Work**
take dictation of letters and reports	load packages onto truck from warehouse
file documents	drive a large van or truck
type letters and reports	steer around narrow city streets
answer telephone	park in difficult places
make appointments for supervisor	unload packages for delivery
separate office mail	deliver parcels to homes and apartments
photocopy documents	

Write a paragraph in which you contrast the different abilities needed for secretarial work and parcel post delivery work. Consider such qualities as physical strength, personality, punctuality, language ability, and special skills. Include a main idea sentence that clearly states the topic and the contrast about which you will be writing.

2. **Composing a Paragraph.**

   a. Think about a traditionally male occupation such as fire fighting, construction work, or dentistry. Write a paragraph about why a woman could or could not do *one* of those jobs as well as a man.

   b. Think about a traditionally female occupation such as elementary school teaching, nursing, or telephone operating. Write a paragraph about why a man could or could not do *one* of those jobs as well as a woman.

CHAPTER NINE A

FOCUS ON THE FAMILY

PREREADING

Class Discussion.   Modern family life is hard for divorced parents and their children. It may also be lonely for older people whose relatives live far away. A recent *New York Times* article told of a divorced mother of two children who found a way to involve older people in child care. She advertised for Grannies—grandmothers and grandfathers—to help single parents care for their children. Read her advertisement for the Granny Emergency Service. Then answer the questions that follow.

> Through your help three generations can find new trust in each other. Children need love and care to grow up healthy. They are the future. If we are ready to accept this mutual bond and responsibility, life can be more meaningful and harmonious for you, the older generation, and for parents and children.

Do you agree with the statements in this ad? Would you prefer a young or an older person to help with your children? In what ways can older people help in caring for small children? How might each generation benefit from this arrangement?

New Words.   Try to understand the meanings of these words as they are used in the reading passage. Use a dictionary when necessary.

mature (verb)	companionship	dignity
provide	generation	industrial
permanent	survival	
adapted	urban	

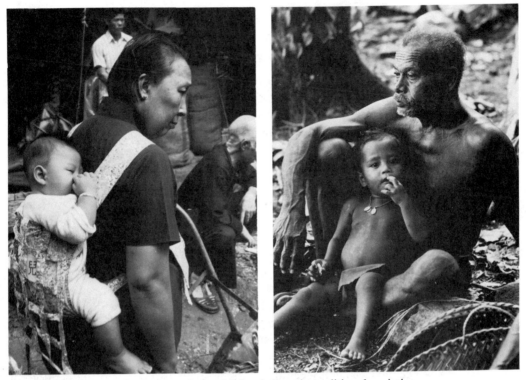

Grandparents play an important role in children's lives in traditional societies.

READING

The Family: Past, Present, and Future

[1]   A baby elephant can walk shortly after it is born. Only a few weeks after they are hatched, birds can fly away from the nest to find their own food. Animals mature rather quickly. A human baby, however, is helpless for a long time. Its slow development makes it dependent on adults for many years. Adults must cooperate to provide the food, warmth, and protection necessary for a child's growth to maturity. They must provide some kind of family for the human child.

[2]   Thousands of years ago men and women lived by hunting animals and gathering wild plants. People had few possessions and no permanent home. They had to move from one area to another in search of food. They lived in small units of a mother, a father, and children. Social scientists call this the elementary, or nuclear, family. The nuclear family was well adapted to this hunting and gathering society. Even with several children, it was small enough to move easily from place to place. Each family was independent, but sometimes several related families

camped together for companionship and the chance to communicate their ideas and experiences.

[3]   As time passed, people discovered how to plant food and to tame wild pigs, goats, and other animals. With farming, a new type of family structure developed: the extended family. Several generations of the same family lived together in a permanent place. This arrangement provided many workers for the family farm. When older members died, the farmland continued in the hands of the younger generations. Many healthy children were important for the survival of the family and the land.

[4]   Both the nuclear family and the extended family exist today. Extended families follow the economic and social traditions of the past. Most of them live on farms or in villages, mainly in Asia, Africa, and South America. Some have moved to cities and started family businesses. The marriage union is important, but blood ties between the generations are still very strong, so that the family continues through time as a permanent economic unit. But the extended family is more than a business affair. It offers companionship, as daily activities are carried out by a number of relatives working together. When a family member becomes too old or too sick to work, he or she still participates in family decisions. Older people don't lose their sense of dignity or purpose. Children who grow up in this environment are naturally respectful and caring toward older people. The majority of the world's people live in this way and have these ideals.

[5]   The modern nuclear family, living in an industrial society, has a different set of ideals. In North America and Europe economic success often depends on the ability of people to move from one city to another. The nuclear family today is adapted to apartment living in urban centers, small homes in suburban areas, or individual farmhouses. Such a family may live far from relatives. Some children don't have a close relationship with aunts, uncles, or grandparents. Their interests and activities lie more with those of the same age group than with those of other generations. In the nuclear family, children are educated to become independent and follow their own careers. A person is expected to be economically and socially independent in old age.

[6]   There are weaknesses in the nuclear family structure as its exists today. It can be broken easily by divorce or the death of a parent. Even with two parents, children sometimes don't get enough attention or love. Then, too, there is the problem of caring for the elderly without strong family support. Loneliness can be a problem for young and old alike. Nevertheless, the nuclear family will survive. In fact, social scientists predict that there will be more independent nuclear families in the future because extended families will separate into basic nuclear units. They say that as the world becomes more and more industrialized, there will be little place left for extended family farms and businesses. But perhaps some of the extended family ideals will survive and give renewed strength to modern family life.

Summary Completion.   Choose the correct word from the columns following the paragraph to fill in each blank space in the paragraph.

Two types of family structures (1) _____ in the past. The nuclear family was adapted to a life of (2) _____ and gathering. The members of the (3) _____ family lived together in a permanent place. Both types of families (4) _____ today. The extended family is an (5) _____ unit as well as a social unit. There is companionship for the workers and dignity for (6) _____ members. The nuclear family has a different set of (7) _____ . Children in a nuclear family are educated to become (8) _____ in their own careers. In the future there might be (9) _____ in the structure of the family, but family life will survive.

(1) gathered, approached, developed, rested
(2) planting, growing, arranging, hunting
(3) nuclear, extended, broken, divorced
(4) exist, control, depend, decide
(5) economic, active, American, interesting

(6) literate, ideal, older, personal
(7) people, ideals, units, ages
(8) weak, lonely, independent, elderly
(9) parents, predictions, scientists, changes

VOCABULARY

1. **Expanding Vocabulary.**   Circle the number of the item that explains the meaning of the italicized word.

   a. My friend is staying with us at present, but the arrangement isn't *permanent*.
      Permanent means

      (1) short-lived   **(2)** well furnished   **(3)** long-lasting

   b. Polar bears are *adapted* to living in a cold climate.
      Adapted means

      (1) unsuited   **(2)** adjusted   **(3)** allowed

c. The sun *provides* warmth and light on the earth.
To *provide* something means to

(1) supply it   **(2)** feel it   **(3)** warm it

d. My daughter enjoys the *companionship* of her cousins.
Companionship means

(1) easy life   **(2)** daily schedule   **(3)** close company

e. Although they were poor, my grandparents lived with a sense of *dignity.*
A sense of *dignity* is a feeling of

(1) worthiness   **(2)** brotherhood   **(3)** hardship

f. People have a better chance of *survival* in a car accident if they use seat belts.
Survival means

(1) getting hurt   **(2)** being careful   **(3)** remaining alive

g. Fruits taste best when they *mature* on the tree.
When something *matures,* it

(1) falls easily   **(2)** develops fully   **(3)** grows poorly

h. Many grandparents communicate well with members of the younger *generation*.
A *generation* is

(1) an age group   **(2)** a national group   **(3)** a social group

i. The city of Pittsburgh is the heart of an *industrial* area of Pennsylvania.
In an *industrial* area there would be a lot of

(1) farms   **(2)** factories   **(3)** clean air

j. Would you rather live in an *urban* center or in the countryside?
Urban refers to

(1) farmlands   **(2)** villages   **(3)** cities

2. Using Vocabulary.   Follow the directions for each item.

a. Write a complete sentence for each item. Use the italicized words in your sentences.

(1) Why would *survival* on the moon be difficult?
(2) Name two things public elementary schools *provide* for the children.
(3) Do you get along well with people of your parents' *generation*?
(4) Is *urban* living more expensive or less expensive than living on a farm?

(5) Where in your neighborhood can older people go to find good *companionship*?

b. Fill in each blank space with an appropriate word from the New Word list.

(1) My cousin is unfit for an office job; he is more _____ to outdoor work in construction.

(2) I have only a temporary address. I'll let you know my _____ address when I find an apartment.

(3) There are government buildings, art museums, and historic monuments in Rome, Italy. Rome is not an _____ city.

(4) My doctor is a man of warmth and understanding. He treats all his patients with _____ .

c. The word *mature* is a verb. It is also an adjective. The noun form is *maturity*. Fill in the blank space with the correct verb, adjective, or noun form, depending on the sentence.

(1) A _____ student sits quietly in class and listens to the instructor.

(2) When a person _____ , he or she is called a young adult.

(3) Doctors say that females _____ at an earlier age than males.

(4) My children are only nine and eleven years old; they have not yet reached _____ .

3. **Word Families.**   A prefix is a syllable at the beginning of a word that changes or adds to the meaning of a word. If you know the meaning of a prefix, it will help you understand word meanings and build your vocabulary.
   Follow the directions for each item.

a. *di-* = apart, separate: *divide, divorce, distance*
   Choose the correct word with the prefix *di-* to fill in the blank spaces.

(1) When a husband and wife separate permanently, we say they get a

   _____ .

(2) You should _____ a birthday cake equally so that each child gets a part of it.

b. *sub-* = under, secondary: *subway, substitute, submarine, subject, suburban*

Choose the correct words with the prefix *sub-* to fill in the blank spaces.

(1) A ship that can travel underwater is called a _____ .

(2) The place that is secondary to a main urban area is referred to as a _____ area.

(3) A _____ is an underground transportation system.

(4) If your teacher is absent, you may get a second, or _____ , teacher in his or her place.

c. *co-, col-, com-* = together, with: *communicate, common, cooperate, company, collection*

Choose the correct words with *co-, col-,* or *com-* to fill in the blank spaces.

(1) When people work well together, we say they _____ with each other.

(2) If you gather together a number of stamps from different countries, you will have a fine stamp _____ .

(3) When people talk together and understand each other, we say they _____ well.

d. *ex-* = out of, from: *exit, existence, extended, express*

Choose the correct words with the prefix *ex-* to fill in the blank spaces.

(1) When a family stretches out to include two or three generations, we call it an _____ family.

(2) If there is a fire in your school, you should go out of the building by the nearest _____ .

e. *pre-* = before, in advance: *prefix, prediction, prefer, prepositions, premature, prepare*

Choose the correct words with the prefix *pre-* to fill in the blank spaces.

(1) Before you eat, you must _____ the food and set the table.

(2) A _____ is a syllable that comes before the other parts of a word.

(3) People who tell something in advance are making a _____ about the future.

(4) The words *in, on, to,* and *from* are placed before nouns; they are called _____ .

READING COMPREHENSION

1. **Understanding the Text.**   Circle the number of the correct answer.

   a. In Paragraph [1], the development of animals

      (1) is described as similar to that of human children.

      (2) is contrasted to the development of human children.

      (3) is said to be slower than that of human children.

   b. Hunters and gatherers

      (1) sometimes lived with related families on farms.

      (2) lived permanently in small villages.

      (3) depended on wild plants and animals for food.

   c. According to Paragraph [3], the extended family was a benefit to people who

      (1) were lazy.

      (2) farmed the land.

      (3) wanted a private life.

   d. The extended family is

      (1) both an economic and a social unit.

      (2) only an economic unit.

      (3) primarily a social unit for the care of the aged.

   e. In the fifth sentence of Paragraph [4], the phrase *so that* signals the reader to expect

      (1) a contrast.

      (2) an example.

      (3) a result.

   f. The extended family continues as a permanent economic unit because

      (1) farms and businesses are handed down from generation to generation.

      (2) all the members have companionship.

      (3) the older generation has a sense of dignity.

   g. Movement, distance from relatives, and independence are typical characteristics of

(1) the majority of the world's families.

(2) the modern nuclear family.

(3) extended families in cities.

h. In Paragraph [5], the sixth sentence, the first word *Their* refers to

  (1) aunts and uncles.

  (2) grandparents.

  (3) children.

i. In Paragraph [5], the last sentence, the words *A person is expected to be* mean the same as

  (1) a person must be.

  (2) a person is supposed to be.

  (3) a person will be.

j. Social scientists predict that

  (1) there will be fewer divorces in the future.

  (2) the nuclear family won't survive.

  (3) the extended family structure will change.

Extended families follow the economic and social traditions of the past. Most of them live on farms or in villages, mainly in Asia, South America, or Africa, as does the family pictured here.

2. **Answering Information Questions.**   Write the answers to the following questions in complete sentences.

   a. Name three things that adults must provide for a child.

   b. In the hunting and gathering society, did people live in nuclear families or in extended families?

   c. In which areas of the world do most of the extended families live today?

   d. How do children who grow up in extended families behave toward older people?

   e. In what type of homes do nuclear families live today?

   f. Do modern nuclear families usually live close to or far from their relatives?

   g. In the nuclear family, is an old person expected to be dependent or independent?

   h. Will there be fewer or more nuclear families in the future?

3. **Following Key Words.**   In reading a paragraph you must look for the key, or main, topic words that the writer uses all through the paragraph. These words may not always be exactly the same. The writer may use synonyms, paraphrases, specific parts of a topic, or pronouns in place of the topic word(s). Study Paragraph [4] of the reading passage. This paragraph is about the extended family. The main idea is stated in the second sentence. The key topic words in that sentence are the following: *Extended families, economic and social traditions*. By following these key words, the reader can divide the paragraph into the economic and social benefits of extended family life as follows:

Economic	**Social**
live on farms	marriage union important
started family businesses	blood ties strong
family as a permanent economic unit	offers companionship
a business affair	old members participate in decisions
working together	older members have dignity
	children respectful and caring

Now read the following paragraph carefully. It tells how a young Italian man manages family life. The key topic phrases in the first sentence are italicized. In the blank spaces following the paragraph, fill in the key words or phrases that are appropriate for the headings. The first ones are done for you.

   Carlo Caperna manages to combine *modern family living* and *traditional family ties*. Carlo lives with his wife and two children in a small apartment in Turino, an industrial city in northern Italy. On weekends he drives with his family up to the mountains near Turino where his wife's parents have a farm. Other relatives do the same. Three generations gather there to make an extended family for the weekend. For Carlo, whose own relatives live far away in the south, the closeness between generations is basic to his feelings of pleasure and happiness. He knows that the ties between his children, their aunts, uncles, and grandparents will develop stronger generations for the future.

Modern Family Living   **Traditional Family Ties**

Carlo, his wife and two children   *wife's parents have a farm*

_____   _____

_____   _____

_____   _____

_____

WRITING EXERCISES

Complex Sentences with *Before* and *After*

Complex sentences sometimes include activities that happen at different times. One part of the sentence happens *before* or *after* the other. The part of the sentence that begins with the time word *before* or *after* is called the *dependent clause*. The dependent clause must be joined to a main, or independent, clause to complete the sentence.

> **Before my grandfather ate lunch, he read the newspaper.**
>   (dependent clause)   (independent clause)
>
> **He took a short nap after he ate.**
> (independent clause)   (dependent clause)

Note that when the dependent clause begins the sentence, it is followed by a comma.

Related Verb Tenses in Complex Sentences with *Before* and *After*.   The main verbs in both parts of a complex sentence must be in the same or related tenses.

Simple Present   **Simple Present and Future**

Babies *make* a lot of different sounds before they *learn* to talk.
After my cousin *graduates*, he *will work* in his father's business.

Simple Past   **Simple Past and Past Continuous**

After my brother *entered* school, my mother *went* back to work.
Before the instructor *arrived*, the students *were talking* loudly.

---

1. **Sentence Combining.** Join the two sentences in each set by adding the word *before* or *after.* Make whatever small changes are necessary for sentence correctness. Rewrite each new complete sentence. The first one is done for you.

   a. **(1)** I go to work in the morning.
      (2) I take my child to school.
      Before I go to work in the morning, I take my child to school.

   b. **(1)** Many older people find interesting things to do.
      (2) They retire from their regular jobs.

   c. **(1)** My grandmother used to read me a story every night.
      (2) I went to sleep.

   d. **(1)** We were living near my aunt's house.
      (2) We moved next door to my grandparents.

   e. **(1)** My baby brother learned to walk.
      (2) My mother had to watch him all the time.

   f. **(1)** My daughter finishes her homework.
      (2) She will play outside with her friends.

   g. **(1)** Some families move many times.
      (2) They finally find a suitable place to live.

   h. **(1)** My aunt had a baby.
      (2) She didn't go back to work for a few years.

   i. **(1)** People lived mainly by hunting animals.
      (2) They learned to plant food.

j. **(1)** Related families camped together for companionship.
(2) Their work was done.

2. **Sentence Building.** Use each pair of items in a complete sentence with the time word *before* or *after.* You may use the items in any order and add as many words as you like to make a complete, interesting sentence. You may use the verbs in any tense, or in the negative. The first one is done for you.

a. finish this exercise, do another

After we finish this exercise, we'll do another one.

b. open the window, go to bed
c. get a job, answer an advertisement
d. graduate, pass my courses
e. eat, get thirsty
f. go swimming, play
g. buy my ticket, pack
h. give my opinion, read
i. write a paragraph, proofread

3. **Sentence Composing.** Follow the directions for each item.

a. Tell what you will do after this class is over.
b. Tell what people need before they can drive a car.
c. In two separate sentences, tell two things the astronauts did after they landed on the moon. Now combine the two sentences into one, making all the necessary changes.
d. In two separate sentences, tell two things you should do before you write a paragraph. Now combine the two sentences, making all the necessary changes.
e. In two separate sentences, tell what children like to do after they come home from school.
f. In three separate sentences, tell three things you do after you get home from school or work. Then combine the three sentences into one complete sentence, using a series of items.

Adverb Use

1. **In What Manner.** Adverbs describe how, or *in what manner,* verb action is done.

> **The children are playing *quietly*. (Children *are playing*. How are they playing? *quietly*)**

Rewriting Sentences.   Rewrite each sentence changing the italicized phrase into an adverb that tells how the verb action is done. Use the space provided. The first one is done for you.

   a. Animals mature *in a rapid way,* but human babies develop *in a slow way.*

      Animals mature rapidly, but human babies develop slowly.

   b. Hunters and gatherers didn't live *in a permanent way* in any one place.

      _____

   c. In cold climates they dressed *in a warm way* in animal skins.

      _____

   d. The baby rested *in a comfortable manner* in its mother's arms.

      _____

   e. After children learn to walk, parents must watch them *in a close way.*

      _____

   f. Children in extended families always behave *in a respectful manner* toward their elders.

      _____

   g. Many older people are living *in a modest way* on small incomes.

      _____

   h. Some of them live with relatives and others live *in an independent way.*

      _____

   i. Carlo works *in a successful way* at keeping his family together.

      _____

2. Extent or Degree.   Adverbs tell *the extent or degree* of an adjective or adverb. Some common adverbs of degree are *very, too, extremely, rather, quite,* and *fairly.*

> **Animals mature *rather* quickly.**
> **I had a *fairly* pleasant time at my cousin's house.**

Note that in English the adverb *too* usually has a negative meaning: You smoke *too* much (you should smoke less). *Too* is not a synonym for *very*, which may be used in either a positive or negative way.

Sentence Completion.   Read the first statement in each pair. Then choose one of the given adverbs of degree to fill in the blank space. (More than one adverb may be correct in some cases.)

extremely   completely   fairly   too   very   quite   rather

a. The doctor told my aunt that she must rest more. She works _____ hard around the house.

b. My grandmother lives about four miles away. I'll take the bus because it's _____ far to walk.

c. As far as we know, there isn't any water on the moon. It's _____ dry.

d. It is fifty degrees below zero in some parts of the north. That's _____ cold.

e. I got 78 on the last exam and 75 on the one before. I think I'm doing _____ well in English.

f. My mother was from a poor family. She was _____ happy that she was able to go to college.

g. We have a few more sentences to complete. We're not _____ ready to begin the next exercise.

h. Spanish and Italian are related languages. An Italian could learn Spanish _____ easily.

i. I went out this morning without much breakfast. I feel _____ hungry now.

3. **Comparative.**   Comparative adverbs compare the different degrees in which verb action is done. To use adverbs for comparison, one must normally add the word *more* before the adverb.

People drive *more carefully* when they see a police car.

Note some common exceptions in the comparative adverb form:
hard——→harder; well——→better; badly——→worse; fast——→faster

Sentence Composing.   Write a complete sentence to answer each of the following items. Use the sentence pattern in the example.

> **Do animals or human beings mature more rapidly?**
>
> *Animals mature more rapidly than human beings.*

  a. Do airplanes or spaceships travel faster?
  b. Did hunters or farmers live more dangerously?
  c. Do men or women act more emotionally?
  d. Can birds or mosquitoes fly higher?
  e. Did Etruscan women or Roman women dress more modestly?
  f. Do cats or mice behave more intelligently?
  g. Does an electric light or a match burn more brightly?

Punctuation: Quotations

Quotations are the *exact* words spoken by someone. These quoted words and their punctuation are written within quotation marks (" "). The part of the sentence that tells who is speaking is called the narration. The quoted part of a sentence and the narration are separated from each other by a comma.

> **Carlo Caperna said, "The family will survive."**
> **"The family will survive," said Carlo Caperna.**

Some common verbs used in the narration are *said, stated, remarked, commented, added,* and *answered.*

Punctuating Quotations.   Ellen Lenz, a writer living in West Berlin, interviewed Tina Breitinger, the divorced mother who started the Granny Emergency Service. Ellen (E) asked Tina (T) several questions. Punctuate Tina's quoted answers correctly.

  a. E: "How did you start your service?"
  T: **(1)** I announced it on local radio stations she answered
  (2) I gave my phone number and business hours on interview programs she added

b. E: "Did you get many responses at first?"

T: **(1)** At first the service got off to a slow start said Tina

(2) Then she remarked I wasn't sure it would be a success

c. E: "Has the service been working well?"

T: **(1)** Tina responded it's been quite successful in a small way

(2) We have seventeen women and two men registered so far she stated

(3) They range in age from fifty-five to seventy-five she added

d. E: "Where do these 'Grannies' take care of the children?"

T: **(1)** Tina answered they go to a family's home and care for the children there

Social scientists predict that extended families will separate into basic nuclear families like this one. The smaller nuclear family is more adapted to modern industrialized society.

(2) We pay them for their carfare or gasoline she said

(3) They do it more for love than money she commented

COMPOSING

1. **Developing a Paragraph.**

   a. The following paragraph about a woman's childhood memories of her grandparents has been broken up into short, simple sentences. Combine the sentences into longer, more interesting statements. Use connectors, signal words, and pronouns where necessary. Leave out all the unnecessary words, but do not omit any of the important ideas or details. Work right in the book for your first draft. Then write your complete new paragraph on a separate sheet of paper.

   (1) My grandmother was kind-hearted.

   (2) My grandmother was loving.

   (3) My grandmother took care of me all day.

   (4) That was when I was small.

   (5) Both my parents worked.

   (6) My grandmother wasn't strong.

   (7) She worked hard.

   (8) The work was around the house.

   (9) My grandmother played games with me.

   (10) The games were interesting.

   (11) That was after the housework was finished.

   (12) My grandmother also made dolls for me.

   (13) The dolls were from pieces of material.

   (14) The pieces of material were colorful.

   (15) My grandmother didn't need a lot of money.

   (16) My grandmother did everything in an economical way.

   (17) My grandmother, my grandfather, and I ate dinner together.

   (18) That was when my grandfather came from work.

   (19) My grandfather always told stories.

   (20) The stories were funny.

   (21) That was while we were eating.

   (22) After that, my grandfather took me back to the house.

   (23) The house belonged to my parents.

   (24) I will always have memories.

(25) The memories are beautiful.

(26) The memories are of my grandparents.

b. The beginning of a paragraph about single-parent families is given to you. Unscramble the five sentences that follow. These will tell you some details about being a single parent. Rewrite the entire paragraph including the final sentence on a separate sheet of paper.

> In today's small nuclear families, due to death or divorce, many men and women are raising their children without a mate. Many of these single parents do not have their own families close by to help them out. There are many problems for single parents in this situation.

(1) working parents   their children   .   at home alone
must leave   after school

(2) nervous   .   may   the parents   very   feel

(3) cannot   the children   .   give   a lot of attention
the parents   perhaps

(4) guilty   about this   feel   .   parents   may

(5) may not   time   have   parents   their   own
social life   .   for

> Yet many single parents do a wonderful job of raising their children.

2.   Composing a Paragraph.

a. Write a paragraph that describes a special relationship you have with a member of the older generation in your family, such as an aunt, an uncle, or a grandparent. Describe the person, tell where he or she lives, and how the relationship developed. Tell what the advantages are, and how both of you benefit. If the relationship is past, use the appropriate tense and time expressions. Begin your paragraph with a main idea sentence that includes a feeling or opinion about this relationship.

b. Different cultures have different ideals for raising children. Imagine yourself as the parent of either a boy or a girl child. Describe some of the things you would do to raise this son or daughter. Be specific about the kinds of toys, clothes, activities, and other things you would provide so that your son or daughter would become the kind of man or women you would be proud of.

c. Some parents think an older person is better able to care for small children than a younger person. If you were a parent who needed help with your children, whom would you choose? Give specific reasons for your choice.

CHAPTER NINE B

DUAL-CAREER FAMILIES

PREREADING

Class Discussion. Read the following poem with your instructor. Then answer the questions about the poem.

> The Bear's Song
> (Haida: Queen Charlotte's Island, British Columbia)
>
> I have taken the woman of beauty
> For my wife;
> I have taken her from her friends.
> I hope her kinsmen will not come
> And take her away from me.
> I will be kind to her.
> Berries, berries I will give her from the hill
> And roots from the ground.
> I will do everything to please her.
> For her I made this song and for her I sing it.

A man from the Bear clan of the Haida tribe of Native Americans is singing this song for a special occasion. What is the occasion? What are the man's feelings about the woman? What gifts will he give her? What do you think these gifts mean?

Discuss the kinds of gifts that are exchanged as part of the engagement and wedding ceremonies in your culture.

New Words. Try to understand the meanings of these words as they are used in the reading passage. Use a dictionary when necessary.

odd	available	expect	supervise
conference	standard	jealous	proud
opportunity	apply	cooperate	cope (with)

READING

One Household: Two Careers

[1]   In an increasing number of American families both the husband and the wife have careers in which they will spend their working lives. These careers often require them to work more than the nine-to-five, five-day-a-week schedule of most people. For example, men and women in sales, or those who own their own small business, may have to work weekends or evenings. Men and women in the medical or police field may work odd hours, or be on call at any time. Teachers, hairdressers, or computer technicians may have conferences or educational programs to attend that take them out of town for several days at a time. Male and female workers who are active in their labor unions may have many meetings to attend that take up a great deal of time. When both the husband and the wife in a family are involved in these types of careers, theirs is known as a dual-career family.

[2]   The number of American dual-career families is steadily rising. There will be more of these families in the future. There are several reasons for this. First, the women's liberation movement has given women the desire and opportunity to work outside the home and enter new occupations. More husbands are sharing the household and child care responsibilities with their wives, and more day-care services are becoming available. Therefore, wives have more time for the requirements of higher level jobs. Second, in today's inflationary situation, both the husband and wife in many families must work in order to provide the basic necessities. Furthermore, if American families want to enjoy a high standard of living, two good incomes are often needed. If families want to buy more goods, own their own homes, and take interesting vacations, the wife's income is often essential.

[3]   In some dual-career families the husband and wife are both in the same field. This may make it easier for them to understand each other's needs and

Physicians Anna and William Fisher are both pursuing careers as scientist-astronauts.

requirements. Dual-career couples in the same field can communicate well because they are interested in the same things. Married astronauts Dr. Anna and Dr. William Fisher are an example of one such dual-career couple. They both developed an interest in space and medicine when they were children. Dr. Anna Fisher says, "When I was twelve or thirteen, I knew that by the time I grew up there were going to be space stations and they'd need doctors." Both Anna and William became physicians. Then they applied together for work in the Space Agency. Today they train together as specialists in space travel. After they train for four or five years, they expect a team assignment on a space shuttle or rocket plane.

[4]   Drs. Anna and William Fisher have no children. What happens in dual-career families where there are children? A recent article in *Harvard Magazine* discussed this problem. One doctor stated that children raised in dual-career families may feel angry, fearful, or jealous. But if dual-career parents cooperate with each other and arrange leisure time activities with their children, then the children may not suffer these emotional problems.

[5]   Professors Ravinder and Serena Nanda are a dual-career family with two children—Raj, 14, and Jai, 12. In their careers as university professors both parents must attend many meetings, do a lot of writing, and occasionally speak at conferences out of town. But they try to spend as much time as possible with their children. They try to arrange their schedules so that one parent is home while the other is away. They bring some of their work home so that they can supervise the homework of their two boys. Their two boys take on some of the household responsibilities such as doing their laundry and cooking simple meals. The boys are equally proud of their mother's and father's work. When they grow up, they will be able to cope with dual-career marriages themselves.

Guided Summary.   A summary tells about the most important ideas of a passage. A summary may also include the most important details or examples used by the writer. Follow the directions for each item to write your summary of this passage. Write the sentences in correct paragraph form.

a.   Complete the following sentence with the main topic of the reading. This will be the first sentence of your summary.
     This passage discusses . . .

b.   Compose your second sentence by choosing the best item to complete the given words.
     Paragraph [2] tells why

  (1) it is difficult to choose a career.

  (2) dual-career marriages are increasing.

  (3) children should share household responsibilities

   c. For your third and fourth sentences, complete the following statements.

      (1) Dual-career couples in the same field . . .

      (2) Astronauts Anna and William Fisher are an example . . .

   d. For your fifth sentence, choose the best statement about Paragraph [4].

      (1) *Harvard Magazine* contains important articles.

      (2) An article in *Harvard Magazine* discusses the advantages of dual-career families.

      (3) A *Harvard Magazine* article tells about the problems of children in dual-career families.

   e. For your sixth sentence, complete the following statement.
      But the example of the Nanda family shows that . . .

VOCABULARY

   1. **Expanding Vocabulary.** In the blank space in Column A write the letter of the synonym from Column B.

A		B	
odd _____		**a.**	look forward to
conference _____		**b.**	handle
opportunity _____		**c.**	ready for use
standard _____		**d.**	unusual
available _____		**e.**	level
apply _____		**f.**	envious
expect _____		**g.**	good chance
cooperate _____		**h.**	look over
jealous _____		**i.**	meeting
supervise _____		**j.**	compete against
proud _____		**k.**	emotional
cope with _____		**l.**	work together
		m.	strongly satisfied
		n.	ask for

2. **Using Vocabulary.**   Follow the directions for each item.

   a. Choose the correct verb for each blank space.

      are coping   expected   cooperated   applied   supervises

      In 1978 over eight thousand people (1) _____

      to the Space Agency for astronaut training. Drs. Anna and William

      Fisher both (2) _____ to be chosen. But only Anna

      was accepted. So Anna (3) _____ with William so

      that he could get extra training. The Space Agency (4) _____

      the training for the space program very carefully. Now both Anna

      and William Fisher (5) _____ well with the difficult

      training program of the Space Agency.

   b. Circle the items of behavior that would make a parent *proud* of his or her
      child.

      breaking a window   getting high grades in school
      losing the house keys   listening to TV all day
      playing the piano well   calling up a sick friend

   c. Write a complete sentence for each item. Use the italicized words in your
      sentences.

      (1) At what hours is your English instructor *available* for *conferences*
          with students?
      (2) Does the Space Agency have high or low *standards* for astronaut
          training?
      (3) Explain why a nurse, a department store salesperson, or a police
          officer might have to work *odd* hours.
      (4) Name two things you might have the *opportunity* to do this summer.

3. **Word Families.**   The word *dual* is used as a prefix meaning "two." Two
   other prefixes meaning "two" are *bi* and *di*.

   My brother is *bilingual;* he speaks French and English.
   Two students read a *dialogue* in front of the class.

Other prefixes that show number are the following:

mono 1	quint 5	oct 8	cent 100
tri 3	sext 6	nov 9	mille 1000
quad(t) 4	sept 7	dec 10	

Answer the following questions in the space provided.

a. *Logue* is a part of a word that means "speech." If a dialogue is the speech of two people, how many speakers are there in a monologue? _____

b. *Ped* is a part of a word that means "foot." Is a horse a *biped* or a *quadruped*? _____ Is a human being a *biped* or a *quadruped*? _____ What kind of insect is a *centipede*? _____

c. Why would a mother with *quintuplets* find it difficult to have a career?

_____

d. If you played the drums in a *sextet,* how many other people would be in your band? _____

e. September, October, November, and December are the number-names of months taken from the early Roman calendar. These months are correct in that calendar because the Roman year did not start in January, but in

_____ .

f. A *decade* is a period of _____ years. A *century* is a period of _____ years. A *millennium* is a period of _____ years.

g. On July 4, 1976, the United States celebrated its *bicentennial* birthday. How old was the United States on that date? _____

READING COMPREHENSION

1. **Understanding the Text.** Circle the number of the correct answer.

   a. In a dual-career family
      (1) the husband and wife share one full-time job.
      (2) the husband and wife both have long-term careers.
      (3) only the husband has a long-term career.

Dual-career families like the Nandas appreciate the leisure time they can spend together.

b. Paragraph [1] gives medical and police work as an example of

   (1) careers that are mostly for men.

   (2) careers that offer normal eight-hour work days.

   (3) careers that require long or unusual hours.

c. In the last sentence of Paragraph [1] the word *theirs* means the same as

   (1) this family.   **(2)** these careers.   **(3)** these meetings.

d. According to the passage, the number of dual-career families

   (1) is rising.   **(2)** is decreasing.   **(3)** will remain about the same.

e. In Paragraph [2] the words *First* and *Second* signal the reader to expect

   (1) a negative statement.

   (2) a list of additional items.

   (3) a statement of contrast.

f. In the sixth sentence in Paragraph [2], the word *Therefore* signals the reader to expect

   (1) a negative.   **(2)** an example.   **(3)** a result.

g. Buying more goods, owning your own home, and taking interesting vacations are examples of

   (1) a low standard of living.   **(2)** a high standard of living.

   (3) the standard of living in most of the world.

h. According to Paragraph [3], husbands and wives who work in the same field

(**1**) compete against each other. (**2**) earn extraordinary incomes.

(**3**) can communicate easily with each other.

i. Dr. Anna Fisher's quotation in Paragraph [3] shows that

(**1**) she became a doctor after she got married.

(**2**) she always wanted to work in the space and medical field.

(**3**) she is a better astronaut than her husband.

j. The last sentence in Paragraph [3] tells us that

(**1**) long training is necessary before astronauts go into space.

(**2**) long training is necessary after astronauts go into space.

(**3**) the training to be an astronaut is not difficult.

k. In Paragraph [4], the third sentence, the phrase "this problem" refers to

(**1**) the difficulties of writing for *Harvard Magazine*.

(**2**) the difficulties of holding two jobs.

(**3**) the difficulties of children in dual-career families.

l. According to Paragraph [4], parents in dual-career families should

(**1**) spend free time with their children.

(**2**) take frequent vacations away from home.

(**3**) suffer emotional problems.

m. Paragraph [5] is an example of which sentence in Paragraph [4]?

(**1**) the fourth (**2**) the last (**3**) the first

n. The Nanda boys have probably been taught to cook simple meals because

(**1**) their parents don't like to eat out.

(**2**) their parents are not always home for dinner.

(**3**) the parents want the boys to become restaurant workers.

o. The Nanda boys will probably be able to cope with their own dual-career marriages because

(**1**) they can do their own laundry.

(**2**) they take vacations with their parents.

(**3**) they have lived in a dual-career household.

2. **Answering Information Questions.** Write the answers to the following questions in complete sentences.

    a. What kind of schedule do most people work?

    b. What kind of people may have to work weekends or evenings?

    c. If a person is active in a labor union, will he or she have many or few meetings to attend?

    d. Is the number of dual-career families increasing or decreasing?

    e. How many incomes are often needed for a high standard of living?

    f. Are day-care centers becoming more or less available?

    g. Why can dual-career couples in the same field communicate well?

    h. When did Anna and William Fisher develop an interest in space and medicine?

    i. Did the Fishers apply separately or together for work in the Space Agency?

    j. What do the Fishers expect after four or five years' training?

    k. How many children do Professors Ravinder and Serena Nanda have?

    l. Do the Nandas do a lot or a little writing in their careers?

    m. What are two household responsibilities that the Nanda boys take on themselves?

    n. How do the Nanda boys feel about their mother's and father's work?

3. **Following Key Words.**   In reading a paragraph you must look for the key, or main, topic words that the writer uses all through the paragraph. These words may not always be exactly the same. The writer may use synonyms, paraphrases, specific parts of a topic, or pronouns in place of the topic word(s). Study Paragraph [5] of the reading passage. This paragraph is about the Nanda parents and children. The key topic words in the first sentence are the following: *Professors Ravinder and Serena Nanda, dual-career family, two children.* The topic is referred to in later sentences by the following words:

Sentence 2	their careers, both parents
Sentence 3	they, their children
Sentence 4	they, one parent . . . the other
Sentence 5	they, their two boys
Sentence 6	their two boys
Sentence 7	the boys, their mother's and father's work
Sentence 8	they, they, dual-career marriages, themselves

Now read the following paragraph carefully. The key topic phrase in the first sentence is underlined. Circle the other words in the paragraph that refer back to this key phrase. The first one is done for you.

    Because of the high divorce rate in America, one California high school has begun a <u>course in marriage training.</u> In this class, students are matched up as husbands and wives for the semester. The course offers these couples various marriage problems to solve throughout the semester. In it the student-couples may have to cope with such difficulties as the husband's or wife's loss of a job, the arrangement of child care schedules in a dual-career family, or even the death of a child. The creator of this new approach to premarriage counseling hopes that it will make young people more thoughtful about marriage. Students who take this marriage training course should be able to make wiser decisions about their future marriages. Perhaps this instruction will lower the American divorce rate.

WRITING EXERCISES

Complex Sentences with *Before* and *After*

Complex sentences sometimes include activities that happen at different times. One part of the sentence happens *before* or *after* the other. The part of the sentence that begins with the time word *before* or *after* is called the *dependent clause*. The dependent clause must be joined to a main, or independent, clause to complete the sentence.

Before my sister got married, she worked as a private nurse.
    (dependent clause)   (independent clause)

She became a hospital nurse after she married.
    (independent clause)   (dependent clause)

Note that when the dependent clause begins the sentence, it is followed by a comma.

Related Verb Tenses in Complex Sentences with *Before* and *After*.   The main verb in both parts of a complex sentence must be in the same or related tenses.

Simple Present   **Simple Present and Future**

Many mothers *go* back to work after their children *are* in school.
Most couples *will open* a joint bank account after they *get* married.

Simple Past   **Simple Past and Past Continuous**

> Before my niece moved to New York, she *was living* in California.
> After she *finished* school, she *moved* to New York with her husband.

---

1. **Sentence Combining.**   Join the two sentences in each set by adding the word *before* or *after.* Make whatever small changes are necessary for sentence correctness. Rewrite each new complete sentence. The first one is done for you.

   a. **(1)** I went back to work.

      (2) My daughter began kindergarten.

      I went back to work after my daughter began kindergarten.

   b. **(1)** Dr. Anna Fisher was a physician in California.

      (2) She applied to the Space Agency.

   c. **(1)** Dr. Fisher's application was accepted.

      (2) She took many physical and mental tests.

   d. **(1)** The Fishers expect to work in space.

      (2) They have four or five years' of training.

   e. **(1)** The Space Agency assigns people to rocket planes.

      (2) They give them long, difficult training.

   f. **(1)** The Fishers relax by skiing.

      (2) Their work for the week is done.

   g. **(1)** The Nanda boys do their homework.

      (2) They come home from school.

   h. **(1)** The boys go out to play on Saturday.

      (2) They must do their laundry together.

   i. **(1)** Mrs. Nanda cooks many meals in advance for her family.

      (2) She goes out of town to a conference.

   j. **(1)** The Nandas all go on vacation together.

      (2) School is over in June.

2. **Sentence Building.**   Use each pair of items in a complex sentence with the time word *before* or *after.* You may use the items in any order and add as many words as you like to make a complete, interesting sentence. You may use the verbs in any tense or in the negative. The first one is done for you.

a. work hard, feel tired

After I work hard all day, I feel very tired.

b. leave my house, lock the door

c. have a test, review my notes

d. eat dinner, see a movie

e. take a course, see an advisor

f. quit my job, save money

g. get married, think

h. graduate, apply for work

i. finish work, go bowling

3. **Sentence Composing.**   Follow the directions for each item.

a. In three separate sentences, tell three things you do before you leave the house each morning. Then combine the three sentences into one complete sentence, using a series of items.

b. In two separate sentences, tell two things you must not do after a test has started. Now combine the two sentences into one, making all the necessary changes.

c. Tell where you lived before you came to this city.

d. Tell where you plan to live after you finish school.

e. In two separate sentences, tell two things you do before you buy a new pair of shoes.

f. In two separate sentences, tell two things you must do before you can get a passport. Now combine the two sentences, making all the necessary changes.

Adverb Use

1. **In What Manner.**   Adverbs describe how, *in what manner,* verb action is done.

> **Most people plan their vacations *carefully*. (People *plan*. How do they plan?** *carefully*)

Rewriting Sentences.   Rewrite each sentence changing the italicized phrase into an adverb that tells how the verb action is done. Use the space provided. The first one is done for you.

a. Dual-career parents have to plan their schedules *in a careful manner.*

Dual-career parents have to plan their schedules carefully.

b. Men and women both work *in an active manner* in labor unions.

_____

c. Children from dual-career families may suffer *in an emotional way.*

_____

d. They may behave *in a fearful manner.*

_____

e. They may speak *in an angry way* to their parents.

_____

f. But if parents and children work *in a cooperative manner,* a dual-career family may work well.

_____

g. The number of dual-career families in America is increasing *in a steady manner.*

_____

h. Dual-career couples can communicate *in an easy manner.*

_____

i. Children in dual-career families often speak *in a proud way* of both parents' work.

_____

2. **Extent or Degree.**   Adverbs tell the *extent or degree* of an adjective or adverb. Some common adverbs of degree are *very, too, extremely, fairly, rather, quite.*

Some people plan their vacations *very* carefully.
I had a *rather* difficult schedule last term.

Note that in English the adverb *too* usually has a negative meaning: You work *too* hard (you should work less). *Too* is not a synonym for *very,* which may be used in either a negative or positive way.

Sentence Completion.   Read the first sentence in each pair. Then choose one of the given adverbs of degree to fill in the blank space. (More than one adverb may be correct in some cases.)

fairly   very   extremely   extraordinarily   quite   rather   too

a. I've read that chapter three times. I know it _____ well now.

b. That was a dull, uninteresting movie. I was _____ bored by it.

c. My daughter is five feet, four inches. That's _____ tall for a ten-year-old girl.

d. Our Russian friend has been here just three months. She's still _____ shy about speaking English.

e. That tree has more apples than any other in the yard. It produces _____ well every year.

f. Our new piano is over seven feet long. It's _____ large to fit in the elevator of our building.

g. My neighbor's three children are so well behaved. They play _____ quietly in the evenings.

h. John often drives at eighty miles per hour. I don't like to drive with him because he goes _____ fast.

i. Chinese characters are _____ difficult to learn. But the verbs have no tense endings, so they are _____ easy to remember.

j. Dinosaur bones may break at the first touch. They are _____ fragile.

k. I'm not going to buy those theater tickets. At $17.50, they're _____ expensive for me.

3. **Comparative.** Comparative adverbs compare the different degrees in which verb action is done. To use adverbs for comparison, one must normally add the word *more* before the adverb.

> **People communicate *more easily* when they have things in common.**

     Note some common exceptions in the comparative adverb form:
hard⟶harder; well⟶better; badly⟶worse; fast⟶faster

Sentence Composing. Write a complete sentence to answer each of the following items. Use the sentence pattern in the example.

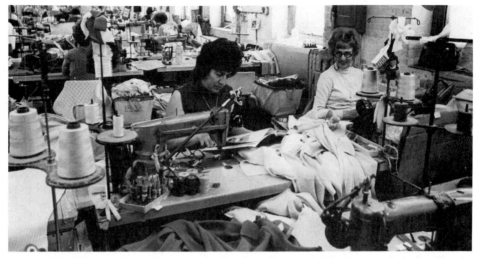

Many immigrant women today, as in the past, bring needed income to their families by working in factories. Dual-income families of all kinds are on the increase today.

Do teenagers or older people drive more safely?

Older people drive more safely than teenagers.

---

a. Do older children or younger children cooperate better?
b. Do men or women work more actively in labor unions?
c. Do boys or girls play more roughly in the gym?
d. Do fathers or mothers work harder at home?
e. Do apes or human beings learn language more easily?
f. Can turtles or rabbits run faster?
g. Do deer or elephants run more gracefully?

Punctuation: Quotations

Quotations are the *exact* words spoken by someone. These quoted words and their punctuation are written within quotation marks (" "). The part of the sentence that tells who is speaking is called the narration. The quoted part of a sentence and the narration are separated from each other by a comma.

> **One working mother said, "I ask my children to help around the house."**
>
> **"I ask my children to help around the house," said one working mother.**

Some common verbs used in the narration are *said, stated, remarked, commented, added,* and *answered.*

Punctuating Quotations.   A magazine reporter interviewed Dave and Martha Harper, a dual-career couple. Dave has his own insurance business, and Martha runs her own travel agency. The reporter (R) asked Dave (D) several questions. Punctuate Dave's quoted answers correctly.

    a. R: "Why did your wife start her own business?"
       D: **(1)** My wife was a gal with a lot of talent he said
          (2) She wanted to do a real service for people he added

    b. R: "How did you feel about your wife working?"
       D: **(1)** Dave said at first I didn't like it
          (2) But now I've changed he stated

    c. R: "Do you help your wife with the housework?"
       D: **(1)** I hate most of it commented Dave
          (2) I do damn little of it he added
          (3) Then he remarked but I do feel a little guilty about that
          (4) Marty's always helped me do what I wanted he said
          (5) He told the reporter I took a long while to do the same for her

COMPOSING

1. Developing a Paragraph.

    a. The following paragraph about a student's immigrant parents has been broken up into short, simple sentences. Combine the sentences into longer, more interesting statements. Use connectors, signal words, and pronouns where necessary. Leave out all the unnecessary words, but do not omit any of the important ideas or details. Work right in the book for your first draft. Then rewrite your complete new paragraph.

       (1) My mother was short.
       (2) My mother was fragile looking.

(3) My mother was proud of her appearance.

(4) My mother was a seamstress.

(5) My mother sewed dresses.

(6) The dresses were for other people.

(7) My mother had a sewing machine.

(8) The sewing machine was in a house.

(9) The house belonged to us.

(10) My mother was always at the sewing machine.

(11) That was every day.

(12) The housework was done.

(13) My mother got a lot of work.

(14) My mother sewed very fast.

(15) My mother sewed very neatly.

(16) My mother's skills were excellent.

(17) My father worked in the garment business.

(18) He delivered sewing materials.

(19) His deliveries were to the homes.

(20) The homes belonged to the workers.

(21) My parents worked together.

(22) They worked for a better life.

(23) The better life was for their children.

b. The following paragraph tells something about the economic situation of dual-career couples. The first three sentences are given to you. Construct the next five sentences from each set of items provided. Do not change the form or order of the given items. Rewrite your complete new paragraph including the given conclusion.

Many two-income families are looking for new ways to manage their money. It is true that dual-career couples have a double income. But the bigger income can bring bigger expenses too.

a. two-career couples   often   housekeeper   home

b. if   children   spend   day-care

c. spend   more   luxuries   clothes   vacations

d. dual-career   entertain   eat out   more than

e. married   higher taxes   single

According to most writers on the subject, there will be more dual-career couples in the future, and each will eventually learn what kind of money management works best for them.

2. **Composing a Paragraph.**

   a. Write a paragraph that tells about a family in which both parents work or go to school. Tell about the kinds of jobs the parents do and the hours they work. Tell something about how they share the household jobs. Tell about the role of the children in the family: who takes care of them and what responsibilities they may have. Begin your paragraph with a main idea sentence that includes a feeling or opinion about this family.

   b. It is important for all types of families to spend some leisure time together. Write a paragraph about a pleasant day or vacation that you spent with your family. You may write about a time you remember as a child, or you may write about some current experience. Describe some of the activities you and your family did together and how you felt about spending the day as a family.

UNIT THREE REVIEW

1. **Sentence Completion.** Fill in the blank spaces with the appropriate word(s) as directed by the Key following the paragraph.

Until 1976 Ted Koppel (1) _____ in a high pressure job as a television news reporter (2) _____ ABC. In the first thirteen years of his marriage, (3) _____ wife, Grace Ann, stayed home with (4) _____ four children. But then Grace Ann wanted her own (5) _____ . So she (6) _____ to law school. (7) _____ she was accepted, Ted agreed to give up his job for a year and take the (8) _____ for the housework and children. Ted didn't change roles (9) _____ . One of the (10) _____ things he had to learn was that his time was no longer his own. He had to make a daily schedule (11) _____ gave (12) _____ time to write, take care of the house, and (13) _____ the children. (14) _____ a child got sick, Ted couldn't cope with all his work. In many ways his new job kept him (15) _____ than his high pressure job in television.

Key

1. Past continuous tense of the verb *work*
2. Preposition of place
3. Singular male possessive pronoun
4. Plural possessive pronoun
5. Synonym for "a responsible job that a person will keep for most of his or her life"
6. Simple past tense of the verb *apply*
7. Time word showing that one event happened later than another
8. Synonym for *duties*

9. Adverb form of *easy*
10. Superlative form of the adjective *important*
11. Relative pronoun for nonhuman items
12. Singular male object pronoun
13. Synonym for "watch over"
14. Word that introduces the conditional part of a sentence
15. Comparative form of the adjective *busy*

2. **Word Forms.**   Fill in the chart with the correct forms of the given word. (Some parts of speech may have more than one word.)

	Verb	Noun	Adjective	Adverb
1	X		typical	
2	involve			X
3	X	responsibility		
4	X	loneliness		X
5	enrich			X
6		conferences	X	X
7	apply			X
8	X		jealous	
9	X		proud	
10	cooperate			

Word Form Completion.   Fill in the blank space in each sentence with the correct form of the word from the same numbered item on the Word Form chart. Use verbs and nouns in their singular or plural forms as necessary. For dictation with blanks close your book.

1. American women _____ earn less money than men.

2. A teacher's _____ with her students in very important.

3. Working parents must teach their children to act _____ .

4. Even children in large families may suffer _____ .

5. A job helping others offers true _____ .

6. _____ often take place in New York City.

7. Did you fill out an _____ for your promotion?

8. Children are sometimes _____ of their parents' work.

9. A husband should be _____ of his wife's work.

10. Members of a dual-career family must work _____ .

3. **Paragraph Composition.** Write a paragraph that includes five to eight words from the Word Form chart. Select one of the following topics to write about, or choose one of your own.

A Successful Student
A Strong Personality
An Ideal Job

APPENDIX A

BASIC TERMINOLOGY FOR ENGLISH LANGUAGE STUDY

1. Parts of Speech

Noun: A word that names a person, place, thing, quality, idea, or action.

Peter Rodriquez, girl, country, chair, attention

Verb: A word that expresses a state of being, feeling, or appearance.

You *seem* ill today.
I *am* nervous about my exam.

A word that expresses physical or mental action.

I *thought* about you yesterday.
My friends *play* soccer very well.

Adjective: A word that describes a noun. Articles (a, an, the) and numbers are adjectives.

***Many* students find English *a difficult* subject.**

Adverb: A word that tells us how often or in what way verb action is done.

Young people *often* have part-time jobs.
New Yorkers speak *rapidly.*

A word that tells us the degree to which an adjective is true.

My cat is *very* healthy.

Preposition: A word that generally has some meaning of place, direction, time, or connection with a noun.

Please put the book *for* John *on* the table *in* the hall.

Conjunction: A word that joins related words, phrases, or clauses of similar form.
and, but, or connect independent clauses.

Many women work outside the home, *but* they still have household responsibilities.

---

if, because, when, while, before, after, although begin dependent clauses. These clauses must be connected to independent clauses.

***Because* you speak French, you may learn Spanish rather easily.**

---

2. **Phrases**
   A group of two or more words forming a thought unit.
   Prepositional Phrase: A phrase that begins with a preposition.

> **The United Nations is located *in New York City.***

Infinitive Phrase: A phrase that begins with *to* and is followed by the basic form of a verb.

> **Archeologists like *to explore* ancient cities.**

3. **Clauses**

   A group of words with a subject and a complete main verb.

   Independent Clause: A group of words that can stand by itself as a complete sentence.

> **Last week he saw a white tiger at the zoo.**

Dependent Clause: A clause that cannot stand by itself as a complete sentence because it begins with such words as *if, because, when, while, before, after, who, which,* or *that.*

> **It is difficult to live on the moon *because there is no water.***
> **Professor Jones knows *which students will pass the course.***

4. **Punctuation**

   Period: Closes off a finished thought that can stand by itself as a complete sentence.

> **I enjoy this class.**

Comma: Separates parallel items in a series.

> **Many words from German, Latin, and French are found in English.
> Computer science is a new, interesting, and important field of study.**

Follows a dependent clause that begins a sentence.

> **When you have finished your exam, leave your paper on the desk.**

Marks off signal words and expressions.

> **Some languages do not use a Latin alphabet. Russian, for example,
> uses the Cyrillic alphabet.**

Precedes *but* in a compound sentence.

> **Weight lifting used to be a sport only for men, but today many women
> are lifting weights.**

Quotation Marks: Surrounds direct speech, that is, the exact words spoken
by someone.

> **At 12:00 the professor said, "The exam will begin."**

5. Articles

Indefinite Article: a, an

Placed before a singular countable noun when the noun is mentioned for the
first time and represents no specific person or thing.

> **There is *a* cat in my backyard.**

When the noun is an example of a class of things.

> **A bicycle has two wheels.**

Placed with a noun complement.

> **She is *an* interesting person.**

Definite Article: the
Placed before a singular or a plural noun when someone or something is mentioned a second time.

> **I saw a man in the park. *The* man was walking his dog.**

When someone or something is made definite by the addition of a clause or a phrase.

> **The women that I met were very friendly.**
> **The boy in the blue sweater is my son.**

When there is only one of something.

> **The sky is blue. *The* weather is fine.**

Placed before names of seas, oceans, rivers, groups of islands, mountain ranges, and geographical areas.

> **She lives in *the* West near *the* Rocky Mountains.**

Placed before countries representing a union.

---

the **United States,** *the* **Soviet Union,** *the* **Dominican Republic**

Placed before the superlative degree of adjectives.

Paul is *the* **best student in the class.**

Placed before singular nouns that represent a class of objects.

The **rose is a beautiful flower.**

---

6. **Verb Summary**

   Basic Form: Simple verb, no endings for person or tense.

---

hold   study   speak   write

Infinitive: to + basic form of verb.

The movie is going *to begin* **at noon.**

Simple Present: Basic form of verb, except for Third Person singular, which adds *s*. For habitual or general action.

Every summer I *visit* **my family in Haiti.**
Both girls and boys *need* **physical exercise.**

Present Continuous: am, is, or *are* + *ing* form of main verb. For actions that are taking place "right now."

> **Two people *are waiting* to use the telephone.**

For actions that suggest continuous activity.

> **When *I'm studying*, I like peace and quiet.**

Simple Past: Basic form of verb + *ed,* or irregular form. For actions that were completed in the past.

> **Yesterday I *finished* my work by dinner time.**
> **Traffic *was* slow because a car *broke* down in the middle of the highway.**

Past Continuous: was or *were* + *ing* form of main verb. For continuous action in the past.

> **The class *was practicing* verb forms all last week.**

For interrupted past actions, usually with another clause in the simple past.

> **Our team *was playing* very well until our best batter injured his arm.**

7. **Modals**

   Modal forms are used to express certain conditions of ability, possibility, probability, or advisement. The main verbs following the modal are always in the basic form.

   Can: present ability; possibility

> **I *can* drive a car very well.**
> **I *can* do it later.**

Could: past ability (complementary clause in Simple Past)

> **My father *could* swim well when he was young.**

Will: future certainty

> **I *will* meet you tomorrow at noon.**

Would: conditional probability (complementary clause in Simple Past)

> **If I spoke French fluently, I *would* study in Paris for a year.**

Should: advisability; obligation; expectation

> **You *should* take three semesters of English.**
> **I *should* write a note of thanks to my hostess.**
> **She *should* be here soon.**

Must: necessity; strong probability

> **I *must* pay my rent by the tenth of each month.**
> **You *must* be tired after working so hard.**

May: possibility; probability; permission

> **I *may* go to California next summer.**
> **She is absent. She *may* be sick.**
> ***May* I leave now?**

List of Commonly Used Irregular Verbs

Basic Form	Simple Past	Basic Form	Simple Past
arise	arose	forget	forgot
awake	awoke	freeze	froze
be	was	get	got
beat	beat	give	gave
become	became	go	went
begin	began	grind	ground
bend	bent	grow	grew
bet	bet	have	had
bite	bit	hear	heard
bleed	bled	hide	hid
blow	blew	hit	hit
break	broke	hold	held
bring	brought	hurt	hurt
broadcast	broadcast, broadcasted	keep	kept
build	built	kneel	knelt, kneeled
burst	burst	knit	knit, knitted
buy	bought	know	knew
cast	cast	lay	laid
catch	caught	lead	led
choose	chose	leap	leaped, leapt
come	came	leave	left
cost	cost	lend	lent
deal	dealt	let	let
dig	dug	lie (to recline)	lay
do	did	(not to tell the truth)	lied
draw	drew	light	lit, lighted
dream	dreamed, dreamt	lose	lost
drink	drank	make	made
drive	drove	mean	meant
eat	ate	meet	met
fall	fell	mistake	mistook
feed	fed	overcome	overcame
feel	felt	pay	paid
fight	fought	put	put
find	found	quit	quit
flee	fled	read	read (*pronounced* "red")
fly	flew	ride	rode
forbid	forbade	ring	rang

Basic Form	Simple Past	Basic Form	Simple Past
rise	rose	steal	stole
run	ran	stick	stuck
say	said	sting	stung
see	saw	stink	stank
seek	sought	strike	struck
sell	sold	swear	swore
send	sent	sweep	swept
set	set	swim	swam
shake	shook	swing	swung
shoot	shot	take	took
shrink	shrank, shrunk	teach	taught
shut	shut	tear	tore
sing	sang	tell	told
sink	sank, sunk	think	thought
sit	sat	throw	threw
sleep	slept	understand	understood
slide	slid	wake	woke, waked
speak	spoke	wear	wore
speed	sped, speeded	weave	wove
spend	spent	weep	wept
spin	spun	win	won
spit	spit, spat	wind	wound
split	split	withdraw	withdrew
stand	stood	write	wrote

APPENDIX B

PARAGRAPH CORRECTION SYMBOLS

ap.	Apostrophe error (Marias sister is a doctor in the Dominican Republic.)
cap.	Capitalization (My daughter enjoyed her visit to the united nations.)
∧ (caret)	Something left out (∧ French language is very beautiful.)
frag.	Fragment: incomplete sentence; dependent clause used as a sentence (Because the United States is very large.)
℘ (omit)	(I received the good instruction in English last year.)
pl.	Plural error; disagreement in number between plural nouns and related words (There are many good reason for students to continue his education.)
punct.	Punctuation error: comma, period, or question mark misused (Because, I live a long way from the school I am often late to class.)
RO	Run-on sentences: two independent clauses incorrectly joined by a comma (I enjoy reading English newspapers, I get a lot of information from them.)
sp.	Spelling (Their are many bilingual people in New York City.)

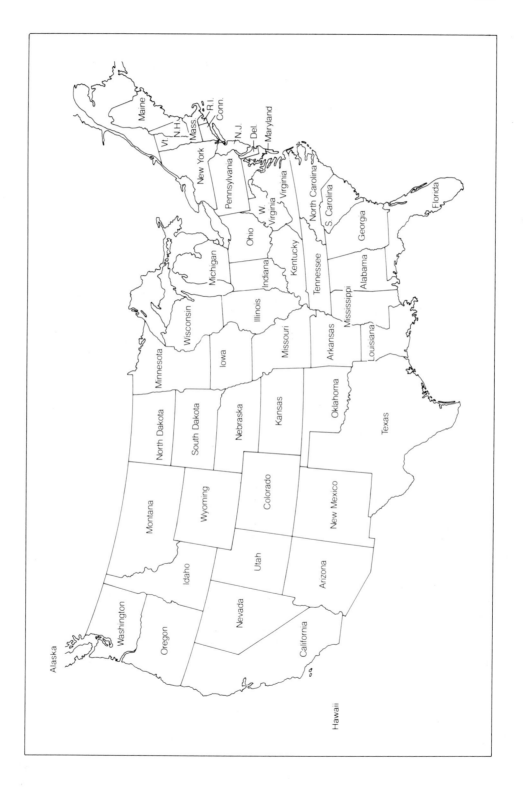

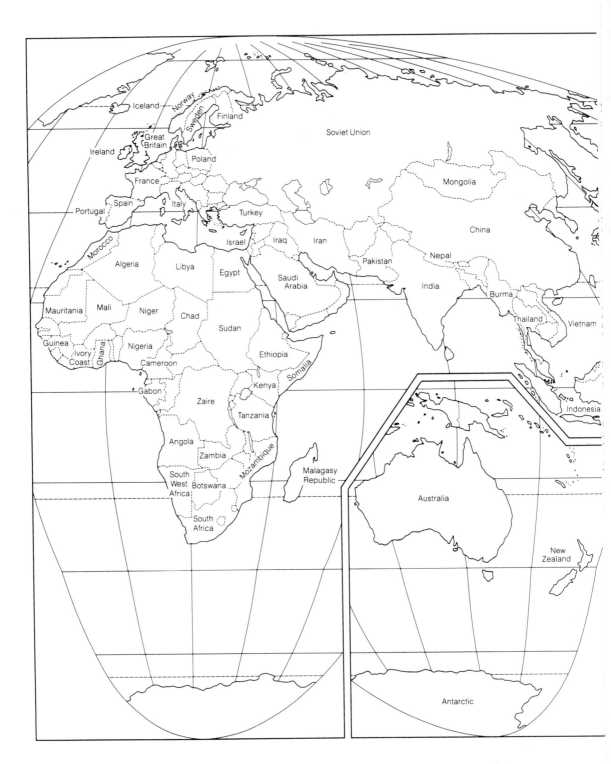

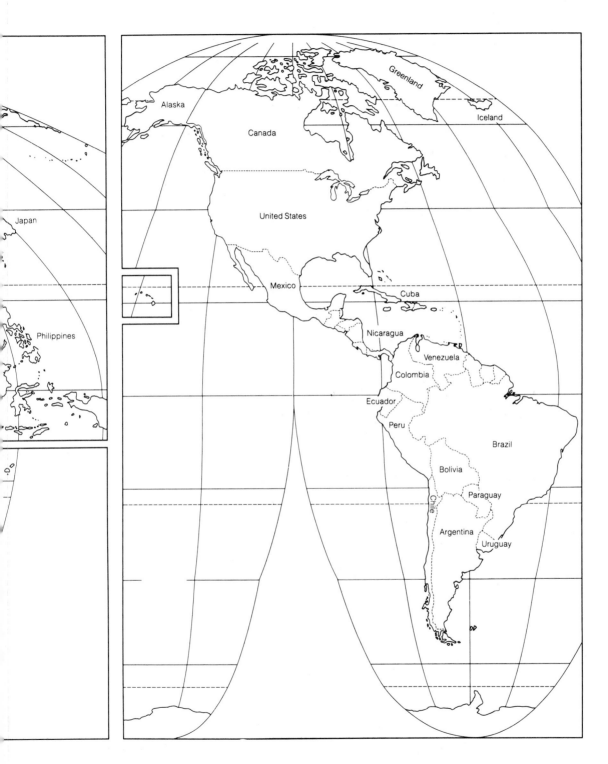